THE MAN WHO WOULD NOT DIE

A catalogue record for this book is available from the British Library

ISBN 978 1 84425 510 8

Library of Congress catalog card no 2008926359

Published by Haynes Publishing,
Sparkford, Yeovil, Somerset BA22 7JJ, UK
Tel: 01963 442030 Fax: 01963 440001
Int. tel: +44 1963 442030 Int. fax: +44 1963 440001
E-mail: sales@haynes.co.uk
Website: www.haynes.co.uk

Haynes North America Inc., 861 Lawrence Drive, Newbury Park, California 91320, USA

Designed and typeset by James Robertson
Printed and bound in the UK by J. H. Haynes & Co. Ltd, Sparkford

THE MAN WHO WOULD NOT DIE

The remarkable story of 'Lucky' Herschel McKee
Barnstormer, war hero, test pilot, motor racer, scoundrel

Stephen Olvey

Haynes Publishing

CONTENTS

AUTHOR'S PREFACE

I never knew Herschel McKee personally. I learned of him from my wife Lynne, McKee's granddaughter. His early exploits were quite well documented, his auto racing days especially, but during World War Two the documentation gradually diminishes. After the war it disappears altogether, and only a few facts are known for sure: he was a decorated hero of both world wars; he was issued a Dade County, Florida, driver's license in late 1945 and listed his residence as the Biltmore Hotel; even though he is buried in Arlington Cemetery, he is not listed as being so on its Internet website; and he is also not listed as being a member of the 44th Bomb Group of the US Army Air Corps, even though his discharge papers have him serving in that unit for the majority of World War Two. His whereabouts during most of this period are unknown – even his closest relations had no idea where he was much of the time. Public records were destroyed or conveniently lost. Only a vague reference is made regarding his intelligence activity for the government. Yet he was promoted to Lieutenant-Colonel just as the war ended.

Certain references were used to create believable scenarios in McKee's colorful and daring life. Among these were Jeff Shaara's book entitled *To The Last Man*, describing what life was like during World War One. Likewise, Patrick Bishop's *Bomber Boys* provided background information on World War Two. Information regarding the 44th Bomb Group's activities was obtained from the 44th Bomb Group's Veterans Association, and

Ron Mackay and Steve Adam's book *The 44th Bomb Group in World War II: The 'Flying Eight-Balls' over Europe in the B-24*, which was published in 2003.

Technical information regarding the B-24 was obtained from Hess, Johnson, and Marshall's treatise on *Big Bombers of WW II*, published in 1998. Early information on the Indianapolis Motor Speedway was verified by Al Bloemker's *500 Miles to Go*, written in 1961.

McKee's later escapades, based largely on speculation, were woven into events known to have taken place in and around Cuba following WW2. These events are well described in Inigo Guevara's *Central and Latin America Database from 2003*, and Document 0156 in the Cuban Information Archives. Who else would be flying a B-24 from Miami to Cuba in 1947? Also assisting me with information-gathering for this story was the very knowledgeable nephew of Betty McKee, John R. Treat. Mr Treat, by the way, still has the flag presented to the family at Arlington Cemetery when Herschel McKee was buried.

Dedicated to Linda Jean McKee, daughter;
and Lynne Vittorio Olvey, granddaughter

PROLOGUE

The granddaughter tugged at the sleeve of the old man. Perhaps she should have punched him in the stomach, as he paid her no mind. He had arrived at the house the day before. The child's parents brought him home from the hospital where he had been for two months. As the girl looked at him, she noticed his mouth drooping some toward the right-hand side. Saliva wetted his chin. He didn't move his left arm at all, the one she was tugging on. They had placed him before the window of an upstairs bedroom in the small bungalow on the southwest side of Indianapolis. His left hand was resting on the wooden arm of the old wheelchair. His eyes stared west, out the rounded window overlooking the small garden. It had snowed earlier in the day, a freak mid-April storm. The sky was clearing now and a pink glow surrounded everything outside. The sun settled on the horizon. As the little girl watched intently, the old man's left eye suddenly appeared to sparkle a bit. She caught the hint of a smile. The old man slowly moved his good hand to grasp the girl's. Together they watched as the sun slowly disappeared and it turned dark.

PART
I
WORLD WAR ONE

Chapter 1

DOWNED OVER GERMANY

The pilot had been flying for nearly two hours. He was lost over Germany, not far from the French border. His goggles were forever fogging over. The air was thick, reminding him of his hometown in summer. He was sure he had seen shadows in the thin clouds above. There they were again. There were two, no there were three. Yes, three of them were flying east in a tight formation. They were flying slowly, unaware of the stalker below. He applied full throttle and began to climb as the German planes vanished into a more dense body of cloud. He wished his comrades were with him. It was still unclear how he had become separated from them. He checked his magazine and made sure the cartridge belt could run freely. His right hand gripped the powerful gun; he extended his index finger toward the trigger. He prayed the timing mechanism would not fail this time and cause him to destroy his own propeller. As the enemy planes broke into the clear he smiled, for he had guessed right. He was at their same altitude and within close range just behind them. He took aim and fired.

The plane to the right and just behind the leader erupted in flames and nosedived precipitously, trailing thick black smoke as it fell, first gently, then at a much steeper angle and with greater speed. *Number 11*, thought the pilot as he turned the gun's muzzle toward the plane to his left. He was spotted now and the advantage of surprise was gone. He fired a short burst and the second plane followed the first to the ground below. *Number 12!* By this time, the lead German had dived and turned his plane so that he was coming at the American from below and just ahead. The pilot went into a steep nosedive, to escape the attack. The strain on the wings pushed their limit. He leveled off in thick cloud at 8,000ft. The German leader was nowhere in sight. He breathed a sigh of relief and turned to head toward France, hoping to rejoin his comrades en route.

He hadn't gone half a mile when he flew into a barrage of heavy artillery fire. He grabbed the throttle, applying full power to the engine, and climbed to 10,000ft hoping to escape the lethal flak. The metal fragments hit him all at once, ripping through the canvas-covered port wing. A piece of the engine tore bone-deep into his left arm just below the shoulder. Blood spewed from the wound, covering the front of his flight jacket. Smoke and flames encircled the cockpit as the plane did a slow roll and plummeted toward earth. As he sped to his certain death, the pilot thought to himself *I sure hope to hell somebody was watching what I did today.*

He tried desperately to regain control of the plane. It wasn't possible. Catching a glimpse of the ground just before impact, he shifted his weight a bit and what was left of his plane leveled off as it crashed belly-first into a newly plowed field. Little of the plane was left intact as an old farmer pulled the body from the burning wreckage.

Chapter 2

A DAREDEVIL IS BORN

Herschel Jessup McKee burst feet first from his mother's womb on November 19, 1897. His initial screams could be heard clear to the end of the small city block on West Washington Street, near downtown Indianapolis, where his parents lived.

He was the second child born to James M. McKee and his attractive wife Laura Raiden McKee. James was a veteran locomotive engineer for the New York Central Railroad. Laura was a housewife. Mom and Dad soon realized that Herschel was not an ordinary child. He walked before he was nine months old, took apart fairly complicated toys and put them back together again when he was a year and a half, and was caught by the neighbors strolling down the street alone at the age of two. When asked where he was going he simply said: "Away."

Young McKee wasn't a sad child at all, he was just restless. Attention deficit disorder wasn't a diagnosis back then, but if any child had it, he did. He worshiped his father, especially loving the stories he told about the unique trips he had been on and the characters he had met. Like the time he drove the train over the mountains during a full-scale blizzard with Teddy Roosevelt on board. Young McKee especially liked his Dad's fancy uniform.

Herschel would often accompany his father to Union Station and was happiest when he was sitting in the cab of the mammoth black locomotive with a too big engineers' hat on his head. When James McKee wasn't working, he would hang out with his pals at the local firehouse. They would often talk for hours on end,

14

playing dominos, and drinking coffee. The firehouse was located just down the street from home, and young Herschel soon learned to ride his tricycle there to visit his Dad and the other men. He would listen intently as they told exaggerated stories of their various manly exploits. His mother offered little resistance to these forays, but did enlist the neighbors as "spies" to watch that young Herschel did not stray off course.

Grade school proved a major challenge to the young McKee. Often, in the middle of the teacher's instructions, he would leave his desk and walk obliviously over to the big window to peer outside. When angrily summoned back to his seat, he would reluctantly turn away with grand imaginings reeling in his brain of what might lay beyond the city's limits. His teacher would often remark to her colleagues: "That McKee child, he always seems to be somewhere else."

Grades were average for the most part, but he excelled in anything mechanical and took an early liking to history. Comments on his report card would invariably include "Fails to pay attention", "Seems bored", and "Often appears preoccupied". He would make the short after-school walk home much longer than it needed to be, often stopping to pick up odd-looking rocks or small creatures.

When he was ten he built a rudimentary car of sorts from old planking he found lying in the garage. He fitted a set of wooden wheels with hard rubber tires onto two wooden axles made from two-by-fours anchored to the frame. Propulsion came from a 2hp washing machine engine that his grandfather had given him. The steering mechanism he devised consisted of a piece of clothesline tied to each end of the two-by-four that acted as the front axle. The axle was anchored in the middle of the car by a three-inch steel bolt placed through the floorboard. Control of the vehicle was maintained by grasping the free end of each rope and making the car turn left or right by applying the appropriate amount of tension. There was no suspension and the throttle control was a piece of used fishing line strung from the motor's speed control mechanism, through a screw eye, to a block of wood hinged to the front of the vehicle that acted as the accelerator pedal.

Young McKee crashed his pride and joy on its maiden voyage. He was attempting a fast downhill run on the big hill the next block over. He lost control when he hit a bump. Becoming airborne, the car turned on its side, tossing him like a rag doll into a thick hedge, but not before he had first made hard contact with the cement curb. Luckily, he escaped with only a small cut above his left eye and a very large bruise on his buttocks.

Undeterred, he made repairs with the help of his uncle – his mother forbade his father to assist in any way. He fearlessly negotiated the hill a couple of days later, only to run afoul of the law. Zooming past the patrol car stationed on a daily basis at the intersection in front of his school, he was apprehended when the racer eventually lost steam and rolled to a stop. His parents were called. Herschel's creation was immediately impounded by Mom and Dad and the young daredevil was relegated to his bicycle with a stern warning not to pedal too far from home.

Boredom frequently haunted McKee by the time he was 16, especially during the gloomy and long winter months in Indiana. During that dark time of the year, he would keep himself occupied by reading stories of far-off lands, building small mechanical devices in his room, and listening to his Dad's tales during dinner. He became fascinated with man's ability to fly, having read profusely of the Wright brothers' early attempts at Kitty Hawk in 1903.

Rapid developments followed the Wright brothers' daring achievement and planes capable of much longer flights were now being built in both Europe and the United States. He read too about the developing war overseas. His father hated the Germans, calling them "Huns". The original McKees had immigrated to America from Scotland and still harbored a dislike of the early Saxons. Young McKee kept hearing rumors of American boys leaving home to join the war effort in France. He had also heard that some of them were actually being taught how to fly.

By this time he had also developed a fond eye for the opposite sex. Wishing to impress a couple of young ladies as they walked home from school one fine spring day, he made an attempt to ride his bicycle down the seven cement steps in the front of his house. The steps led to the sidewalk below. He reasoned that if he pedaled fast enough, he could easily negotiate the steeply inclined steps, ending up a hero and the object of affection of the girls on the opposite side of the street.

He confidently backed his bicycle up to the porch, leaving about 50ft of space to gain the speed he thought he would need. He began pedaling as fast as his 16-year-old legs could go and the steps approached with alarming speed. The girls watched in awe, their mouths agape as Herschel crashed big time. He somersaulted over his handlebars, forming a big "W" with his legs and arms. The girls were not impressed. As he lay unconscious and bleeding on the sidewalk, his mother came screaming from the house. Herschel slowly awoke, bewildered.

"Hi Mom, how did you get in my room?"

The girls hurriedly left the scene. Herschel was confined to his bed for two days by the family doctor. The diagnosis was a mild concussion and he remained generally sore for about a week. Unfazed by the incident, he was a handful to keep indoors. Little did his parents know, but uncalculated risk-taking would become his calling card for the rest of his life.

While recovering from his crash, young McKee began to

formulate a plan for his future. He hated school, seeing no redeeming value in attending class. He quit Manual Training High School against his parents' wishes in 1914 and began to search for a job. He felt ready to make his own way in life and that required absolute freedom, or as much freedom as one could have in the early 1900s. He set his mind in overdrive.

Chapter 3

LEAVING HOME

Herschel McKee truly loved his mother and father, but more than anything else he craved and needed adventure. The war in Europe, he figured, just might be the best way to create a little excitement in his life and to see the world. Talk of local boys leaving their American homes to fight for France and freedom had increased. McKee made his decision. Leaving no note behind, he stealthily climbed from his second-story bedroom window down a makeshift ladder in the middle of one particularly dark night. He briskly walked the two miles to Union Station, located just south of the city's famous "Circle", and, crouching in the dark shadows of the rail yard, he jumped a slow-moving freight bound for New York. For the first time in his young life he felt truly free. Letting out a loud war-whoop in the boxcar, he nearly exceeded the considerable clatter of the train's steel wheels, almost giving himself away.

McKee was nearly broke when he left home, having saved only $55 while working in the pass-book department of the National City Bank. He had no definite plan in mind, but was at least out on his own. He was gangly and a bit awkward, freckle-faced with ill-fitting clothes, and he looked the part of a hobo. He had "borrowed" a suitcase from his father and in it had placed a change of clothes, a shaving kit, a favorite picture of his parents on their wedding day, some dried beef and the wooden accelerator pedal off the car he had built. He kept his money in a small cloth bag tied securely to his belt. The bag was hidden by the length of his well-worn brown leather jacket.

The boxcar he was riding in was cold, musty and damp. It smelled a lot like the outhouse at the home of his grandparents. He shared it with four cows and a mound of hay. He shivered all the way to New York, where the train arrived sometime during the night. McKee jumped from the car as it slowed to a crawl, and, ducking the high beam of a powerful flashlight, he lit out across the rail yard into an unfenced field adjacent to the tracks. The field soon became wooded, and as he hiked into an area of more densely planted trees he could make out several male voices speaking in excited whispers. Not knowing what else to do, he bravely walked right in among the group of five youths roughly his own age.

Surprisingly, he was greeted warmly. The bedraggled band made room for him by the fire they had burning in the small clearing. He was offered a cup of steaming hot coffee in a dented tin cup and a bowl of stew made with some suspicious-looking ingredients. The five boys, like McKee, had all left their homes and were talking about going to Quebec to join the Canadian Army. Rumor had it that the French Canadians were sending troops to Europe in order to help France's fight against Germany. The small group of mercenaries talked well into the night. With virtually no sleep, they hiked into town at sun-up, heading straight for the docks and a steamer bound for Montreal.

The fare for the boat trip took the better part of his $55, but McKee had enough left over to buy some food and a heavy woolen sweater before getting on board. He had taken a particular liking to one of the other boys in the group by the name of William Hennessy. Will, as he liked to be called, was from Ohio, having grown up on a farm near Dayton. Like Herschel, he was tired of the Midwest's dullness and wanted to venture out on his own to see some of the things he had read or heard about, especially airplanes. The two boys combined their paltry resources at the dock and headed for the nearby recruiting station.

It was a pleasant day in Montreal and they marveled at the number of beautiful women walking through town alone. They entered the recruiting station and were warmly greeted by a uniformed receptionist. She led them into a small room. There they waited patiently for several minutes before a young male doctor finally arrived. Both boys were given a cursory examination and promptly rejected with no explanation given.

They would later learn that their respective parents had both alerted the authorities to their sons' attempts to gain freedom. Feeling little obligation to the parents, the Canadians rejected the boys from military service but did not offer to return them home. Returning them to their parents was not the responsibility of the Canadian government. Dejected but not thwarted, the lads headed back onto the street. Feeling uncomfortable in Montreal, partly because neither of them spoke any French, they returned to New York and eventually hitchhiked their way to Rhode Island.

Broke by this time, they went to work for the Colt Arms Company in Providence. Will had a cousin who worked there and he helped them land the jobs. McKee and Hennessy both had the attraction to guns that was so common among young boys, and assembling small arms for Colt paid reasonably well. Tales of the war in Europe permeated Providence as everywhere else, and the boys remained determined to somehow get over there. They rented a tiny flat near the Colt factory and it was there that each lad lost his virginity.

Susan and Mary waited tables at the diner across the street from the Colt factory and were enamored with the boys' boastful tales of their future adventures. The twin sisters were the pretty and petite young daughters of the diner's owners, Walter and Maria Sullivan. The eating establishment was called Walt's Diner, and it was where the two boys ate most of their meals.

On a carefully arranged evening in early June of 1916, the

twins left work as they had always done right at closing time, but instead of going straight home they headed in the opposite direction, toward the boys' apartment. At dusk, they sneaked up the stairs and into the flat occupied by McKee and Hennessy. Its two rooms served the four of them well and this dalliance became a habit throughout the first half of the summer. All good things come to an end, however, and so did these escapades when the girls' father became suspicious about mid-July. His blood boiling, he formulated a plan to catch them in the act.

Walter Sullivan stationed himself beneath the stairs the following evening and waited for the twins to arrive. After allowing an appropriate amount of time to elapse, he burst through the front door with his Colt 45 pointing the way. At the sight of the four naked youths entangled in their ecstasy he became apoplectic. He mumbled incoherently while at the same time violently stomping his feet, then took aim and unloaded his Colt into the slowly revolving ceiling fan directly above them. Chaos reigned. Quickly untangling themselves the boys grabbed their clothes, dove for the porch, leaped the railing to the street below and ran as fast as they could in the direction of the trains.

Fortunately, they had each kept the money they earned in the bags tied to their belt loops, and between them there was enough for two train fares to New York with a reasonable amount left over. They made it to New York after a miserable night spent on the train. The space they were allotted was cramped and the old man next to them kept spitting tobacco juice into his shirtsleeve. The boys hit the wharf as soon as they arrived, looking for passage to Europe. The first night they met a man in a pub who suggested they make contact with the French Consulate. He said that he had heard the Consul General was helping young Americans leave for France to help fight the war. It would still be some time before America officially entered the conflict.

The two adventurers thanked the man, downed their whiskies like they had been drinking all of their lives, and headed for the Consulate. To their surprise, no questions were asked as they were handed fake passports and a booking on the SS *Santa Barbara* to Bordeaux. Once there, they would go to Paris and join the French Foreign Legion to fight against the "Huns", as McKee called them. Ultimately they wanted to learn to fly, and this, they were assured, was the necessary first step.

The trip across the Atlantic was pretty grim. All they could afford was steerage, and what with poor food, rats and North Atlantic storms the trip was miserable. A warning given by the Captain when they embarked suggested that there was also a threat of German U-boats possibly attacking, but most such activity had been further north, near the coast of Ireland. The crew did not appear concerned, which set most of the passengers' minds at ease.

McKee lost several pounds as they crossed due to a bad case of mal-de-mer. He was rarely far from the toilet or the ship's leeward rail. Upon arrival in France he tipped the scales at a scant 136lb. Hennessy didn't fare much better. When they disembarked they looked like two skeletons in dirty clothes. The *Santa Barbara* would later see service in the US Navy, bringing American troops back home when the "war to end all wars" finally ended. She was eventually sunk by a German torpedo off Honduras in 1942 while engaged as a passenger vessel plying the Caribbean during the next "great war".

With their money running dangerously low, the boys went straight to the French military headquarters in Paris. Even though they looked like a tragic end to a short life, they were welcomed into the Legion as infantrymen and hastily shuttled off to Algiers for basic training. The training was rapid and superficial, as troops were desperately needed on the front line.

Neither the Germans nor the French thought much of offense, causing the two armies to face each other defensively for years on end. Both armies were dug into permanent trenches and killing each other off at a rate never before seen.

McKee and Hennessy were returned to France after spending only four weeks training in Algiers. They were now referred to as "Greenies", and assigned to the Western Front and their initiation into what they hoped would be a marvelous experience. The boys were ready for some camaraderie and real excitement. They arrived at their assigned station in early fall. The dank and miserable trenches of a full-scale world war would be their home away from home for the foreseeable future.

Chapter 4

THE LAFAYETTE FLYING CORPS

McKee and Hennessy were each handed a uniform, a backpack, rations, a rifle, some ammunition and a rudimentary bit of additional training on how to survive in the trenches and what to do if they were taken prisoner. Before they knew it they were up to their eyeballs in thick, slimy mud. It was now late fall, and the warm spring and summer nights had long been replaced by nearly constant drizzle. The boys had to endure the cold winter darkness, an almost total lack of sanitation, a steady diet of cold rations, the nearly constant rain of artillery shells, and vermin. Worst of all were the vermin.

When the rats first came, the boys had fed them. Initially these feedings provided a bit of amusement, but they were a big mistake. Soon there were hundreds of the mangy pests scurrying into and under everything. There was no way to keep them out. They seemed to multiply exponentially and could fit into holes less than half their size. They ate everything that was unsecured. In addition to the rats there were the "to-tos". To-tos were a variety of squirrel. The only real amusement for the men in the trenches was to shoot to-tos. Some of these animals grew to an enormous size, the size of a large armadillo. Between the rats and the to-tos, sleeping was only manageable in short stretches. Sleep deprivation to the point of hallucinating became a way of life.

When they were not being shelled, the infantrymen took shifts staring through rolls of barbed wire at the enemy's lines in dreaded anticipation of the next attack. The enemy was less than

300 yards away. Grave-digging became their most frequent diversion and was rapidly becoming an almost constant pastime. The majority of the war's dead would come from the trenches. Depression quickly settled over the entire regiment.

What seemed like such a great idea back in Indiana and Ohio now seemed to have been a huge mistake. Water seeped continuously from the endless line of soggy sandbags used to fortify each trench. Nothing was ever dry. Constant sores developed on the boys' feet, a malady the doctors named "trench foot". Their joints ached incessantly. Maybe the Colt arms company hadn't been such a bad deal after all. Constant bickering replaced their usual good-natured joking around. It would not have taken much for either of them to shoot the other.

After a particularly rough period of not talking to one another for two days, McKee became aware of a steady drone in the air above them during a brief lull in the shelling. Rare for a French winter, the sky was crystal clear as he gazed upward. What he saw immediately set his mind spinning. There, right above him, were four beautiful biplanes flying in a tight formation. His buddy was asleep during this interlude so McKee rudely awakened him.

"What the fuck?" was the response.

"Look up there, Will, that's us!"

The boys inquired immediately and discovered that these planes were called Caudron G-IVs, the original planes of the famed Lafayette Escadrille. Each plane was adorned with an Indian head somewhere on the fuselage. An elite group of mainly American pilots, the Escadrille was formed through a combined effort of some wealthy Americans living in Paris at the time the war broke out, a handful of idealistic young American men and a few farsighted French officials. Originally named the Escadrille Americaine, the name was changed to Lafayette Escadrille. The name change was due to political sensitivities brought to bear on the United States by the German government, since America was not yet involved in the war. Germany was diplomatically, and wisely, trying to keep America neutral.

The Escadrille pilots were handpicked by the French Air Service and did strategic bombing runs as well as observation work. It had only been 13 years since the brief flight at Kitty Hawk, but rudimentary dogfights were already taking place. The planes were made of wood and canvas and could soar to heights greater than 15,000ft. The Lafayette Escadrille had 38 of these elite pilots and was considered to be at full strength. Turnover, however, was high due to the ever-increasing fatality rate.

The boys could not stop thinking about the Escadrille. As soon as the opportunity presented itself, they asked their commander if they could join the Air Service. Commander La Fontisee had taken an immediate liking to the boys when they arrived and told them he would see what he could do. The shelling, the cold and the rats continued unabated. It was during this period of constant misery that two other young men in an adjoining trench, very much like McKee and Hennessy, suffered a direct hit. They were blown to bits by an artillery shell. Blood and body parts showered the emaciated, sickly and dumbfounded Midwesterners. Their collective depression hit bottom. Food had become scarce of late, and both boys were suffering from high fevers they acquired the day before their mates were killed.

Rendered useless as infantrymen, they were thankfully dragged behind the lines by medics after the shelling ceased and transported by ambulance to the group's medical tent. There, they made a slow and agonizing recovery from a virulent form of pneumonia. Not expected to live, they had each been given the last rites by the unit's priest. A month later they were pronounced fit to fight and simultaneously received word they were being transferred to the aviation field near Avord.

Unable to hold back the tears, they hugged the medical staff, danced a little jig to the ragtime being played on the old gramophone, and quickly gathered what few belongings they had managed to salvage. They traveled by truck over picturesque French country roads, none having any resemblance to the rather stark roads McKee was used to back home. Some of the houses were still bedecked with leftover fall blooms. They traveled with seven other lucky recruits to the airfield. With little additional training, they soon found themselves working as ground crew for the Escadrille's pilots, far removed from the miserable trenches. Life for McKee and Hennessy was about to change significantly.

McKee, always the affable sort, met an American pilot within a few days of their arrival. The pilot's name was Mike Flynn and he agreed to give Herschel a shot at flying. McKee and his new best friend headed out to the flight line on one particularly cold and drizzly morning. Flynn painstakingly described the airplane's basic operations and showed McKee the controls. He was describing the plane as if it were a lovely woman. Each pilot in the Air Service was assigned his own airplane for the duration of his tenure and each painstakingly cared for his plane as if it were family.

The craft, coddled by its ground crew, was rolled into take-off position. McKee jumped into the front seat, grabbing the controls. He took off after some brief pre-flight instructions had been shouted by Flynn from the back seat. He had to shout loudly to overcome the roar of the engine. This was how you learned to fly while stationed in France during WW1. No formal training, just befriending someone who already knew the ropes, and off you went under their tutelage.

On his first attempt at landing, McKee managed to bowl over a brazenly daring French photographer who had moved in too close trying to get a good picture for the town's newspaper. The man's left arm was broken in several places and the picture was lost as pieces of the camera scattered in every direction. But McKee had performed well while he was actually flying so Lieutenant Flynn was able to get him assigned to the flying school. McKee said his goodbyes to Will and began to learn how to fly in earnest. Poor Hennessy had not yet developed a friendship with any of the pilots, but his time would come.

McKee was given his own plane on the first day of school. After only two flights with his instructor, he was allowed to go up alone. On his second solo flight he crashed again. This time he had forgotten to set a lever of some sort before landing and the plane did a slow somersault onto its back as it touched down. Only his pride was hurt and he was allowed to continue his lessons. The damage to the plane was virtually nil, and was easily repairable. He was back up the next day.

He gained competence quickly and was soon able to pass the first series of required tests. Designation as a French Air Service pilot followed and McKee received his coveted wings. He took the time to write his first letter home. His mother, describing the letter to an Indianapolis reporter, said that it "bubbled with brashness, enthusiasm and self assurance". In it, McKee described how he had gradually improved his flying skills and that he was now "ready to seek out and kill the Boche", a disparaging term used by the Allies for the Germans. He did not particularly want to kill anyone, but if that was what you had to do in order to fly then that is what he would do.

Upon receiving his wings, McKee was immediately sent on solo scouting missions over France and occasionally into Germany. He continued to improve and was soon asked by his superiors to enter the aerobatic school. This form of advanced flying was required before you could ever hope to become a designated fighting pilot. He had never been happier. He learned how to do nosedives, half loops, wing slips and barrel rolls, all maneuvers that may be required in a dogfight. He later told a newspaper reporter that learning barrel rolls was "no child's play".

He did so well in aerobatic school that his ultimate goal became reality. He was admitted with much pomp and circumstance into the famed Lafayette Flying Corps. With the original Escadrille at full capacity, the French funneled new, promising American recruits into several other squadrons that formed the official Flying Corps. Over 250 pilots would eventually serve France in this way.

The Lafayette Escadrille had been operating since April, 1916. It was now late spring of 1917. McKee was only 19 years old when he gained acceptance into the elite Corps and he was the youngest pilot in his squadron. New planes had recently entered the service. These were called Nieuports and each was equipped with a 110hp motor and improved climbing capabilities. A machine gun for the pilot was mounted on what was called the glare shield of the airplane. The gun's mechanism was timed so that the bullets would not hit the spinning blades of the plane's propeller, located in the direct line of fire. Repeated failures would eventually move the gun to the top of the wing with an extension into the cockpit for the trigger. Capable of 115mph, these planes could climb 1,000 to 1,300ft per minute. McKee was in ecstasy. He was assigned Nieuport number 24.

His squadron had originally been located in Luxeuil, France, but by the time McKee entered the service they had moved to Bar-le-Duc, an airfield closer to the front lines at Verdun. The Escadrille pilots were provided with the best aircraft and equipment available. The accommodations for the pilots were also a major step above life in the trenches. McKee was placed in a luxury hotel and assigned a staff car and driver to take him to and from the airfield for his missions and training exercises. The pilots referred to their planes as "machines". Each pilot was assigned his own machine and a crew of three dedicated mechanics. The pilots were allowed to adorn their machines with whatever personal insignia they desired and paint them whatever color took their fancy. McKee chose dark blue and silver.

To be designated as a fully trained fighter pilot, it was necessary to pass a few more difficult tests. These consisted of one flight in a straight line to a distant point and return, covering a distance of at least 100 miles, then a second flight passing two designated points covering 200 miles. As a final test, you had to climb to 7,000ft and stall your machine followed by a full recovery. In addition, you had to again demonstrate your ability to perform the previously described aerobatic maneuvers. Once these three phases were accomplished you were designated as a "Fighting Pilot". Those chosen to be fighters were given the faster machines. They were also taught to shoot moving targets and small stationary balloons. This advanced training took the better part of six months. For McKee, the training was thrilling and fun. When the day's flying was over, or if you were weathered in, life on the base was one big party. Whisky and champagne flowed freely and hangovers were the rule.

One morning, feeling as if he was still three sheets to the wind, McKee went up to practice some difficult maneuvers. Shortly after take-off he developed engine trouble directly over the base. Smoke began pouring from his engine and it soon quit running altogether. The plane began a rapid nosedive. McKee was able to correct the plane's attitude, somewhat slowing the descent. The more gentle descent did not help his headache at all, and he crashed – for the third time – into a grassy field. The impact caused some structural damage to the undercarriage that upon inspection was deemed repairable. "Lucky" McKee, as he soon became known around the base, was spared injury once again.

Released from the medical station sporting a large ice bag on his head, he was pronounced fit to fly.

As far as McKee was concerned, life in the Flying Corps was nearly perfect. Unlike the soldiers consigned to the trenches, where all they saw was carnage, mud, rats and disease, the Flying Corps was a stage set for grand adventure. Parties were scheduled for almost every evening, beautiful girls were available, and the press was always clamoring for interviews. The pilots became local celebrities. It was still war, and death was commonplace, but none of them would trade it for the world.

Most of the crashes that occurred were tragically fatal, due either to structural failure, engine failure or a strategically placed bullet compliments of the German air force or ground artillery. Even so, not one of the French/American pilots thought it would happen to them. Most of these incidents were unwitnessed, so few of the pilots gave any serious thought to the not-so-unexpected consequences of flying wooden and cloth airplanes in combat 15,000ft over artillery-laden Germany and France.

An anachronistic form of chivalry and honor reigned among the pilots on both sides. Reportedly, the famous Red Baron once went in for the kill during a very intense dogfight. He could have easily shot down his adversary. Instead, he saluted the surprised American pilot because the poor guy's machine gun had jammed. The Baron did not consider it sporting to shoot at a man whose equipment was not performing properly.

Sadly, and often, one's buddy simply did not come back. Fighting pilots to a man exhibited the fatalistic personality seen throughout history among thrill-seeking adventurers. The Roman charioteers had it, the fabled knights of old had it, and so did the early explorers. The prevailing attitude among men who willingly and voraciously challenge death on a daily basis is simply that it was not going to happen to them.

McKee, in his second letter home, said: "The only things we can hunt over here are Boche, and they are getting scarce. I attacked a Boche the other day and he fell too far behind his own lines for the observation post to see it, so I did not get credit for bringing him down. A few days latter I swooped down on a German battery and emptied my 500 rounds on them. Forget me, as I am old enough to take care of myself. Don't be afraid of any Germans as they are a mere trifle."

The letter was signed "Herschel J. McKee, Sergeant Pilot Aviator".

New planes to replace the old arrived almost daily, giving the base at Bar-le-Duc a Christmas-like atmosphere. The latest plane added to the squadron was the SPAD. Faster, more sturdily built and supposedly more – but actually less – maneuverable than the Nieuport, the SPAD was reported by McKee to hit speeds of over 190mph in the air and would land at nearly 90mph. He also said: "It flew like a streamlined brick."

Interestingly, the first SPAD was delivered not to the French Air Service but to Italy, in March of 1917. It was presented to the famous Italian ace Francesco Baracca. It was from the logo of a black horse on Baracca's plane that Enzo Ferrari would later adopt an almost identical prancing horse for his famous fiery red racing cars.

Bar-le-Duc was routinely described by the media as a modern-day Camelot, with the pilots playing the part of the knights. When not engaged in battle or on some other mission they were free to do whatever they wished within the confines of the base. Visitors were allowed on a daily basis, so it wasn't long before McKee met his second female companion. Her name was Saloua, a French girl of Moroccan descent. Her skin was the color of dark caramel, and at six feet she seemed to tower over McKee, who was only five feet ten. A year older than he, she fell for his good looks and his devil-may-care attitude. To be having an affair with a member of the Flying Corps was quite a feather in one's bonnet.

When not flying, the pilots enjoyed playing cards, drinking, dancing, and sex – not necessarily in that order. Herschel and Saloua became a hot item on the base. Baby Herschel, another nickname given McKee because he was the youngest of the Escadrille's pilots, was making some of the old guard quite jealous. Fights rarely broke out in the Corps, however, as life on the base was just too good.

Throughout the Corps' history, only one of its pilots was ever asked to leave. Bert Hall, one of the 38 original American pilots, has that dubious distinction. Prior to being dismissed, Bert shot down four enemy planes – only one short of Ace designation – but reportedly he was just too much of a braggart and basically a pain in the ass to be around. He did not fit the one for all, all for one code of conduct enjoyed among the other pilots.

Much of 1917 was taken up with becoming a fighting pilot. By mid-summer, McKee had developed his skills to the point that he was allowed on sorties with the other fighters. His first battle mission was in August. He and three other pilots were sent over the Lorraine front. They had a marvelous flight but saw no Boche and returned to base dejected. McKee longed for his first "kill".

On January 27, 1918, that opportunity presented itself. He and four other pilots were flying a sortie just over the German lines when they encountered a group of six German Albatrosses. A raging dogfight ensued. McKee later described the fight as "a real mix up" and "the most nervous I have ever been". He placed several rounds into one of the German planes after sneaking up on the unsuspecting pilot from behind a large cumulus cloud, attacking from the rear being the preferred method of killing.

The German plane spewed the customary billow of black smoke as it nosedived into a nearby forest.

McKee was later informed that not only had he killed the pilot but he had killed two passengers as well. He would go on to shoot down four more planes witnessed by observers. History will say that he destroyed another seven that went unwitnessed. McKee certainly deserved the moniker "Lucky", and his life did seem to be charmed. He was the youngest American pilot to achieve the designation of Ace, and was still in one piece after crashing three times, having suffered nary a scratch.

By the winter of 1918 the war had really picked up. Battles were being fought on several fronts. America was in the war now, and had established its own group of combat squadrons. Famed auto racer Captain Eddie V. Rickenbacker had arrived in the spring of the year and was engaged in battle as soon as the Americans could get their hands on some machine guns. Weapons and supplies had lagged woefully behind America's official entry into the war – the American Air Force arrived ready to fly but in need of ammo and guns. Rickenbacker was a member of the famous Hat-in-the-Ring squadron and would eventually become America's leading Ace. He would shoot down 26 German planes and be called the "Ace of Aces". He and McKee would cross paths in the very near future.

As the war escalated, casualties rose, and the mood around the base took on a much more somber tone. Several of the elite pilots had been lost, including McKee's old friend Hennessy and his original instructor Flynn. Some of the stories surrounding these deaths were so gruesome that each pilot asked for, and was issued, a handgun to carry in the cockpit. The idea was that one could end one's life quickly rather than be burned alive in a fatal crash or taken prisoner and tortured by the Germans. The frolicking, pampering and heavy drinking that had gone on almost non-stop during the early days of the war had now basically ceased. Everyone involved was getting exceptionally war-weary and frightened.

On February 8, 1918, McKee took off with three of his buddies on a routine sortie over Château-Salins, south of Metz. The day was partly to mostly cloudy. The mission was the usual one, to seek out and destroy as many enemy aircraft as they could find. The men were cruising at 8,000 feet, enjoying the control they had over their machines. The enemy was nowhere to be found. Less than an hour into the flight McKee became separated from the other pilots. He had lost them in a particularly thick bank of clouds and was trying to find them when he caught the hint of a familiar shape in the corner of his eye. It was the shape of the new German Fokker.

The War Department sent a man to Indianapolis with the grim news: "Your son, Herschel McKee, was shot down over Germany and killed in action. He is a hero of the war and an Ace. The Commander in Chief wishes to express his sincere condolences to you and your wife during this time of grief and sorrow. Let us know if you have any questions or needs."

The man turned sharply and walked away. Laura McKee sobbed hysterically and James hugged her tightly, saying: "He was a good young man, my dear, and we can be very proud of him."

Chapter 5

INCARCERATION

McKee woke up in a German hospital nine days later. He was under heavy guard. He spent six weeks in bed nursing several injuries, including a moderately severe concussion. He was in a deep coma for the first two days. Shrapnel was still embedded in his arm and it was horribly infected, constantly draining foul, yellow pus. It was a miracle he was alive. He had received quite good care from the physicians and nurses.

He learned that the farmer who pulled him from the wreckage had brought him by horse-drawn cart to this hospital, where he was admitted and placed in a single room to die. A nurse by the name of Anne passed the room one day as she completed her morning rounds and realized he was beginning to stir a little. She noted that he was attempting to care for himself in a primitive and feeble sort of way. His tenacity caused her to take him on as a personal project and he began a painful recovery. He did what Anne told him to do and progressed slowly. It wasn't long before he took a more than a casual interest in Anne.

The Germans had other ideas. When he was well enough, he was marched out of the hospital and taken on a forced tour of Germany, paraded about as "a horrible example of what Americans looked like". This degrading method of embarrassment was frequently used by the German authorities to boost citizen morale while at the same time humiliating the enemy. McKee felt like a sideshow performer.

He was paraded barefoot in what was left of his tattered uniform through most of Germany's principal cities. When his feet were ground nearly raw by the pavement, he was given Dutch-style wooden shoes to wear. He was described in the German press as "a damnable American in a French uniform". Back home his parents were still dealing with the horrible news. They were only partially relieved when the French government eventually informed them that he was reportedly alive, but in a German prison camp, his condition unknown.

He spent time in at least five different German prisons. During his incarceration he saw many prisoners shot to death for merely hinting about an escape. Undaunted, McKee managed a near escape on one occasion. He teamed up with the famous polo player, Tommy Hitchcock, and the two of them managed to break through the wire fencing surrounding their prison. They were found by dogs three days later, hiding under a loading dock without food and with only a small quantity of saved rainwater.

Following his recapture McKee was sent to Bastatt Prison, where he was placed in solitary confinement and fed only bread and water for more than a week. He never found out what they did to Hitchcock. The only reason he wasn't executed was the fact he was a pilot. Celery soup was eventually added to his diet but not before he lost so much weight that he looked like a skeleton. He slept on a wooden platform and was given only a thin sheet of tissue paper to use as a blanket. The nights were cold and he was constantly shivering. There was nothing to wash with and vermin were everywhere.

He tried in vain to ignore the body lice that invaded his skin. There was no light in his cell so he never saw the myriad of other creatures. He only heard and felt them crawling incessantly about. He was eventually placed back in regular confinement and on that very day witnessed the horror on an Italian officer's face as he was shot to death while trapped in barbed wire during a failed attempt at escape through the prison's perimeter.

McKee remained under lock and key for nine more months. He lost a total of 56lb but never lost his resolve. He felt as if he was constantly sick but was afforded no medical care. Fevers came and went. Every day was the same. The prisoners were allowed out of doors for only an hour a day. The rest of the time they were confined to their cells. They were allowed to read but there were only a few books, mostly written in German. McKee couldn't stand it; he built up his strength as much as he could and planned another escape.

The prison he was in was located relatively close to the Swiss border. The grounds were surrounded by a rusting barbed wire fence and patrolled around the clock by armed sentries. When outside in the yard the prisoners were shackled in lines of ten or more to discourage any thoughts of escape. The prison itself had been hastily constructed of brick and wood taken from dilapidated homes soon after the war started. The entire place had literally been thrown together in anticipation of a German victory.

For more than a month, McKee painstakingly chiseled away enough mortar in his cell to loosen an area of bricks large enough to squeeze his now very thin body through. He used a flat piece of steel he had found in the yard. He waited patiently until just the right night. If he failed this time, a public execution in the yard was inevitable.

The perfect time came on a cold drizzly night with ghost-like patches of fog drifting about. The floodlights surrounding the field had suddenly grown dark, the result of some massive electrical failure. The guards making their rounds had just passed McKee's cell when the lights went out. Mass confusion reigned in the yard, centered about the main electrical box. McKee summoned all the courage he could muster, remembering the agony on the face of the entangled and dying Italian officer, and launched his daring escape.

Two weeks earlier, a local repairman had inadvertently dropped a pair of shears from his wagon as he was leaving the facility. No one noticed them fall to the ground. They landed right at McKee's feet. He had been briefly freed from his shackles earlier to do some trimming of a tree in the yard whose branches threatened the phone lines. Dropping from this tree as the repairman lumbered by, he hastily bent over, grabbed the shears, and pushed them inside his tattered flight jacket. Moving swiftly, he was not detected. He stuffed the shears halfway into his pants and managed to walk almost normally. He faked a limp to escape discovery as he was re-shackled to his group and returned to his cell. Walking past a couple of inattentive guards, he thought to himself that they must be nearly as miserable as he was.

With his opportunity now at hand, McKee quietly removed the bricks he had loosened, exposing just enough of an opening for him to wriggle into the yard. Using his elbows, he dragged himself to the rusted fence about 30 yards away. He was repeatedly stabbed by the shears stuck in his pants. Once during his arduous crawl he had to flatten himself beyond what he thought possible and lie perfectly still as the now functioning beam of the searchlight passed dangerously overhead. When he reached the fence, he cautiously withdrew the shears, being careful not to reflect the searchlight. He cut the barbed wire as rapidly and quietly as he could, and, pushing himself through to freedom, he took off at a dead run and kept running until his heart begged him to stop. He spent the rest of the night on the ground covered with wet leaves.

He was awake before sun-up the next morning and took off running again. He didn't hear any dogs so he felt he was in the clear. The only food he had managed to take with him was some hard biscuits he had stuffed in his pockets. He had collected these over the past two weeks and they were full of mealworms. For water, he drank out of the several small streams he encountered as he ran. Miraculously he remained undetected and reached the Swiss border tired and tattered on the third day.

He rested for a bit and then made his way to a road he hoped would lead to a safe haven. He had walked for about two miles when an official-looking vehicle came squealing round the bend before him. His urge was to run back into the woods, but he stood still instead, his heart pounding, seeming to clog his throat. The vehicle was Swiss. The guards almost fired at him as he slowly raised his hands in surrender. He was saved only because one of the guards recognized the tattered jacket of the Lafayette Flying Corps.

He climbed into the truck laughing and was warmly received by the Swiss troops. They were anxious to hear where he had come from and what he had been through. He told them of his daring escape. Their collective mouths dropped. The coffee and fresh biscuits they provided hit the spot. Lucky Herschel McKee had survived yet another one.

He was briefly interrogated by Swiss intelligence personnel and then transported to a nearby United States Army base. Once on the US base, word quickly spread that he was alive and well and had managed to escape a German prison. A letter was sent to his parents from the War Department. Tom Connolly, one of the pilots on McKee's ill-fated mission, was chosen to pick him up and fly him back to Bar-le-Duc and a hero's welcome. Saloua met him at the plane. Their embrace lasted a full five minutes before McKee was whisked away on the shoulders of his fellow pilots. The bar was opened early that day and within an hour not a single pilot was fit to fly.

At the celebration, McKee was introduced to "Ace of Aces"

Captain Eddie V. Rickenbacker. The two hit it off immediately. They promised to look each other up in Indianapolis if they survived the war.

Three days later the war ended. The date was November 11, 1918. Twenty million people had died in the war. The German, Austro-Hungarian, and Ottoman empires had all fallen. A revolution had enveloped Russia. With the exception of money and lives, the net effect on the rest of the world was nil. The turning point in the war, and victory for the Allies, was attributed to the involvement of the United States. The 269 members of the Lafayette Flying Corps had shot down and destroyed 199 German aircraft. Their reputation as superb, brave, and flamboyant pilots was so widespread that news accounts after the war revealed as many as 4,000 other pilots falsely claiming to have been in the famous Corps.

Every day the war was fought, 5,000 servicemen had died. One-third of all serving American pilots were killed. Old military tactics, formations, and attitudes on both sides would be laughable if it were not for the tragedy inherent in all wars. Tremendous advances in technology took place during the destruction. The airplane, the submarine, the machine gun, poison gas, hand grenades, and flamethrowers were all introduced on a large scale during World War One, thus providing a clear explanation for the huge loss of life.

For his heroic service, Lucky Herschel McKee was awarded the French Medaille D'Evade, the Croix de Guerre with four palms, the Combat de Voluntaire, the Croix de Combat, the Lafayette Medal, the French Victory Medal, and the highest award given by France for valor, the Medaille Militaire of France. McKee bid goodbye to Saloua and left for the United States by ship immediately after the armistice was declared.

PART

II

THE SPEEDWAY YEARS

Chapter 6

A Lifestyle Emerges

McKee went straight home to his family following the war. His parents still lived in the small bungalow on West Washington. The seven cement steps had cracked a bit, but otherwise things looked much the same as they did when he left. He arrived just in time for the holidays and for a while was comfortable and happy to be back. He was welcomed as a war hero and spent much of his time telling people what it had been like "over there". He was not one prone to embellishments, often somewhat droll. Even so, the truth was thrilling enough. The fact he made it home at all seemed a miracle to most who listened to his tales.

Winter was spent renewing acquaintances, telling war stories, and looking for a job. He wasn't sure what to do with himself. By this time he was thoroughly bored. He scoured the newspaper ads, listened to his parents, who desperately wanted him to return to school, and spent a lot of time just nosing around. For him, a return to school was out of the question. He now thought of himself as a man of the world, a kind of soldier of fortune. What could he possibly learn in school? Nothing in Indianapolis seemed to strike his fancy.

Then one day, in the early spring, he rode his bicycle out to the famous Indianapolis Motor Speedway. Rickenbacker had mentioned it to him when they met in France. The Speedway was now almost nine years old. The track had been conceived by a fellow named Carl Graham Fisher, an entrepreneur and former bicycle racer who envisioned a facility that would allow car companies to test cars at speeds not allowed on the nation's highways. Indianapolis was the hub of the American automobile industry at the time, with Duesenberg, Cord, and Stutz all being built there. Fisher felt he could make the track profitable with an occasional automobile or motorcycle race to supplement the almost year-round testing by the automobile industry.

Opened in 1909, the first race at the Speedway was held on August 19. Summer in Indiana was usually hot and sticky and this summer was no exception. The main event was a balloon race with a short five-mile automobile race thrown in as an afterthought. It took only two laps around the mammoth facility to cover the five miles. The car race, as a consequence, lasted less than 15 minutes. It was won by Louis Schweitzer, a driver of considerable note.

Even though short, the race was a disaster. The surface of the track broke into large clumps almost immediately and indirectly caused the deaths of two drivers, two riding mechanics, and two spectators. No one was safe anywhere near the racing surface. Consequently spectators were not seen in great abundance. Undaunted, Fisher continued to host both motorcycle and automobile races, but with only limited success. Always the visionary, he now conceived the brilliant idea of staging one truly big race each year instead of the multiple small ones he was currently promoting. He planned to make the event international in scope and therefore attract all of the world's most famous racing drivers. He would have to spruce the track up a bit and improve spectator safety, but it could be done.

The Indianapolis 500 Mile Race was born two years later. It was an instant success. Over 80,000 spectators jammed the mammoth facility for the first spectacle, held on May 30, 1911. Word of the big race soon spread throughout the world. McKee heard about it while he was stationed in France. The famous French driver André Boillot, a fellow member of the Lafayette Flying Corps, went on and on about the race during one of their evening binges. Eddie Rickenbacker likewise expounded on the event during McKee's "return from prison" party.

McKee turned his bicycle right, off the now famous stretch of 16th Street that parallels the short chute between Turns 1 and 2, and pedaled through the main gate of the Speedway. He immediately fell in love with the place. The track was rectangular in design, not really an oval, with four distinct turns separated by two long straightaways and two short ones. Each turn was banked 9° 12′. The entire 2.5-mile track was paved with large, red bricks. McKee could easily picture himself racing there in spite of the fact that he had not yet driven an automobile. As he was riding around marveling at the facility, he ran into a man who introduced himself as a racing driver. The man lived in a small house just down 16th, and invited McKee to his home for lunch.

McKee ended up spending most of the afternoon listening intently as the man talked about how dangerous and exciting automobile racing was. Indianapolis, it turned out, wasn't the only racetrack around. Tracks were being built all over the country. While the Speedway was paved in brick, most of the other tracks were either dirt surfaced, or paved with wooden boards. The board tracks were usually built as high-banked ovals and were much shorter in length than the super speedway at Indianapolis. The thrill level at these smaller tracks was just as high as in Indianapolis, said the driver, and so was the death rate. They were often called "splinter tracks" or "bull rings". McKee asked the man how he could get started.

"Look me up in May and I'll introduce you around," stated the young Howdy Wilcox.

All McKee could think about during his ride back home was the big race in May. As a practical matter he still needed a job, and luckily managed to land one the following week at the Stutz Automobile Co. Located on the near west side of Indianapolis, the Stutz Co built racing cars in addition to some of the finest road cars of the day. Word of McKee's war exploits had helped him land the job, and the bosses agreed to support his burgeoning racing career. McKee kept himself busy working, and the year flew by. He quickly learned to drive, being taught in a Stutz roadster by one of the company's pretty blond secretaries.

On May 1, 1919, the famous track opened for practice for the first time since the armistice. In 1916 the race had been shortened to 300 miles in deference to the war, and it was cancelled altogether in both '17 and '18. This year's race was renamed the "500 Mile Liberty Sweepstakes" as a tribute to the US servicemen who had fought and lost their lives in World War One. On the first day of practice McKee was at the track just after sun-up. Again he ran into Howdy Wilcox, who told him that the best way for him to get started in racing was to become a riding mechanic.

Later that same day McKee fortuitously bumped into his old flying comrade, André Boillot. As luck would have it Boillot was without a riding mechanic, having just arrived from France. He offered McKee the position on the spot. McKee told him he had never done it before and Boillot said not to worry, he would show him all he needed to know when he got in the car. Boillot was lead driver for the famous Peugeot team at the time, having performed well in Europe the previous season.

McKee shrugged his shoulders and told the Frenchman he guessed if he could learn to fly, he could certainly learn to be a riding mechanic. At least this would get him in the race. The press referred to riding mechanics as "mechanicians". The name sounded good to McKee and he told everyone he knew that he was going to be a "mechanician". His parents weren't thrilled.

The riding mechanic's job was primarily to maintain the fuel pressure in the engine. He did this via a hand-pump located on the side of the car. In addition he acted as a lookout, provided balance if needed and, if necessary, would occasionally climb out of the cockpit to make rudimentary repairs while the car continued to race. For a thrill-seeker like McKee, this was a great job.

Riding mechanics and drivers shared equally in the risk of death and injury. It was not uncommon for a hapless mechanic to fall out of, or off of, a car at speed while performing his duties. This made him a sitting duck for other speeding racers. Through 1937, riding mechanics and drivers were level-pegging when it came to being killed at Indianapolis. This, of course, did not deter McKee. He was once quoted in an Indianapolis newspaper as saying: "If it goes fast, I damn sure want to be in it."

Boillot and McKee qualified next to last for their first race together. Race day was to be May 31. At the start of the race they were nearly overcome by the choking cloud of engine smoke as 31 other cars expelled their exhaust gases in front of them. McKee's observational skills were immediately called into play due to the poor visibility. Their dismal qualifying time was not at all a reflection of Boillot's driving ability, nor was it due solely to the car's performance. The track conditions had progressively deteriorated during the day, and were exceptionally poor by the time Boillot made his qualifying run due to the accumulation of oil spilled by earlier drivers.

The two men found themselves passing cars at will after the third lap. They had reached the top 20 on lap 45 when two cars suddenly collided in front of them. The crash was in Turn 3. Well-known driver Arthur Thurman swerved to avoid the two crashing cars as they attempted to regain control. He failed, and went headlong into the wooden retaining wall that surrounded the track. His car erupted in flames and both he and his riding mechanic, Nicholas Mollinard, were killed instantly. Boillot and McKee continued their charge unabated.

On the 97th lap, American driver Louis LeCocq had his gas tank explode on the main straightaway. Flames engulfed the cockpit and both he and his riding mechanic, Robert Bandini from Los Angeles, were also killed in the ensuing fire, both men burned beyond recognition. The team of Boillot and McKee continued to improve their position and moved into third with only five laps remaining. McKee was beside himself with glee. Covered in oil and rubber, all you could see of either man was his toothy smile.

Fate intervened on lap 191. Boillot, pushing too hard, lost control of the Peugeot in Turn 2. The rear right wheel collapsed under the pressure, causing the car to flip upside down. Both occupants banged their heads together as the car rolled over again. It then slid on its side for nearly 100 yards before finally careening over the wall in flames. Seat belts were non-existent in the 1920s, not coming into play until the 1960s. As a result both drivers were ejected as the burning car sailed over the fence, saving them from being burned. They landed spread-eagled on the ground. Miraculously, neither of them was seriously hurt. In those days it was actually better to be thrown out of a crashed car than to stay in it. Like being dumped from a motorcycle, as long as you were not run over by another vehicle or thrown into a solid object you could fare pretty well.

They were awarded 15th place for their effort, as only 14 cars finished the grueling race. No prize money was given for 15th. Asked by his family if he wanted to do it again, McKee's reply was a quick "You betcha!"

The race was won by new acquaintance Howdy Wilcox, who was also driving a Peugeot. His share of the $50,000 purse was $20,000, a lot of money in 1919. McKee didn't really care that much about the money. He had a good job with Stutz, had no big financial obligations, and he was able to satisfy his thrill-seeking cravings. After the race he and Boillot sadly parted company. Boillot went back to race in France, where he was quite successful and a real celebrity. McKee went back to testing cars for the Stutz Co.

He was part of a team of young, single men hired by the company to try and destroy its cars. The wannabe race drivers would take the company's new models out after hours and drive them as hard as they could on some of the deserted roads around Indianapolis. They would mercilessly try to break them. Frequently they had great success. The management at Stutz could think of no better test for their automobiles than to have these young men play racing driver with their cars.

When not testing new models for Stutz, McKee would spend time on his newly acquired Harley-Davidson motorcycle, a pastime he shared with his father. Ignoring his mother's pleas, he soon mastered wheelies, slides, and jumps. It wasn't long before he booked himself as a one-man motorcycle thrill show at the Indiana State Fair. To awe the crowd, he would ride his bike over a homemade wooden ramp just under five feet tall and crash through a flaming wooden wall. Several crashes and a few minor burns had occurred while he experimented with just how thick to make the wall, and out of what kind of wood. Once he had it perfected, the show caught on and became one of the highlights of the Fair's midway.

All thrill shows of this type need a pretty girl and McKee's was no exception. The girl's name was Susan Donovan. McKee had met her at a party thrown by some of his buddies following an evening of car testing. She had ebony hair and was pleasantly rounded in all the right places. Her job was to throw water on any fires ignited by McKee if he happened to crash while going through the flames.

Standing ready, she wore a sexy low-cut dress with the hemline just above the knees, a very risqué outfit for Indianapolis in 1919. A gramophone would play a military build-up and McKee would take off for the ramp dressed in patriotic attire. This very effective entertainment model would form the basis of motorcycle thrill shows for decades to come.

After the show, the daredevil and his able-bodied assistant would go get ice cream and then relax either at his house or hers. Both of them still lived with their parents. This arrangement was not conducive to intimate encounters and because of that the young couple grew quite frustrated. McKee began looking for his own place. He soon found a small single-story home not far from his parents. He was comfortable that it was far enough. Susan helped him pick out the furniture and they began a steamy live-in relationship.

Still only 21, McKee had done more in the short time he had been alive than most men did during their entire lifetime. Even so, he was not at all ready to settle down. Far from it. He craved adventure and thrills as much now as he ever did. He grabbed Susan after work one day and told her they were headed to California. She wasn't hard to convince. He wanted to find a permanent position on a racing team. Stutz management supported the famous war ace and told him that a job would always be waiting when and if he ever returned.

Susan's parents weren't too thrilled with the announcement, even though McKee was a war hero and would be looked upon as a fine catch for their young daughter. Reluctantly, they acquiesced. McKee's parents had already given up trying to keep him contained so they simply wished him well. After all he had been through, in his mind at least, he was as much an adult now as any man could be.

The young couple left for California the next morning. It was September, and racing in the Midwest was finished for the year. Everyone involved in the sport had left for the West Coast and the winter season there. If McKee was going to land a racing job, he too would have to head west. The two young lovers packed the dilapidated Ford truck they had just purchased with what few belongings they had, strapped the motorcycle down in the bed, and took off on Route 40 headed toward St Louis.

Chapter 7

MARRIAGE

Herschel and Susan ran out of money somewhere in the middle of Missouri. They hadn't reached Kansas yet and already they were scrounging food from whoever would give them something. State Fairs everywhere were finished for the season and the weather had turned much colder, making the motorcycle useless as a money-maker. When life looked its bleakest the two bedraggled travelers happened upon a sign advertising for a pilot. It read: "Pilot Needed. Must fly sober. No dependents. Good living to be had."

McKee made a sharp turn off the main highway onto a rutted dirt road that led back to a rickety old farmhouse. He pulled the truck up at the porch, raising a thick cloud of dust as he did so. An elderly man appeared from inside and introduced himself as Clem Higgins. He wore bib overalls and a red flannel shirt. The air was dead still, allowing the man to blow a couple of perfect smoke rings from his corncob pipe. He glared with suspicion at the young couple.

"Howdy! I just saw your sign."

"Yeah," said the man.

"I'm a pilot, just got back from the war."

The man looked at the pair, smiled a bit and said: "You're hired, son."

Higgins invited the two travelers inside and offered them some lemonade and a piece of cherry pie. He said he had an SE5 airplane, the only one in the United States. He went on say it was built in 1916 by Curtiss Aircraft from a British design and that he couldn't fly it any more due to his failing eyesight. He said he needed someone to keep the business going.

"As a barnstormer, it's a great airplane, reliable as they come."

The man told McKee he could take it anywhere he wanted as long as he made some money with it. McKee could keep 30 per cent of the take and send the rest back. When he was tired of it, he could turn the plane back in and be on his way.

It took McKee about two seconds to say yes. He and Higgins drew up an agreement and signed it with Susan as the witness. Feeling some much-needed financial relief, the pair decided to accept Higgins's kind offer to spend the night. They would take off for California early in the morning.

After a simple dinner of pork chops and corn-on-the-cob, the two travelers had a meeting of minds. They decided that she would drive the truck while he did his best to fly directly overhead. They would stop to take passengers for rides if and when the opportunity presented itself. Barnstorming was a big draw in those days, allowing the general public a chance to experience the thrill of flight – if they were brave enough. Barnstormers frequently crashed with the inevitable results.

Herschel and Susan, following a rowdy night in bed, left for points west after a large breakfast of country fried steak, biscuits and gravy. They thanked Higgins profusely, hoping to see him again before too long. The plane's engine started right off and McKee taxied from the barn onto the grassy strip separating two cornfields. Higgin's wife had died unexpectedly the year before from a massive heart attack, leaving him alone on the farm with only a few chickens and two cows to take care of. Unlike his airplane, the farm was in miserable disrepair. An old tractor, missing one of its wheels, sat next to the barn, the axle propped up on a small stack of logs. Weeds grew everywhere. McKee waved goodbye to the old man as the wheels of the biplane left the ground. He circled and picked Susan and the truck up about two miles down the highway. Their destination was Los Angeles, California.

Business was good for the couple through Kansas and into Colorado. The weather held for the most part and McKee found several small towns with suitable landing strips to ply his newfound trade. As he flew into a town, he would do a couple of snappy barrel rolls, gun the engine, and then fly as low as he dared over the town square to attract a crowd. Everyone from children to grandparents wanted a ride. He would often accept gasoline in lieu of cash to guarantee a full tank when he left town. Higgins was faithfully mailed his rightful share of the take. Things were going exceptionally well until the couple hit the rugged mountains of Colorado.

The weather had taken a sudden turn for the worse with an early snowfall grounding McKee in Denver while Susan had two flat tires in the middle of nowhere just short of the city. Night was nearly upon her and things were looking grim. Luckily, a Mexican truck driver happened along with a load of old tires. He sold her two of them and helped her get them onto the truck. She was able to meet up with McKee at a small airfield on the east side of town just before dark. They spent the night huddled together in the cab failing to keep each other warm. Both bordering on hypothermia, they headed south at first light toward Colorado Springs and hopefully warmer weather.

Taking the longer southern route, the two still planned to be in Los Angeles by Christmas. There was little chance to make any more money except in New Mexico, where they experienced a streak of really good weather and did quite well. The plane continued to perform flawlessly and Susan had no further difficulties with the truck. McKee landed in Los Angeles, with Susan following close behind, on December 1, 1919.

After securing the plane, they went straight to the Los Angeles Speedway. McKee's game plan was to talk to anybody that would listen and hopefully get a ride lined up for the next year's Indianapolis 500. All of the nation's top drivers were there in preparation for a fledgling series of races scheduled for the board tracks of California during the winter. The races held to date had been a huge hit, attracting very large crowds.

Susan went with him as McKee combed the garage area. He talked to the likes of Jimmy Murphy, Tommy Milton, and Gaston Chevrolet. They already had their riding mechanics signed up. Getting discouraged toward the end of the day, he was turning a corner for the parking lot when he ran smack into a driver by the name of Roscoe Sarles. Sarles was a fellow Hoosier, having been born in New Albany, Indiana. He was a very promising driver and had won his first three races that year. He had previous experience racing for a short time in Europe and had gained a reputation as a steady hand at the wheel.

Older than McKee, Sarles had come into some good financial backing while in California from a wealthy man by the name of Bandini (not related to the mechanic of the same name killed at Indy in May). Sarles had ample sponsorship money behind him, but had not yet been able to secure a ride for the 1920 race. He and McKee struck a chord right off. Sarles had heard good reports about McKee from André Boillot and agreed to let him be his riding mechanic for the big race as soon as he secured a ride. They shook on the deal and Herschel and Susan headed back to Missouri.

They dodged several snowfalls along their way and made it back to Higgins's home with enough money to go on to Indianapolis in reasonable comfort. McKee thanked Higgins over and over for the use of his airplane. After some more country cooking, he and Susan jumped in the truck and headed for home. McKee drove the whole way with Susan curled up beside him asleep.

It was another long Indiana winter with no warm days until mid-April. McKee took up where he had left off with Stutz and Susan got a job as a waitress in a small diner downtown. The idea of marriage came up as both parents were having a difficult time with the live-in arrangement. Living in sin, as Susan's mom called it, was just not done by proper people. Plans for a wedding were soon made. If Herschel was reluctant he did not show it.

The wedding took place in the Scottish Rite Cathedral on North Meridian Street, not far from the city center. Several racing people showed up along with some boyhood friends and immediate family members. The service was functional and brief, the way McKee wanted it, and the couple honeymooned in Carl Fisher's new hotel on Miami Beach. Fisher, continuing to venture where no one else had gone before, was instrumental in developing Miami Beach as a winter paradise. He built the hotel and adjoining casino there early in 1919. Several of the drivers had already enjoyed the hotel and were raving about it. Access to Miami Beach required traveling on Henry Flagler's railroad. One could get there by boat, but the route could be treacherous in winter.

Allowed only a week to frolic, the newlyweds were now at least legitimate.

May arrived and the famous racetrack opened for practice. The sprawling facility looked more like a massive park than it did a racing venue. There was a large expanse of grass, Midwestern green in color, dotted with trees. Some local citizens swore it was the greenest grass in the world. New whitewashed grandstands outlined the entire main straightaway as well as the first and fourth turns. Tall hardwood trees lined the backstretch. A five-foot wooden fence surrounded the track. The fence was perpendicular to the ground as it encircled the modestly banked turns, making it more of a ramp that a barrier. Errant racecars were easily launched up and over it, into the hinterland beyond. You could fit all of Vatican City, Churchill Downs, and several other sporting arenas inside the facility with room left over for the garage area.

Sarles had managed to garner a spot over the winter as part of Louis Chevrolet's seven-car team, one of the most formidable in racing. Chevrolet had been born in Switzerland in 1878. He moved to the United States in 1900 and began working as a mechanic, first for De Dion-Bouton, and then for Fiat in New York. While working at Fiat in 1905 he entered his first automobile race as a driver and won. In doing so, he set a new one-mile world record at the then blistering speed of 109.7kph. From that moment on he was smitten by the racing bug.

In 1906 he left Fiat to devote his time to building racing cars. Passenger cars bored him to tears. His first job was with a fellow named Walter Christie. With Christie, he helped design the first front-engine racer, called the "Big Bear". The car was only modestly successful. He continued to experiment with Christie but left him in 1911, joining up instead with a fellow named William Durant. Together he and Durant founded the Chevrolet Motor Company. Reportedly they tossed a coin to see whose name they would use for the company's title.

Louis was not the easiest person to get along with and soon got into an argument with his new partner over some design issues. He left the company in a huff. His name stayed behind, however, due to some complicated contractual verbiage. Durant would later expand the business to form a small company he would call General Motors.

Chevrolet, now working alone, concentrated his efforts on building his own signature racecars. He called them Frontenac Specials. He was one of the first car builders to use aluminum parts for weight reduction and he designed the first locking differential for the rear axle. His original racing team consisted of himself and his brother Gaston along with drivers Joe Thomas, Joe Boyer and Bennett Hill. In the 1919 500 Mile Race, Louis finished seventh and his brother Gaston finished tenth. The team was a strong favorite to win the race in 1920, having added both Sarles and well-known driver Art Klein to their already formidable line-up. McKee felt he could be on no better a team.

Memorial Day 1920 rolled around with the usual pre-race hoopla. Bands played, multi-colored helium-filled balloons were released, and the mayor gave a long-winded welcoming address. People from around the world were in attendance. Just before the start of the race, McKee was asked by a local reporter whether he had ever been afraid. McKee's answer was quick and to the point.

"Sir, a man in the air or in a racing car is too damn busy to be afraid."

The 1915 race winner Ralph De Palma was on pole in his Ballot Special, with Joe Boyer, the fastest of the Frontenac team, qualifying second. Louis Chevrolet qualified third, Klein was fifth, Gaston Chevrolet sixth, Sarles seventh, Hill eighth and Thomas nineteenth. McKee, as was his custom, jumped into the seat of the number 5 Gregory Special long before the drivers were summoned to their cars. He just couldn't wait to get going.

The race started with De Palma grabbing the lead. Even though it was a small field of only 23 cars, visibility at the start still approached zero due to the usual heavy cloud of exhaust smoke. McKee likened it to dogfighting in the clouds over Germany. Louis Chevrolet quickly passed Boyer for second, while Sarles tucked in behind Klein for fourth. Bennett Hill was behind Sarles. The race remained hotly contested throughout. De Palma continued to lead the early laps, with Gaston Chevrolet jumping into second by the halfway point when his brother Louis's car suddenly began to falter. Louis rapidly fell back to the middle of the pack, eventually dropping out of the race altogether.

On lap 54 disaster struck the Sarles-McKee duo. Sarles lost control while trying to pass Klein in Turn 4, and their car, with both men clinging to their seats, bore straight through the wooden fence. Splinters flew in every direction. Once through the fence, both drivers were ejected, landing on the grass in the usual spread-eagle pose. Once again neither man was seriously injured. Only their pride was dented as they were taken back to the garage area in an official vehicle. But it had been a good run while it lasted, and the two teammates decided to continue their partnership throughout the rest of the 1920 season.

The race was eventually won by Gaston Chevrolet, who passed a hapless Ralph De Palma on the 187th lap. For some inexplicable reason, De Palma's car burst into flames going down the backstretch. Rather than stop, the determined De Palma continued to race as his riding mechanic and nephew, Peter De Paolo, climbed out of the speeding machine's cockpit and crawled into the rising inferno. Kneeling on the hood, his hair whipped by the wind as the car faltered, De Paolo bravely fought the vicious flames with a small hand-held fire extinguisher. The over-cooked engine eventually sputtered to a stop, allowing Chevrolet the win.

No one died during the 1920 event and for that everyone was thankful. Gaston Chevrolet's win broke an eight-year foreign hold on the race. He was the first American to win since 1912. Sarles and McKee, licking their wounds, joined their wives afterward and headed straight downtown to seriously tie one on.

Chapter 8

BOARD TRACK RACING AND A
LOVE LOST

McKee continued to race with Sarles throughout the summer of 1920. When he wasn't risking his life as a riding mechanic, he was riding his motorcycle through flaming walls. When he wasn't risking his life on the bike, he was in the air flying the mail from Chicago to St Louis and back. He had taken on this additional job with the United States Postal Service on a whim. He flew a biplane similar to what he had flown in France. The pay wasn't that great but it helped defray some of his thrill-seeking expenses and it allowed him to fly for free. If the weekend weather was going to be good he and Susan would also barnstorm around central Indiana giving people airplane rides, having saved up enough money to buy the plane he had flown for Clem Higgins. Higgins had given up on his farm and moved into an apartment in St Louis. He and McKee would often dine together during mail-run stopovers.

Getting a license to fly for the Postal Service wasn't as easy as McKee thought it would be. When he flew for Higgins, he wasn't licensed; but Uncle Sam wanted him to be legitimate. McKee wrote a letter in April appealing to Indiana Senator Harry New. New was then Chairman of the United States Senate Committee on Territories. As the senior Senator from Indiana, McKee felt that New could convince the War Department to issue a flying permit without having him go through all of the hassle and red tape normally required. McKee, being a World War One ace, thought it beneath him to prove that he could safely fly an airplane.

He received a reply from the Senator on April 12, 1920. In his letter, the senator wrote: "There is no question at all in anybody's mind about the facts of your extraordinary record and service, and the War Department is only endeavoring to find a way to permit them to except their general rule in this connection and allow you to fly."

McKee's license arrived in the mail two weeks later. With the barnstorming, the racing, and the motorcycle thrill shows in full swing, McKee no longer needed his job at Stutz. He bid his buddies on the testing team farewell and he and Susan began a life filled with pure adrenaline. At least, it was for McKee. Susan mainly observed, frequently turning ashen as he went through his nerve-shattering antics.

Racing with Sarles was not too productive following the race in Indianapolis. Louis Chevrolet let Sarles go shortly after, feeling that seven cars were just too many to try to manage and campaign all season, especially following the extensive damage sustained at Indy. As a result, Sarles and McKee were left with various single-car entries fielded by low-budget operators. They bounced from one car to another with only limited success. Occasionally they would place in the top three at one of the lesser tracks, but they failed to win any important events. Breakdowns were frequent and they both became extremely frustrated. They parted company as good friends in the early fall, both seeking the change of luck that sometimes comes with a new partnership.

The State Fair season was closing down about the same time and the weather would soon turn colder. McKee and Susan packed up, closed their house and headed to California and the new season there. Life had been good and the young couple still appeared to be very much in love. Their trip to Los Angeles was uneventful and they arrived in early October. A big race was scheduled for the brand new Beverly Hills Speedway on

Thanksgiving Day and McKee wanted desperately to be in it. All of the top teams were entered. With only six weeks to go he was in a hurry to find a suitable driver.

The Beverly Hills Speedway was a new one-mile oval covered entirely with four-by-fours. Wood was cheap, and a board track didn't have the problem of dirt, and sometimes rocks, flying into the drivers' faces. Another problem inherent to dirt tracks was the constant dust cloud created by the cars. This and the ever-present exhaust smoke robbed spectators of seeing much of the thrilling in-fighting that occurred. Complaints to the promoters were frequent.

The Beverly Hills track was conceived by a man named Jack Prince. Prince purchased a burned-out lima bean field for $1,000 an acre and built a fine facility. The first race scheduled for the new track was to be a 250-miler. At the time, the wooden speedway in Beverly Hills was ranked second only to Indianapolis as far as racetrack amenities go. Seating capacity was in excess of 70,000 and every seat had an excellent view of the track. A crowd that big or bigger was anticipated for the first event, to be held on Thanksgiving Day.

McKee's only hope for a seat in the race was with a driver named Riley Brett. Brett was new to the game as a driver but was a well-known car builder. McKee liked him. Brett would be considered a "rookie" at Indianapolis come spring, but the gossip among the other drivers had him reaching elite status soon. These expectations were based on some stellar performances at the smaller venues.

The car they hoped to race was being built at Harry Miller's shop at the request of Kansas City oilman C. L. Richards. It was one of two so-called "Junior Specials", named after Richards's son. The engine, a Miller 181-cubic inch straight six, was reportedly the "loudest engine ever built". The two cars had not been very competitive in their first few races but McKee and Brett would at least have a ride if they could convince the owner to hire them. Richards, with little hesitation, nominated Brett to drive one of the cars.

Thanksgiving Day dawned crystal clear and the stands were packed with a rowdy bunch of racing fans. Ralph De Palma, Tommy Milton, Roscoe Sarles, Jimmy Murphy and Gaston Chevrolet were all entered. Brett and McKee qualified in the last row. The track was fast, with average speeds well over 100mph. That speed or more was required in the high degree banking simply to keep the racecar on the track. Any slower, and it would slip to the bottom.

Well into the race, Gaston Chevrolet, driving the Frontenac Special for his brother Louis, crashed into rival driver Eddie O'Donnell while vying for the same piece of track. Both cars ignited and then melded into one flaming amorphous mass. Nothing was left of either when the flames were finally extinguished. A pall came over the crowd as it was announced that both Chevrolet and O'Donnell were killed. O'Donnell's mechanic, Lyall Jolls, was tossed free from his car but died the next day in a local hospital from multiple internal injuries. Chevrolet's mechanic had been able to jump free before the cars collided and was uninjured.

The race was eventually won by Jimmy Murphy, driving car number 14. He had been dominant throughout the event and was a real crowd pleaser because of his daring maneuvers to get by his rivals. Brett and McKee had mechanical failure and failed to finish. Remaining optimistic, they would soon regroup and hoped to compete in a few more events in California before leaving for the Midwest and hopefully Indianapolis in the spring.

The color green had historically been avoided by many drivers, although the roots of this aversion are cloudy. Following this race, and the death of Gaston Chevrolet – one of the most accomplished and respected drivers of the day – in the dark green Frontenac Special, no one drove a green car at Indianapolis again until Britain's Jimmy Clark turned up in 1965.

Louis became disenchanted with automobile racing following the death of his brother and withdrew all of the Frontenacs from further competition for the rest of the California season.

Attendance that day was announced at more than 80,000 people, a new record, but in spite of continued large crowds the glamorous facility was destined to last only three more years, as the land was soon deemed more valuable than the events held on it. It was closed in 1924, making way for the posh new Beverly Wilshire Hotel and the glitzy Hollywood lifestyle that soon followed.

Board-track racing was at its zenith during the 1920s. Racing on public roads was logistically difficult, dangerous to spectators as well as the participants, frowned on by the politicians, and did not generate large enough revenues for the organizers. Stopping gate-crashers was also a difficult task. Spectators in America continually complained that spread-out road-course layouts didn't allow them to see enough action for their money. The closed course, action-packed board tracks seemed to be the answer for both promoters and fans.

Board tracks were normally a mile to a mile and a quarter in length, and each track would usually hold several events a year. Spectators could see around the entire track and the promoter enjoyed having the audience essentially held hostage, greatly adding to his concession revenues. It was because of these board tracks that oval racing became the predominant form of motor sports in the United States and remains so to this day.

A typical wooden track required several million board-feet of lumber to build and lasted an average of only three years. The problem with longevity was the rapid deterioration of the wood.

Treated lumber did not exist then, and the exposure to high speeds also took its toll. The boards would first soften and then decay from wear and tear as well as from infestations of various insects. Eventually the boards would begin to break up. Drivers were often pelted with nails, pitch and small pieces of wood as they rocketed around these highly banked tracks. Driver Eddie Miller was quoted in Griffith Borgeson's *Golden Age of the American Racing Car* as saying: "You used to get hit with some terrific blocks and knots of wood. We all came in with pieces of wood bigger than kitchen matches driven into our faces and foreheads. They'd go in, hit the bone and spread out. Then you had to remove them, of course."

Brett and McKee didn't do well as they continued to campaign in California, losing to better teams at every venue. Thankfully they managed to stay injury-free. When McKee mentioned going back to Indianapolis, Susan balked. She desperately wanted to stay in California for the entire winter in order to avoid another long siege in Indiana during its gloomiest time of year. That sounded like a good idea to McKee. They rented a house in Newport Beach and decided to do nothing constructive until their money supply became critical.

During the winter, McKee had a lot of time to think. One thing was for sure. At some point, he wanted to become the driver. Drivers received most of the accolades when a team won while the riding mechanics often received much of the blame when they lost. The fans were there primarily to see their driving heroes and McKee was getting damn tired of sitting by helplessly while the car he was in crashed. He had been watching his various drivers closely, learning something from each one of them. He felt that if he could settle down with one really good driver for an entire season he could learn to do the job just as well. He began to search for a driver to act as his mentor. When the time came, and he thought that he was competitive enough, he would then tackle the much more difficult job of convincing some owner that he was worthy of driving his car.

The other idea pestering him as he enjoyed the surf, sun and fun of southern California, was really pie-in-the-sky. He harbored a desire to fly across one of the two great oceans of the world with a passenger, preferably a female passenger from Indiana. If Lindberg was going to go around the world alone, he could do it with someone who was simply along for the ride. He envisioned a contest, for women only of course, to select the first person to be carried across the sea by air. Susan would be the most likely choice, but in all their days of barnstorming she had never once wanted to fly. He promised himself a look into the idea as soon as he returned to Indianapolis.

The McKees waited until the middle of April to return home. He had promised Brett that he would stick with him at least through Indianapolis. They didn't expect much of a result and they were not disappointed. Brett qualified 16th in the 23-car field and crashed on the 91st lap having never been in contention. They were awarded 15th place. McKee and his driver were out of the money again. They parted ways immediately following the race.

On his own again, McKee spent another summer flying the mail, crashing his motorcycle and taking people for airplane rides. He kept busy trying to kill himself and put his dream of flying to Europe on hold. His immediate plan was to hook up with a really good driver for the winter season. He heard a rumor that an old friend from Missouri, Frank Elliott, had split up with his mechanic and was looking for a new one. Elliott had never raced at Indianapolis as a driver, but the word around the garages was that he was quite talented. Before becoming a driver he had served for more than a year as Barney Oldfield's riding mechanic.

McKee and Elliott met at St Elmo's Steak House on Illinois Street in Indy and put a deal together. To this day St Elmo's is still a favorite eating establishment among racing personalities. Elliott talked enthusiastically about driving a new car being built in California called the Leach Special. The chassis was being assembled by engine whiz Harry Miller specifically to house his newly designed power plant. The car/engine combination was reportedly nearing completion and would be race-ready soon. Elliott told his new mechanic that Mr Miller had recently been described in the media as "quite simply, the greatest creative figure in the history of the American racing car!"

Miller's customary method of operation was to incorporate his own automotive innovations into tried and true international designs. The engine he had designed in early 1921, that was being fitted into the Leach Special, was a twin-cam, four-valve straight-eight with 183 cubic inches that produced 185bhp at 4,400rpm. Miller called it simply the "183", and Jimmy Murphy had already won the 1921 French Grand Prix at Le Mans with such an engine in his Duesenberg. Miller planned to produce twelve 183-engined Leach Specials for the 1921 season. Elliott was fairly certain that he could get the nod to drive one of them at Indianapolis next spring. He and McKee finished their strawberry shortcake and shook hands on a deal that would form a partnership with the promise of great things to come.

The Leach Special was not going to be completed until October, causing McKee to confine his thrill-seeking to the usual pursuits. With his newly acquired and updated Harley-Davidson he could now reach greater heights before crashing through the wall of fire. A crowd-pleasing, no-handed jump had been thrown into his latest routine and he was considering the addition of a backward flip, much to his wife's chagrin.

He had crashed so often trying to perfect the flip that he looked like the victim of a mugging. Susan was having more and more thoughts that enough was enough and began suffering feelings of impending doom, real premonitions. For Susan, it was only a matter of time before her husband finally did himself in.

McKee, trying his hardest to reassure her, would emphatically state: "I really do lead a charmed life, you know."

"You're the luckiest man alive and you know it," would be her reply. When particularly angry she would add: "You're loony, and you should have been killed long ago!"

Similar conversations were becoming more frequent in the McKee household. Susan watched day after day while her husband tempted fate with cars, motorcycles, bicycles and airplanes. Her nerves were frayed.

"Herschel, why don't you quit all this crap and go back to Stutz?"

"Not on your life," he would say. "If they say it can't be done, I'm the one that can do it!"

Susan asked for a divorce in August. Taken aback at first, Herschel decided he had no problem with her request. *Hell,* he thought, *she wouldn't fly with him, he didn't want any children complicating his life, and there were plenty of other fish in the sea.* In fact, he had been spending a lot of time downtown at the soda shop lately talking to a delightful young girl named Betty. And then there was Liliana, one of the secretaries at Stutz; Rachel, the ticket lady at the Speedway; and Shelly, who worked at the tailors. A divorce was no problem for McKee.

He and Susan separated and the divorce became final in September. Their property was divided, with McKee keeping his toys and Susan getting most everything else. Their house was sold and the money was split evenly between them. Susan moved back in with her parents. McKee found an apartment close to the Speedway and began to entertain in earnest.

After a month of generalized debauchery, he received word from Elliott that the Leach Special was just about ready for delivery. He packed his stuff, deciding to fly Higgins's old plane to California. The trip would take him a couple of weeks, longer if the weather didn't cooperate. He wanted to stop by and see the old man one more time, then pick up Elliott, who lived nearby. The weather held and the newly formed race team, full of optimism, landed in Los Angeles on October 15, 1921. They headed straight to the Miller shop.

The Leach Special was a beauty. Every part of the car had been designed and built in Harry Miller's facility. Engineering drawings, as was Miller's habit, had been created for each and every part of the car. No one else did it that way. Even though he was not Italian, aesthetics were given top priority and his cars and engines were considered by many to be downright artistic. It was said that the assembly of each of his automobiles involved over 6,500 hours of labor. Not until Harry Miller was completely satisfied were his cars allowed into the hands of the crewmen. They were then tested and tuned to perfection at the nearby Beverly Hills racetrack.

The annual Thanksgiving Day race was only a month away and Elliott and McKee were eager to test their newly assigned car. They waited patiently while Miller himself painstakingly went over the finishing details. Finally, on November 1, they headed to the speedway. Racecars in general had been getting faster and there was talk among the officials of a new, smaller engine formula in the works in order to contain the speed. Elliott was anxious to get the car into some races soon, and hopefully into some money, before it became obsolete.

The Leach ran flawlessly as soon as it hit the boards. Elliot broke the existing track record by almost a second. He had to remind himself that there were going to be ten other cars just like it on the track before the week was over. Sure enough, by midday Tommy Milton arrived with his Leach and beat Elliott's time by two-hundredths of a second. It was going to be one competitive race. McKee couldn't wait.

After the test, Milton and his mechanic along with Elliott and McKee went to the quaint little speakeasy across the street from the speedway. There, they managed to get soused telling stories of all their near-misses, affairs and hopes for the future. More and more women gathered around the booth as the men carried on. This was not an unusual occurrence. Racing drivers and pilots were highly revered by the public in the 1920s. They were society's darlings. As a rule they dressed expensively, were clean-shaven, and had a charming, devil-may-care way about them. They looked and talked much like the movie stars of the day. Women were easy pickings for the "Speed Kings", as they were referred to by the news media. Pilots and race drivers, it seems, have had this attraction forever.

After an hour of carrying on, McKee announced to anyone who was listening that they should all go flying and view the lights of the city. It was a glorious night, it didn't seem to matter that the plane was stored several miles away. What did matter was the fact that he was trying to get a particular redhead into bed with him. Elliott, the most sober of the four, managed to corral the would-be flyers before disaster struck, convincing them all to go back to their respective hotels. There is no documentation as to what hotel McKee and the redhead returned to.

With the race now less than a week away, interest had picked up among the local media. A reporter for the *Los Angeles Times* by the name of Alfred Nielsen asked McKee why most of the drivers were also fliers? McKee explained: "A pilot has to have total concentration and a feel in the seat of his pants as to what the plane is going to do. He has to stay ahead of the airplane. It is no different when driving racing cars. You are going so fast there is no time to think about anything else. If a driver reacts to a loss of traction after the car has already changed direction, it is too late. He has to anticipate that he is going to lose control before he actually loses it in order to survive."

Explanations like this enthralled a populace that was still largely on horseback.

The LA racetrack opened for practice the day before Thanksgiving. A large crowd was on hand, with sunny and mild weather promised for race day. Qualifying was held, and McKee's old driver and close friend Roscoe Sarles took the pole position in his Leach number 6. Milton was second in number 2, while Murphy and De Palma made up the second row. Elliott and McKee were on the outside of the third row, qualifying sixth.

The times were very tightly bunched. McKee felt confident that he had finally hooked up with a driver and car combination that would be in the money. His confidence was rewarded. They didn't win the race – it was won by Eddie Hearne in a Duesenberg – but they finished third. In so doing, Elliott set a new one-lap track record of 107.3mph toward the end of the race. In the money and greatly encouraged, the team prepared for the next event, scheduled for December 11 in San Francisco.

The San Francisco Speedway was another of the California board tracks that routinely entertained crowds of more than 70,000. Elliott qualified the car well on Saturday morning and he and McKee planned to celebrate by having dinner and a couple of drinks in town before getting to bed early. They promised each other they would be in bed by 10pm. McKee meant well when he made the promise, but he happened to meet a young socialite in the pit area toward the end of the day. He drove her to the airport after the final practice period and gave her a quick ride in his airplane. They took in the sights of San Francisco Bay on a spectacularly beautiful sunny afternoon. Getting her into bed after the flight was not difficult.

McKee woke up in the girl's apartment at 6am. He was due at the track by 7. Hurriedly dressing, he bid her a quick goodbye and raced to the track, arriving just as Elliot pulled in.

"Get a good night's sleep Herschel?"

"Excellent!" he replied.

The cars were marshaled on the grid, lining up behind the Auburn pace car. More than 78,000 race fans were on their feet in anticipation of the start. Everybody that was anybody was in attendance. Several in the crowd had made the arduous trip from Los Angeles, including some famous Hollywood stars, Douglas Fairbanks among them. As usual, McKee was in the car before the command to start engines had been given. He ran through his usual checklist, anticipating a tough race but with realistic hopes of finishing up front.

Elliot jumped into his seat just before the start of the pace lap. You could cover the field with a blanket as they charged out of Turn 4. Only the first two rows were visible to the audience as the rest of the field was enshrouded by smoke. Elliott craned his neck, eyes focusing through goggles that were already coated with grime. McKee leaned out dangerously from the cockpit, his head only inches from the track's surface as he peered at the cars charging behind them. The green flag dropped.

Jimmy Murphy jumped into the lead with the rest of the field tightly bunched. Early in the race, Elliott, still in sixth, was forced to steer high to dodge an eight-inch hole in the track, not an uncommon maneuver on the boards. The hole had appeared sometime during the weekend and had not been a factor when he qualified. He lost six positions fighting to maintain control of the car. Now running in 12th, he began a charge for the lead. McKee had never seen such determination on a driver's face. Elliott was pushing the car to the limit. The strain on the drivetrain and tires was palpable.

By lap 78 the relentless duo had moved into fourth. As they entered the treacherous North turn, McKee heard a loud *crack* over the growl of the engine. Simultaneously, he felt a shudder rock the chassis. The car skidded wildly. His eyes were glued on the rapidly approaching guardrail as they slammed head-on into it. Splinters of every size filled the air. The still speeding racer dismantled more than 50 feet of fence and flames erupted as the fuel tank exploded. Witnesses gasped in morbid horror, knowing full well that the driver and his helpless mechanic must be dead.

Gradually, the smoke cleared and the debris settled. What was left of the car dangled precariously from the racetrack's edge. It was teetering on the rim, 50 feet above the ground. The engine, torn completely from the chassis during the crash, lay smoldering in ruin at the bottom of the track, the crankcase impaled by a large four-by-four. Eventual winner Jimmy Murphy and runner-up Tommy Milton narrowly missed the engine as it slid ominously across the track in front of them. The huge crowd was hushed. Within a few seconds some of the fans could be heard cheering. The cheering soon grew into a loud roar as two figures clad in white drivers' suits arose ghostlike from the smoking wreckage.

Coming quickly to his senses, McKee had realized that a large piece of fence rail was lying on the racing surface, threatening oncoming drivers. He grabbed the still dazed Elliott by the arm, and the two men pulled the obstruction out of harm's way. Unaware that he was bleeding profusely from a deep gash in his leg, McKee then knelt on the rim of the track to hold what was left of the Leach Special from toppling to the ground below. He was eventually relieved by two stunned security guards who had witnessed the entire incident up close. He and Elliott then rose slowly to their feet to painfully stand together and shake hands at the top of the racetrack. The roar from the crowd could be heard many miles away. McKee had somehow escaped death again.

Elliott and his seemingly charmed mechanic were driven back to the pits by an official car and spent the rest of the day and early evening reliving their big crash with the media. The young socialite had wiggled her way into the throng of newspapermen and would sooth McKee's aching body over champagne and caviar at her place for the rest of the night. In the morning, he and Elliott were at the Miller compound lobbying for a new car. They were optimistically planning an assault on the world closed-course speed record at a nearby track in early January.

Chapter 9

SUCCESS AT LONG LAST

A brand new Leach Special was built and presented to Elliott and McKee shortly after the first of the year. They tested it in Los Angeles in preparation for their assault on the record. Cotati racetrack on the outskirts of Santa Rosa in Northern California was the venue chosen for the attempt. Another of Jack Prince's creations, Cotati was an oval a mile and a quarter in length, with the turns banked a steep 38°. The highly successful track opened in August of 1921 and was operational through 1924, when it was torn down to make way for a more profitable egg farm.

Arriving at Cotati toward the end of the month with their new Leach Special in tow, Elliott and McKee stopped for fuel just short of their destination. While filling the tow-car, the racecar and their spare gas cans they replaced the spark plugs and made some minor adjustments to the engine. McKee asked the station attendant if he had any of the newfangled high-octane fuel recently made available in some parts of the country. The man said no, so they filled their tanks with the regular brand of gas. Weight conscious, they were careful to add only enough fuel necessary for the record attempt. They finished the short drive to the track, planning to leave the car there. McKee told the old man who acted as caretaker to watch over it closely during the night.

Word of the two daredevils had preceded their arrival, and a throng of well-wishers, as well as some local media, jumped them at the hotel. They answered the usual questions: Why do you do this? Aren't you afraid? How fast is too fast? The questioning went on well into the evening. The same questions are frequently asked of racing drivers today. McKee gave simple, one-line answers:

"I do it for the thrill."

"No, I'm not afraid."

"You can never go too fast."

Elliott and McKee finally begged to be released. They hadn't eaten since breakfast, and both men were starving. The certifying team from the AAA (American Automobile Association) had arrived earlier in the day and had prepared the track for the record attempt. It had been carefully cleaned and repaired where possible. Several holes were patched with new wood and the timing lines were carefully laid out. The weather forecast promised a cool, dry, sunny day, perfect for high speeds.

Each man slept soundly and was at the track just before sun-up the next morning. For once Herschel behaved himself, having gone to bed at 8:30. Several townspeople arrived with picnic baskets full of pastries and beverages of one type or another. The certifying team was making last minute preparations and McKee and Elliott were entertaining some young ladies in the garage area. The promised weather was good, with the temperature in the mid 50s. The cool air was conducive to higher horsepower from the engine. The driver and his mechanic made sure the press knew about their inability to obtain the new high-test gasoline, planting that bit of information in their minds as a plausible excuse if they failed to set a new record.

At 11 o'clock the engine was started. Elliot pulled onto the track and made two moderately fast warm-up laps. McKee checked all of the gauges and listened intently for any unusual noises. The engine sounded powerful. After the warm-up lap, a brief stop was made in the pits to ensure there were no leaks and that the tires looked good.

The official, timed lap was to be the third time past the starter's stand. Elliott stood on the gas. The car leaned into the corners with a bit of flame erupting from the exhaust. All eyes followed the brave twosome as they blistered the track. They roared past the timing line. The crowd erupted in loud acclaim as a time of 38.4 seconds was announced. A new one-lap closed-course world record of 117.6mph had just been set. There was immediate speculation by the press that if the new high-test gas had been available they would have easily been over 120, a speed never before thought possible on a closed course of any length.

The new car was truly awesome. The two men hit the town in celebration following a quick debriefing with the press. 1922 promised to be a good year. They parted company the next day, with Elliott returning to his home in St Louis. McKee returned to Beverly Hills for the remainder of the winter, but not before visiting Indianapolis to check on his property and catch up on personal business. While there, he talked Betty – the very attractive waitress who had been much on his mind lately – into going with him to California. He and Elliott planned to meet up again in April for a race in Los Angeles and he was sure she would enjoy it. They would return to Indianapolis in May.

When he arrived in Indianapolis, McKee was surprised to find himself more famous than previously as a result of the new speed record coupled with his miraculous escape from certain death in San Francisco. Even though he was just the riding mechanic, his endless ability to remain alive brought him great notoriety, at least in Indianapolis. Betty was very proud of him and jumped at the chance to go off to California.

The couple headed for Los Angeles in mid-February, flying Clem Higgins's old airplane. It still performed well, and McKee could make some money barnstorming along the way. His personal appearance had matured considerably since returning from the war and he was developing a definite movie-star look. Charismatic and fearless, he had no trouble finding willing passengers. Betty was a good sport and didn't mind the constant stream of young beauties that enjoyed Herschel's piloting. She was along for the ride and happy to get out of Indianapolis for a time.

McKee missed his motorcycle back home and purchased another Harley soon after they arrived in LA. The coast highway offered a challenging drive while providing several good lodges to spend some quality time with Betty. McKee would also take Betty on frequent, hair-raising rides to the top of Mount Wilson – the more frightening the ride, the more she seemed to like it. Betty's real name was Mary Elizabeth, much too long for McKee. He liked her good nature and willingness to share in his high-risk life style.

"A girl like Betty was someone a man could stay with for a long time," he once told Elliott.

Elliott arrived in Los Angeles along with the winds of March. The Leach Special had been pampered, cleaned, caressed and tuned during the winter. They tested her at the speedway and pronounced her ready to race. The event on April 2 was only a short 25-miler but all of the top drivers were entered. Elliott and McKee took the checkered flag handily. It was McKee's first win.

The duo were seemingly on a roll. The 500 Mile Race was just around the corner and they were looking forward to a successful run. While McKee waited, California, with its endless variety of leisure activities, had become one giant playground for him and Betty. They had managed to cover most of the state on the new motorcycle, finding their favorite spot to be Carmel. On a whim they took up horseback riding along the beach – neither of them had ever been on a horse before. They raced each other in the surf, McKee falling off only once. They would return home in the evening, nearly exhausted, and Betty would make a quick dinner, followed on most evenings by a romp in bed before they fell asleep in each others' arms. McKee, of course, had no interest in golf, the predominant Carmel pastime. "Too time-consuming," he would say.

The winter went by quickly and they left for Indy on April 15.

Chapter 10

THE GOOD LIFE

In May of 1922, Indianapolis was undergoing some needed change. The city's leaders announced the annexation of a beautiful residential area on the north side they called Broad Ripple, balancing the city's expansion in all directions. Future novelist Kurt Vonnegut Jr was about to be born, prohibition was in full swing and Elliott and McKee were busily preparing for the big race as soon as they hit town. Rumors over the winter had Jimmy Murphy putting one of Harry Miller's successful new "183" engines in his Duesenberg for the 500. A Miller "183" with Tommy Milton the driver had won the 1921 National Championship in a Duesenberg, and a dozen cars had been built with this engine for the 1922 season.

Frank Elliott and his mechanic Herschel McKee were fortunate enough to have one in their Leach when they won their first race together the month before. They were now concerned that the Duesenberg just might be a better car. Jimmy Murphy had garnered international acclaim with a "Duesy" in July when he became the first American to ever win the French Grand Prix at Le Mans, and he was putting a "183" in this very same car for Indianapolis. The "183" was without a doubt the hottest engine going. McKee, ever the optimist, kept telling Elliott not to worry, that they could beat Murphy with their eyes closed.

Qualifying day rolled around and sure enough Jimmy Murphy placed the Miller-Duesenberg on pole with an average speed of 100.5mph for the ten-lap run. Duesenbergs managed to take the top three spots on the grid. Elliott and McKee qualified a respectable eighth, beating out such notables as Tommy Milton, Howdy Wilcox and Peter De Paolo. The only other driver that concerned McKee in the race was his friend Roscoe Sarles. Sarles qualified sixth in a year-old Frontenac. Still confident, McKee dismissed Sarles's performance as some sort of aberration.

"Find a good place to watch the race, Betty, because Frank and I are going to kick ass!"

It wasn't to be. Murphy basically ran away with the race from the start, beating Harry Hartz in another Duesenberg by almost four minutes. Elliott and McKee took 16th, falling out of the race on lap 195 with a broken differential. They did beat Sarles, who had a connecting rod break on lap 88. He finished 23rd. McKee was out of the money again. Even so, he still had faith in Elliott and felt he had learned much from him during the month. The two of them debriefed after the race, deciding that their car was much better suited to the short tracks that made up the majority of the season. They planned to carry on undaunted.

With rarely more than one race per month in those days, drivers had a lot of free time to do other things. The weather in Indianapolis during the summer wasn't all that bad. There were many hot sunny days and warm nights for the pursuit of happiness. Herschel and Betty took advantage of the warm weather and free time to travel the state, putting on their motorcycle thrill show and giving plane rides whenever they could. With Herschel's charm and Betty's looks business stayed good.

In May, McKee was introduced to famed boat racer Gar Wood, who was attending the 500 Mile Race as a guest of Barney

Oldfield. The two men took an immediate liking to one another. Wood loved airplanes and speed and was a daredevil himself. He was born in Indiana and began his boat-racing career as a young boy in paddle-wheelers with his father, after moving to Minnesota. He built his first racing boat in 1910 and with it started a career of international boat racing that spanned the years from 1917 to 1933. Wood won the American Gold Cup four times as a driver and the European Harmsworth International Trophy eight times. It was often stated that the key to his success was largely his use of aircraft engines. "More reliable," he said.

Between races in July, McKee and Wood, along with their female companions, took a weekend trip to Lake Wawasee in Northern Indiana. A haven for gambling, drinking and general carousing in those days, Wawasee was a favorite place to relax and let one's hair down. The Lilly pharmaceutical family built an enormous compound there, as did many other influential Chicago and Indianapolis residents. The beautiful and expansive glacial lake was an ideal place to open the throttle of a brand new speedboat.

The two couples enjoyed a thrill-packed weekend, buzzing the lake in one of Wood's racy new runabouts. The boat could exceed 50 miles an hour, thereby striking terror into the fishermen and day sailors who frequented the lake. Tearing into a small bay in the middle of the afternoon on their second day, they nearly capsized a trio of unsuspecting local fisherman, their wake swamping the tiny vessel as they passed within five feet of it. The fishermen could be seen waving their arms and mouthing words best not interpreted. Wood's long, sleek craft was powered by two big Allison aircraft engines. The noise was deafening, driving native birds en masse from their nesting grounds.

On Monday, Wood left for the Detroit Yacht Club, where he was commodore and was due to host the 1922 Gold Cup event. During their short holiday, Wood captivated McKee as he discussed the building of the world's fastest express cruiser. He called it the *Gar Jr II*. It was a 50ft, V-bottomed craft that would later become the model for the famous PT boats of World War Two. The first was built in 1921 and was made famous when Wood raced it all the way from Miami to New York. He beat the *Havana Special*, a passenger train of some note, in a match race for publicity. Wood's boat made the 1,250-mile trip in 47 hours 23 minutes, beating the ponderous train by more than 12 minutes.

Wood inspired McKee, starting him thinking about some design ideas of his own. He was sick of hearing about the deaths of fellow pilots when they crashed their airplanes, and lately he had started to worry about his own luck running out. He reasoned that if pilots could be saved by individual parachutes, why couldn't the whole airplane? If a plane could be equipped with one or more parachutes, it could return to earth gently in the event of an engine failure or some form of structural damage. He would have to get to work on that one.

In the meantime, there were still races to be run and fun times to be had. Betty constantly scoffed at most of his ideas, but McKee liked her spirit and her willingness to stick her own neck out with his. She was a good traveling companion and wouldn't fuss too much if he wanted the occasional man's night out. Herschel had been repeatedly warned by his buddies that "Sex is the game and marriage is the penalty." So far, he had been able to successfully avoid that subject with Betty.

Back in Indianapolis, Betty and Herschel began to plan for their winter in California. The western swing was to start earlier this year with a race scheduled at the Cotati track in Santa Rosa on August 6. Elliott entered the record-breaking car. Even though they had set the one-lap closed-course record earlier in the year, no one gave them much of a shot at winning a scheduled race there. The pre-race favorite as usual was the nearly unbeatable Jimmy Murphy. And if Murphy had trouble, Tommy Milton was lurking in the wings. Elliott, though a fun guy to be around and a good teacher behind the wheel, had not had a lot of success in his nearly nine years of racing. He'd had some early wins at small events back in 1914 and 1915 and there was April's 25-miler with McKee, but that was it. He was a steady driver, but had never really set the world on fire. Top-three finishes were rare. McKee remained loyal, however, thinking their day must surely be coming.

Newspaper articles at the time were praising racing drivers in general. They described their "nerves of steel" and explained that "they exhibited a courageous spirit of adventure". Some reporters began to take note of the physical attributes required to drive racing cars. They would mention the reflexes drivers must have in order to race at over 100mph just inches apart. The "Speed Kings" were getting as much publicity as the top entertainers of the day. Deep inside, McKee enjoyed the publicity. Outwardly, he would never let it show. In crowds, he would remain stoic, preferring to let others do the talking. He was no good at self-promotion, a fact that would cost him in the future.

The *San Francisco Chronicle* interviewed McKee in an article dated August 13, 1922, the week after the Cotati race. In it, he refused to talk about himself at all, stating instead that "Frank Elliott is the headiest and cleverest driver on the tracks today."

Elliott and McKee defied the odds makers at Santa Rosa by annihilating the field on race day. They broke the existing

100-mile race record during the first race, averaging just over 117mph. It was the fastest time ever recorded for a completed race on a board track, the best previous average having been 115mph. Spectators interviewed after that event were quoted in the papers as saying "no one will ever be able to go faster than that!"

Elliott and McKee, in fact, won both hundred-milers that day. The *San Francisco Chronicle* printed the following: "Along comes Frank Elliott and takes both races and makes the champion of 1921, Milton, and the leader for the 1922 crown (Murphy) look like amateurs." Their luck did appear to be changing. They basked in the limelight for an entire week in San Francisco, being wined and dined by some prominent local sportsmen. Although thrilled with their success, McKee was internally resentful of the attention Elliott was receiving. After all, was it not he that had kept the engine running at peak performance throughout the race, and was it not he who kept them out of at least two crashes with his timely warnings shouted above the noise of the engine? The itch to drive was spreading over him like a rash, but the opportunity just wasn't there, not now anyway. Consequently he did as much basking as he could.

After their week in San Francisco, Herschel and Betty took an excursion along the coast highway, stopping for a couple of days in Carmel. The next race wasn't until the middle of September so they had some time to kill. The two really did enjoy each other's company. Unlike Susan, Betty was adventurous. She loved riding behind Herschel on the Harley, a feat pretty scary in itself, and she was always egging him on to go faster. They had some close calls but never a big crash. She was beginning to think her boyfriend just might be charmed.

Betty lived an independent life of her own in spite of Herschel's desire for almost constant companionship. She harbored a desire to teach school one day and had recently begun a home study course. A teaching license could be hers within two years. She wasn't sure the two of them would be in any one place long enough, but she was determined. Their relationship continued to blossom as she maintained her petulant, sexy look, highly successful in keeping McKee's fires kindled.

Betty brought the subject of marriage up occasionally, but Herschel would promptly switch to some other topic, usually having to do with racing or flying. He would add the fact that his position as a husband would likely be transient at best considering his avocations. He liked the variety his lifestyle afforded and didn't want the burden of being tied down. Understanding what women were trying to say escaped him most of the time anyway. He and Elliott would spend long hours discussing the fact that men and women seemed to be from two different planets.

What irked McKee most was the fact that he always knew when Betty was upset about something, but when he asked her what was wrong all she ever said was: "Nothing's wrong, I'm fine. What's wrong with you?" A week or more would usually lapse before the truth would finally make itself known. When it did, she would erupt with a vengeance, usually at a time least expected, and often following an unexplained string of cold nights in bed. After such periods, he would appeal to Elliott: "You give 'em what they think they want, and then it's your fault they're not happy. They ain't logical, I tell ya."

These deep and profound discussions would often last well into the night. The conversation would invariably run full circle and the two racers would eventually decide to call it quits. They would toast the fact that life without women wasn't worth living and then stumble off to their respective homes. Betty was still great fun to have around and she satisfied any needs McKee had when it came to female companionship. Marriage was simply not in his long-range plans and his plans were not about to change, not right now anyway.

He and Elliott, brimming with optimism, headed toward Kansas City and their next race. Herschel promised himself: "From this day forward, I will keep any thoughts about how men and women might actually communicate effectively with each other out of my mind forever. Amen brother!"

Chapter 11

DEATH TOO CLOSE TO HOME

In 1922, Jack Prince was building racetracks for anyone who could come up with the cash and a parcel of suitable land. Kansas City, Missouri, was the latest town to get on the bandwagon. Their sparkling new speedway opened for business on September 16. The sprawling facility was built on swampy land not thought suitable for anything else. It cost over $500,000 to build, a huge sum in those days. The length of the track was a typical mile and a quarter and there was seating for 85,000 spectators. With a nearly packed house and the very intimidating 42° banking, the track looked from the air like a giant dessert bowl full of crawling insects. A state-of-the-art loudspeaker system was installed for the first race and there was a radio network similar to the one pioneered in Indianapolis for a lap-by-lap national broadcast.

Prince predicted speeds greater than 120mph. Entries for the inaugural event read like a who's who of racing: Jimmy Murphy, the 1922 AAA champion; Harry Hartz, the runner-up to Murphy at Indianapolis that year; Tommy Milton, the 1921 AAA champ; Cliff Durant, Roscoe Sarles, Al Melcher, Joe Thomas, Jerry Wonderlich and Elliott were all early entries. Barney Oldfield and Ray Harroun, the first winner of the Indianapolis 500, were honored guests along with the State Governor. The race was to be a grueling 300 miles. It promised to be very tough on both man and machine.

Word of the event spread rapidly. Even the *New York Times* had an article about the new track and the race. A purse of more than

$30,000 was promised, with the winner receiving $10,000. McKee could already taste the money. He and Elliott arrived at the track on Wednesday and painstakingly went over every square inch of the car. That evening they enjoyed dinner and several drinks with Herschel's WW1 flying colleague, Eddie Rickenbacker, who was the assigned referee for the race.

He and McKee reminisced about their WW1 days and the fact that both of them had managed to make it out of France alive. Elliot sat and listened, enthralled by the two pilot's tales. The "Ace of Aces" described each and every detail of his kills, the same way a professional golfer describes a winning round he played in the distant past. Talk eventually returned to racing and Captain Eddie asked Herschel when he was going to start driving and quit being the monkey.

"Soon," was the reply.

Again, the odds-on favorites for the race were Milton and Murphy. The two had a friendly but vigorous rivalry going on that was unsurpassed in the history of motor sports. In 1920, while both of them drove for the Duesenberg factory team, they had set almost identical land speed records on Daytona Beach, each surpassing 150mph. Murphy, because Milton made a surreptitious side trip to Havana for some personal business, was officially awarded the record, even though Milton had been originally primed by the factory for the honor. Milton's embarrassment upon returning from Cuba exacerbated the rivalry and caused him to leave the Duesenberg team in anger. Driving for separate teams, the two dominated the AAA series, capturing over half of the 1921 Championship races between them.

As usual McKee paid no mind to the odds makers. He and Elliot had beaten them before so there was no reason they couldn't do it again. Elliot qualified well on Friday, narrowly missing quickest time. He and his reluctant mechanic shunned the evening's social events and got to bed early with little alcohol on board. This unusual demonstration of sobriety the night before a race was testament to the importance both men placed on this particular event.

Each awoke refreshed. After peering out of his hotel window, McKee announced to no one in particular that it was going to be a glorious day. He quickly dressed and met Elliott at their garage, but not before he stopped to chat with his old driver and friend Roscoe Sarles. Sarles had been more competitive of late, still driving the now ancient Frontenac. He was considered a major factor in the race, having finished a very respectable third in the National Championships the year before.

"Don't get in our way, you old coot."

"You'll be lucky to see us at all," Sarles replied.

The two friends reminisced for a time then parted ways, wishing each other well. After Elliot, Sarles was probably McKee's closest friend, at least among the active drivers. He had always admired his honesty and sportsmanship, not to mention his terrific sense of humor. Sarles was nicknamed "The Clown" and was constantly playing practical jokes on the other drivers. McKee truly did wish him well.

Elliot appeared relaxed and somewhat jovial when McKee returned to the garage. There was nothing more to do before race time so they sat down to endure what seemed like ages before the start. It was only two hours away. Betty soon arrived bubbling with enthusiasm. She was carrying something wrapped in a towel. Unveiling it in the garage, they toasted their expected success with a small dram of good Scottish whisky. Both men struggled to resist the urge to tinker with the car.

The race began without incident. Murphy jumped into an early lead with Milton hot on his tail. Elliott was embedded somewhere in the top five. It was difficult to assess anyone's position from third place through seventh due to the dense cloud of smoke and small bits of debris surrounding the tightly bunched group. The race was so close that nearly all of the fans were still on their feet when lap 54 was completed.

Still in the lead, Murphy's car suddenly lost a wheel as he entered Turn 2, which caused him to skid sideways out of control. Pointed toward the inside wall, the car slowed abruptly. Joe Thomas, who had moved into second and was all over Murphy's tail at the time, tried to avoid the now crawling vehicle. He couldn't. He plowed into its side, splitting the frame into two distinct parts. Thomas's mechanic was thrown clear of the crash, sustaining only minor injuries – he was able to jump to his feet and leapt over the inside rail to safety. Thomas wasn't so lucky. He suffered a badly fractured leg as well as several internal injuries. He would be hustled off to the city's main hospital. Elliott and McKee took little notice, concentrating on the job at hand.

With Murphy and Thomas out of the race, Milton jumped into the lead and held it until Eddie Hearne's car abruptly lost a wheel. Traveling at an estimated 110mph, the wheel rolled right into the path of hard-charging Peter De Paolo. De Paolo reacted swiftly, dodging the errant wheel by millimeters, but slammed head-on into the outer retaining wall. Roscoe Sarles, running just behind him when the melee began, was unable to avoid De Paolo and he too clobbered the northeast fence. He hit it so hard, and at such an extreme angle, that his car went right through the barrier, plummeting 60 feet to the ground. The car exploded into a brilliant fireball on impact and the crowd watched in horror as Sarles desperately tried to squirm from beneath the burning car. He was slowly swallowed by the flames and burned alive.

Sarles's mechanic, C. V. Pickup, was in a racecar for the first time in his life. A local barnstormer and World War One fighter pilot well known to McKee, he had been beside himself with happiness at being chosen to ride with as talented a driver as Sarles. He was thrown clear of the car just before impact with the ground but would later die in the hospital from a massive skull fracture.

Over 50,000 spectators stood in silence as a thin column of dense black smoke rose slowly from the wreckage, eventually clearing the top of the press box.

De Paolo, also thrown from his car during the huge crash, was dazed but able to stand on his own. He stumbled clumsily to the aid of Harry Henning, his mechanic. Henning was lying unconscious on the track only a few feet from their crumpled racer. He appeared dead. De Paolo, obviously in pain, helped the medics load him into an ambulance. Henning would also succumb in the hospital, dying of a brain hemorrhage.

Three deaths in one crash drew caustic remarks from the press. Several of the media blamed the track. Oddly, history would show that these were the only fatalities to ever occur at the Kansas City Speedway. The deaths weighed heavily on most of the drivers and mechanics. McKee was no exception. Throughout the years, in all of the major racing series, there have been drivers who seem to be above the danger, who are immortal for a time. The most recent examples are Dale Earnhardt Sr in America and Ayrton Senna in Europe. Sarles was one of these men, a racer who somehow seemed to be above death at the racetrack. His crash made international news.

After a massive clean-up the race continued, as it always does when a death occurs. Within five laps of the restart the crowd was again jolted to its feet when the front axle on Hearne's car finally broke free. The car flipped side over side several times down the front straightaway. The crowd again grew quiet as the errant car came to rest near the infield grass, but thankfully neither Hearne nor his mechanic was seriously injured. Tommy

Milton eventually won the crash-marred race in his Leach Special, at an average speed – in spite of the carnage – of a phenomenal 108mph for the 300 miles. The actual running time was just under three hours. Harry Hartz finished second with Elliot and McKee a well-deserved third.

It wasn't until after they had returned to their garage that they were officially told what happened to Sarles and the others. McKee said he had felt it in his heart. For the first time in his life, he was actually saddened upon hearing the news of a fellow combatant's death. He liked Sarles, and the incident hit a little too close to home. He and Elliot grabbed their girlfriends and headed downtown to hear some blues and get loaded – the same defense mechanism used by the airmen of the French Flying Corps during the war.

"It wasn't our time," they said simultaneously over a large glass of the best whisky the house had to offer.

Elliot's date didn't have a clue as to who Roscoe Sarles was.

Chapter 12

CHARMED

McKee returned home following the fatalities in Kansas City. He had some business affairs to settle and was anxious to see his family. On the trip home, he found himself reflecting on the amazing amount of good luck he seemed to keep having. Betty had been going on and on lately about how often he seemed to defy the odds. Sooner or later, he thought, his number was certainly going to come up.

"You should have died a hundred times!" she would tell him repeatedly.

"Better them than me, I guess," was his reply. "I think I'm charmed, you know. Must be," he added.

McKee was not a religious man. He never went to church. He denied ever having prayed, not even when he was falling from the sky over Germany (although the validity of this assertion may be questionable). The only rational explanation he could come up with for his exceptional luck was that he truly must be charmed.

"How else can you explain it?" he appealed to Betty. "I've crashed three airplanes, six racecars, and I don't know how many motorcycle wrecks I've had. I've been shot at, shot down, jailed and escaped. I've been burned, broken, and found unconscious.

"Hell, I can't die! I'm Lucky Herschel McKee!"

Betty decided she might just as well keep quiet. Herschel was convinced that he led some kind of magical existence and there was no point trying to argue with him. Perhaps he was right. Her life with McKee never lacked for excitement that was for sure, but she questioned how long it could last. She spent as much time by his side as she could. The day would soon come, she thought, when he would no longer be around. He was a true adrenaline junkie, and his lifestyle simply could not be sustained indefinitely. With that, she threw her arms around him as he popped a small wheelie and they took off on the Harley for a ride in the country.

McKee headed south out of Indianapolis to an area of the state known as Brown County. It was the only part of Indiana with hills. A series of winding roads enabled him to try out his latest bike. Betty had no reservations as she clung tightly to McKee's waist. *If he goes, I go*, she thought. He was an accomplished rider and brimming with his usual level of confidence. He twisted the throttle on full as they rounded a particularly tight bend.

"Shit!"

Lying directly in their path was a lumbering, rickety, horse-drawn old hay wagon. The two nags pulling it should have been sent to the glue factory long before now. Traveling at over 40 miles an hour, McKee deftly laid the bike on its side and grabbed hold of Betty's arms. He pulled her tightly to him and they slid off the road as one. Plowing first through an area of high grass, they slid unceremoniously into a fetid pond with a big splash. The pond was used as a watering hole for the pigs and cattle that resided on the farm they had just barged into.

McKee did his usual self-examination, a technique he had perfected over the years to assess personal injury. He found none. He then inquired as to Betty's well-being. She seemed fine but was obviously shaken. Her boots were full of water, her hair was a mess, her blouse was torn open, but she was alive and kicking. She hugged McKee tightly, looked into his deep-set blue eyes, and planted a big kiss on his lips. *Maybe the son of a bitch is charmed and it rubs off*, she thought.

Dripping wet, she and McKee went back to check on the bike. It was dented in a couple of areas, having made contact with some of the rocks on the side of the road, but otherwise seemed to be intact. McKee gave a kick to the starter and it fired right up. The left handlebar was bent some, but the bike was definitely rideable. Betty hopped on the back and they headed toward the little town of Nashville for some much-needed nourishment and to catch their breath.

It was well past noon by the time they got there. Rather than turn right around and head for home, they decided to find a place to stay for the night. As they walked along the main street they stumbled upon a quaint little boarding house near the center of town. It reminded McKee of some he had seen in France. They knocked. The lady of the house opened the door, took a quick look at the bedraggled and still wet pair then abruptly shut the door in their faces. McKee knocked again. After a couple of minutes the lady opened the door wide, but this time she held a butcher's knife in her free hand just in case she might need it.

McKee started to explain why they looked so bad, but before he said two words Betty smiled her best smile and let out a great big "Howdy!"

The lady threw open both arms, the knife barely missing the chandelier as she did so, and invited them inside. Pointing to the kitchen, she offered them some cherry pie left over from lunch and two cold beers from the icebox. She picked up the knife, placed it on the counter, and sat down beside them. She watched as the pair ravenously devoured the pie and beer.

The woman stared at McKee for a time and then blurted out: "I know you!"

She recognized McKee from a newspaper article and picture she had seen after the war. Her husband had died fighting in the

Above: Originally presumed dead after being shot down in a dogfight over Germany in 1917, McKee is pictured being transferred to the hospital by medical personnel. Destined to make a near-miraculous recovery, he was incarcerated in a German prison as soon as he was up and about. Managing a narrow escape, he returned to France for the duration of the war.

Below: Baby McKee at two months of age. The dress was short-lived as McKee's thrill-seeking lifestyle developed at an early age.

Right: McKee at age 16. He had quit school, deciding it was a waste of time, and was already plotting to leave for France and the war. His devilish good looks would serve him well in the years to come.

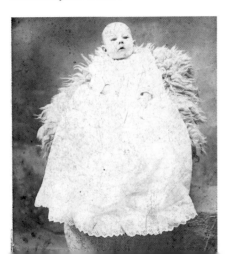

Left: Having just returned from basic training in Algiers, the newly assigned "Greenie" was bound for the Western Front and a life he thought would be fun and exciting. When he hit the trenches his dreams turned to painful reality as bombardment, disease, mud and vermin became the order of the day.

Below: The men of the Lafayette Flying Corps, 1918. McKee is thought to be in the middle of the second-to-last row. The spirit as well as the turnover was high in this group of young gladiators. Without their daring and expertise the war may well have had a different outcome.

Above left: Home from the war and still in uniform, McKee sits on his first motorcycle, a passion he developed upon his return in 1919. Jumping over flaming walls came soon afterward as he developed the model for motorcycle thrill shows that remain to this day.

Above right: Dressed and ready, McKee is about to embark on a career of "mechanician" that spanned the years from 1919 to 1937. His first stint as a riding mechanic was with the Peugeot team and driver André Boillot in the 1919 Indianapolis 500 Mile Race.

Below: André Boillot, the famous French racing driver of the time, and McKee in their Peugeot, ready for the 1919 500 Mile Race. They were passing cars at will until a big crash late in the race ended their hopes.

1 Tom Besset   3. Tom Rooney   5. Fat Inman.
2. Ward Table   4. Lieut. Mack McKee   6. Leo Schaphner.

Tom Rooney and his
going to broadcast
Stutz Motor car famous
Indianapolis Ind.
May, 1925.

Above: The boys at Stutz. What better way is
there to test a new model than with young
men trying to destroy it during after-hour
sorties on public roads? Indianapolis was the
center of automotive production during the
post-war years with the Speedway frequently
used for testing.

Left: Daredevil McKee, ready to jump through
fire as he practises at home for his original
thrill show scheduled for the Indiana State
Fair. When the money grew tight, he and his
first wife, Susan, would hit the road traveling
to local fairs throughout the Midwestern part
of the United States.

Right: An unidentified "barnstormer" waiting to go aloft with the young McKee. Little did she know that she was safer aloft than on the ground as the handsome McKee so often became the object of a pretty girl's affection.

Right: Found among McKee's belongings, this photograph shows a privately-owned Fokker D.VII, similar to those flown by the Germans in World War One. Unadorned and on the ground in Indiana, it looks fairly harmless. That probably wasn't the experience of 'Herschel J. McKee, Sergeant Pilot Aviator', as the young warrior signed off in his second letter home from the Lafayette Flying Corps.

Right: Respected driver Roscoe Sarles with McKee as his riding mechanic are pictured in 1920 before practice for the 500 Mile Race. The car number was changed to 5 for the race. The team was doing well in the event, running as high as forth, before a crash forced them to retire after 54 laps. Sarles and McKee remained close friends after the breakup of their partnership.

Left: McKee with driver Frank Elliott, ready to race in the #9 Leach Special. Of all the drivers he rode with, Elliott was the most successful. They remained close friends until Elliott's death.

Below: Elliott and McKee had their worst crash of all at the San Francisco Speedway on December 11, 1921. The car can be seen teetering on the rim of the Speedway, approximately 50 feet above the ground below. Though injured, McKee kept the car from falling off the edge. The engine can be seen at the bottom of the track impaled by a 2 x 4 thrust through its crankcase. The fuel tank exploded during the crash, causing the car to burst into flames before impact. The hushed audience expected the worst.

Above: McKee and Elliott happy to be alive following the big crash. Lucky Herschel McKee had survived another one.

Right: A stylish Betty atop of Mount Wilson. California, 1922. She and her daredevil lover would ride the twisting mountain road for fun when living in California for the winter racing season. Eventually they married and remained so until the end.

Below: One of two Junior Specials built by Kansas City oilman C.L. Richards. The twin to the car shown was being prepared for driver Riley Brett and McKee for the Thanksgiving Day race held at the new Beverly Hills Speedway in California. The year was 1922. The car reportedly had "the loudest engine ever made". Brett and McKee qualified in the last row.

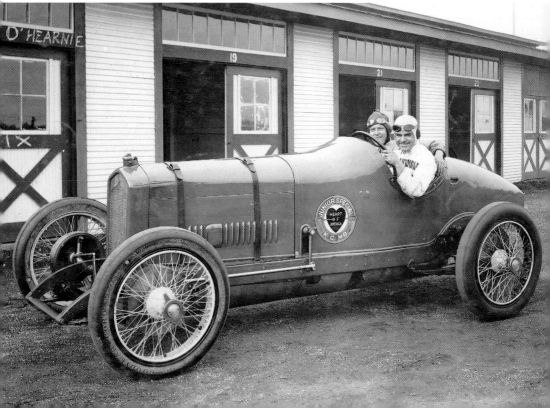

Above: "Splinter" track racing at its finest. Here, Elliott and McKee in car #9, the Leach Special, pass Tommy Milton, who is running the low line. These short tracks, each made of several million feet of lumber, provided spectacular races throughout the 1920s. The thrill level was high and so was the danger. Surviving the era was not easy as deaths and severe injuries were common.

Left: Elliott and McKee winning at the Los Angeles Speedway on March 2, 1922. It was their first significant victory and the two men celebrated in style following the event. Life for a time was truly good and the two men made the most of it.

trenches; she remembered the war all too well. Widowed at age 23, she ran the little boarding house with her son Tom, who had just turned 13. A black man named Jake helped her with odd jobs. Her usual tenants were struggling, itinerant artists who frequented the area. These artists had managed to develop an impressionist style all their own, and Indiana impressionist art would later become much sought-after by collectors.

Staying upstairs at the time was Otto Stark, one of the deans of the impressionist school. He was now 63 years old. He would shuffle more than walk to a place just outside the town limits each morning, painting his interpretation of the spectacular vistas that surrounded the little village. In the fall, the leaves made the hillsides seem on fire.

The lady's name was Celia. Like most Indiana natives at the time, she had never been more than 20 miles from her home. She was intrigued with Betty's story of the day's misadventure, marveling at the fact she would even sit on the motorcycle, let alone ride it. The two women began to talk in earnest after lunch. Their talk eventually led to a discussion as to why some people seem to lead a charmed life while others face nothing but illness, sadness and hardship.

The aging artist shuffled slowly in from his day's painting while they were still talking. Stark appeared much older than his age. His wife had died prematurely earlier in the year from a form of cancer, and his own health was failing. He had some preliminary sketches and showed them to Celia and Betty. McKee had little interest in art, or in the things women talked about, so he went outside to tinker with the motorcycle. He had sat still long enough. It may have been a record.

The women's chatter was sharply interrupted when they heard the bike's engine roar to life in concert with the shrill scream of a 13-year-old boy. Young Tom had returned from his errands, meeting McKee in the yard. He immediately accepted an offer to hop on the bike and take a run down to the end of the street to check out the completed repairs. He was hollering for joy. Celia turned a ghastly pale color. Betty consoled her, telling her not to worry because McKee was one of the charmed ones.

The thrill-show performer and his young passenger returned to the house all smiles. Celia scolded her son only half-heartedly. They all got cleaned up for dinner, inviting Mr Stark to join them. The conversation went on well into the night. McKee even enjoyed himself, as Stark was a gifted conversationalist and kept everyone captivated. Herschel and Betty returned to Indianapolis in the morning. As they left, McKee promised Thomas a job on his race crew in May if his mother would let him come to the big city. That was none too likely.

Herschel and Betty arrived back home in the middle of the afternoon. McKee was due for a meeting at the Miller shop in California in three weeks and still had several loose ends to tie up before leaving for the coast. He spent some additional time with his parents, telling them he was too young to settle down. He and Betty packed up the truck and headed to St Louis, where they planned to meet up with Elliot and take the *Super Chief* train to LA. Barring any unforeseen delays they should arrive well in advance of the meeting.

During the long train ride, Elliott and McKee would have ample time to discuss their respective futures. McKee was itching to take the wheel of a racing car. He planned to break the news to Elliott on the way west.

Chapter 13

THE LUCK RUNS OUT

The *Super Chief* was making excellent time. Once out of Kansas, a land so flat and devoid of substance that you could actually watch your dog run away forever, the train ride became spectacular. McKee had never seen the Rocky Mountains from within. He had only skirted them in the biplane. This season the snow was plentiful and the scenery gorgeous. He and Betty splurged, paying for first-class tickets. On the second day of the journey he met with Elliot in their compartment.

"Frank, I've got to drive. I don't want to be the monkey any longer."

"I can't believe you've lasted this long," replied Elliott, an answer that surprised McKee. "I hear Duesenberg is planning to add another car before the end of the year. Maybe they'll let you drive it in the Thanksgiving Day race."

"You're not sore?"

"I'm not sore at all, Herschel. You lucky bastard, you'll probably win right out of the box."

McKee thought to himself: *All that worrying for nothing*. They shook hands and headed for the lounge. McKee produced a silver flask from his jacket pocket and they toasted their good fortune and the success they had so far enjoyed. The train was almost through Nevada when McKee found himself looking out the window in amazement. "What a desolate godforsaken land," he said to anyone that might be listening. "There's never going to be anything of substance way out here, that's for sure."

The train arrived in Los Angeles on schedule and McKee and Elliott were met by one of the Miller mechanics. It was the end of October. The Thanksgiving Day race was just four weeks away. McKee sat down with the team manager as soon as he could arrange a meeting. He nervously began a wordy explanation as to why he should be added to the team's roster as a driver. The manager stopped him in mid-sentence and said: "McKee, you're hired," just like that.

A test was planned for early the following week. The newest Miller-Duesenberg was to be named "The Shock-check Special". McKee realized then that the car had been prepared especially for him and that his carefully thought-out speech had been totally unnecessary. It wasn't really a new car as he had initially been led to believe. It was, in fact, Sarles's death car. It had been carefully rebuilt from the ground up, the frame having been not too badly damaged in the crash. When informed of its history, McKee just shrugged his shoulders and told the crew to get on with it.

Test day arrived with the sky a bit overcast and the threat of rain. The shiny, rebuilt racer was unloaded from its trailer. McKee had been at the track for nearly three hours. Betty made a new set of white coveralls for the occasion, but he would wear his customary leather helmet, his old flying goggles from the war and the well-worn gloves he'd used since 1919. Since it wasn't a race, a riding mechanic was not required or even needed. Betty pounced on the rare opportunity and asked if she could go along for the ride.

"Hop in, dear."

Within three laps McKee had the car over 110mph. He was in ecstasy. Betty was hanging on for dear life, grabbing hold of whatever she could get her hands on. McKee came within a quarter of a second of the track record on his last lap. The team was enthusiastically patting him on the shoulders before he could climb from the car. What in God's name was he going to do for two weeks? He was ready to race now. That familiar face-wide grin of his was on vivid display.

Herschel, Betty, Elliott and his girlfriend – new since the one in summer – decided to go to the beach for the next ten days while the team prepared their cars. Upon arriving in Laguna Beach, Betty announced that she had entered an amateur bathing beauty contest. McKee showed his usual lack of excitement, women's activities rarely registering on his scale of worthwhile pursuits.

The contest was scheduled for the coming Saturday, with most of the girls entered being local surfers and blond. Betty took second, losing out to a bigger-busted blond girl who everyone in town seemed to know intimately. The trophy was almost as big as she was. McKee was actually quite proud of Betty, although he allowed little in the way of exuberance to show through his manly facade.

The two couples went into town to celebrate. The race was now only a week away. The "rookie", brimming with confidence, told everyone he came into contact with that he was going to win. Elliott told him that second place would be sufficient for his first time out. Deep down he knew that McKee was indeed a formidable threat.

McKee awoke race morning before sun-up. It was pouring down rain. The forecast was for torrential downpours to last well into the next day. He was more than disappointed. The Thanksgiving Day race was officially postponed at noon for the first time in its history. A new race date was announced for one week later. McKee would have to endure seven more days of waiting for his long-anticipated debut. Betty would later describe those days as the most miserable of their relationship.

The interminable week finally ended with the couple making it through largely intact. Although at times despondent, McKee had tolerated the wait fairly well by maintaining a small but effective blood alcohol level. Practice was scheduled for Friday afternoon with the race planned for the next day. Drawing lots for starting positions was held the morning before practice – there was to be no qualifying due to the postponement and the abbreviated two-day schedule. McKee, not surprisingly, was the first driver in line to draw for position.

The press was already heralding his debut. It was generally assumed that he would be an immediate contender based on his experience as a mechanic and airplane pilot, not to mention the caliber of drivers he had served. McKee reached into the bowl, smiling to everyone in the room. He drew number 13. He was immediately surrounded by a cadre of reporters.

"Don't you know you're driving Sarles's car?" yelled one of them.

"Aren't you afraid of the number 13?" yelled another.

"Hey, today is Friday," yelled yet another.

McKee raised both hands in the air, gaining everyone's attention, and calmly announced: "If my Shock-check Duesenberg continues to hit around 120, the number 13 won't matter at all. That's all poppycock! It's the car, not the number, that counts."

He was then asked by the reporter for the *Los Angeles Times* if he would carry any good luck charms during the race.

"No, sir. I won't carry any good luck charms, won't need 'em. The Shock-check Duesenberg is a good enough lucky charm for me to parade around in."

Hugh Curley, McKee's chosen riding mechanic, was standing close behind McKee during the impromptu interview. He echoed the same sentiments: "If number 13 is good enough for the boss, it's good enough for me."

Eighteen drivers drew for starting positions. A lot of whispered talk could be heard following the press conference, and a lot of furtive glances were directed his way, but McKee paid them no mind. His thoughts were focused on the next day's event. He left hurriedly for the garage area to ready himself for that afternoon's practice session. He would show everybody what he thought of the number 13.

The team rolled the car onto the pit apron after lunch. McKee gave Betty a big kiss and then joined Curley, who was already seated and ready to go. Some of the other cars were already lapping the track. Jimmy Murphy, Bennett Hill and Joe Thomas were among the ones at speed. McKee pulled onto the racing surface. Within four laps he was up to 115mph.

"There's much more speed in this baby!" he yelled at Curley.

As McKee entered Turn 3 on his sixth lap, he punched the throttle to the floor. The car responded with a strong burst of speed. McKee made a slight correction of the wheel, aiming to pass a much slower Joe Thomas, who was lumbering along immediately in front of him. Rather than passing smoothly around Thomas, however, McKee's car, according to several observers, seemed to lurch forward abruptly, and for some unexplained reason plowed into the rear of Thomas's machine. The two cars locked wheels for an instant.

Thomas, describing the incident later, said that when he felt McKee's car hit him from behind he floored his own machine. This action allowed him to break free and into relative safety. McKee was not so lucky. His car veered sideways after the impact, shot forward, and then smashed into the retaining wall with tremendous force. The lights went out for both he and Curley.

Forty feet of fence was splintered into thousands of wooden missiles as the errant car cartwheeled and headed for the bottom of the racetrack upside down and in flames. It was later discovered that one of the flying wooden shards had penetrated the fuel tank, spilling fuel onto the hot exhaust. Thomas was quoted in a post-race interview as saying: "I could hear the impact of McKee's car over the roar of my own engine even though I was 200 yards away by the time."

McKee and Curley were both pinned in the wreckage. Their breath came in short gasps. Their windpipes were on fire as they suffocated on the dense, noxious smoke. Ned Charlton, a pit man for Ralph De Palma, sprinted across the track to their aid. As he was attempting to pull McKee free, the car settled abruptly, crushing his leg in the process.

More rescuers arrived. Curley was dragged from beneath the car unconscious and bleeding profusely. McKee wasn't responding appropriately either – according to rescuers on the scene "he was thrashing about like a caged animal".

Both men were loaded into the same ambulance and taken to the track's receiving hospital. One look told the staff that they were beyond the scope of their limited facility. They were transferred to California Lutheran Hospital and admitted in critical condition. Curley was not expected to survive. He had a large depressed skull fracture with his eyes locked in a frozen stare. He also had several internal injuries and was bleeding profusely from a large scalp wound, causing his blood pressure to drop precipitously. The surgeons were called.

McKee started to wake up en route to the hospital. When Betty was finally allowed to see him he was jabbering about some other race, not making any sense at all. She consoled him as best she could. She phoned his parents, telling them that this may just be it. He looked horrible to her and she fully expected him to die.

Mechanic Terry Curley, one of three Curley brothers involved in racing, had been riding shotgun in the same session with his driver Jerry Wonderlich. He finished the day's practice even though he had witnessed his brother's horrific crash first-hand.

A third brother, Ray, also a riding mechanic, was recuperating at home in Kansas City from injuries sustained in that May's Indianapolis 500. Terry Curley was notified of his brother's condition when practice ended. He made a mad dash to the hospital. The Duesenberg team, meanwhile, regrouped in the garage area immediately after the practice period to prepare for the next day's race.

The main event was run the following day as if nothing had happened. It turned out to be a real crowd pleaser. No one was killed but there were a lot of crashes. Late in the event even steady Frank Elliott crashed, flipping side over side several times down the main straightaway. Neither he nor his riding mechanic was injured. He left the track immediately to visit his buddy McKee. Jimmy Murphy finally won the event. Hugh Curley was pronounced dead later that same afternoon.

For the second time in his eventful life, Herschel McKee found himself in what was affectionately called the "crash house" by the drivers. He had awakened fully by evening and was asking to be let out of the hospital. Sore all over, he had a splitting headache and his face was so bruised and swollen that he looked as if he had just lost a bare-knuckle fight. He asked Betty about Hugh Curley and was told: "It doesn't look so good."

"I know he's dead, I could tell that when we crashed. Poor son of a bitch, and he stood by me during all that number 13 horse shit."

The doctors wanted McKee to stay in the hospital for a full two weeks because of the concussion, to let his cuts and abrasions heal somewhat. It took Frank and Betty teaming up with the doctors to convince him to stay. With each passing day he grew more and more restless. Betty would sneak him some whisky now and then, but McKee got to where he could not stand it any longer. He left via the back door on the seventh day. He and Betty returned to Indianapolis to figure out his next move. When asked by the press how he now felt about having the number 13, he told them: "It's still poppycock! If you race cars long enough, you're going to get banged up a little."

He and Betty decided to spend Christmas recuperating in Indianapolis and then go back to California for the remainder of the winter. His mother and father lobbied hard for him to return to the Stutz Co and settle down. McKee paid no attention. He recovered rapidly from his injuries and was raring to find a new car to drive. It would be difficult during the winter, since most of the owners had their drivers already signed up for the next season, but he was going west regardless.

While looking for a ride after his arrival in California, he met a man by the name of W. Elliott Saffell, a former Navy pilot who was planning to fly across the Pacific. It would be the first flight of its kind, and would travel a circuitous route from Los Angeles to Shanghai. It occurred to McKee that if he couldn't find a racecar to drive, maybe he could at least fly to China with Saffell and set some kind of record. Competition had been heating up internationally to become the first country to claim a flight across the world's largest ocean. Britain had already announced a potential flight and some other European countries were looking into it.

Saffell and McKee met for dinner the week after Herschel arrived in LA. Saffell described in detail an elaborate plan to fly a six-legged route to China. The first leg would take them to Seattle, then on to Sitka, Alaska, continuing to Dutch Harbor. After that, they would cross over to the Siberian coast via the Aleutian Islands and go south to Tokyo, with the final destination being Shanghai. The total distance was more than 6,000 miles. They planned to use a Saffell-Hardin triplane with a new Liberty motor. Saffell thought the plane would be capable of sustaining 115mph over the long distance.

Investors were already on board, and the plane was being

readied in a hangar at Los Angeles airport. The British team had announced its intention to depart in April, so there was no time to waste. The deal Saffell and McKee made had each of them sharing equally in the flying duties as well as any profits that might come from the venture.

Before their meeting, Saffell was dubious that McKee had recovered enough from his recent injuries to make such a long and difficult journey. From what he had read in the papers, and from what people had told him, he expected McKee to be significantly impaired. After the meeting, all fears were gone. The two men shook hands, planning to reunite in mid-April to make the final preparations.

McKee left the meeting happy to have a new adventure in the wings. His next stop was to visit a friend he had met the previous spring while doing a thrill show at the Fair in Ventura, California. Edward Malone was a motorcycle racer of some repute. He and McKee would often ride their Harleys together on the coast highway. They planned to ride that afternoon and catch up on each other's lives, since they hadn't talked for over six months. It was a typical sunny California day. Their ride would take them along the coast to an eventual meeting with their significant others for dinner around 8:00pm. Malone had a different idea. When McKee walked in the door, he said excitedly "Herschel, I've been thinking of trying out something new."

"What's that, Ed?"

"I want to try to do that wing-walking thing, pays more'n racing. Do you think you can get us a plane this afternoon?"

"Have you ever tried it before?"

"Nope."

"I'll borrow a plane from Lefty, but I think you're nuts."

McKee liked flying almost more than he liked sex. He called Lefty, a mechanic he knew from a couple of years back, and arranged for a plane. He and Malone hopped on their motorcycles and headed for the airport at Goodyear field. They figured they would still have enough time to hook up with the girls for dinner.

When they arrived, Lefty led them to a biplane owned by Virgil Moore, manager of the facility. McKee did a quick walk around and pronounced the plane fit to fly. Malone jumped into the back seat. McKee got behind the controls. His take-off was effortless and they quickly climbed to an altitude of around 1,000 feet. McKee leveled off and Malone began a somewhat clumsy but determined climb onto the wing. He grabbed one piece of the plane after another trying to find a proper path to the top. They were traveling at close to 80mph.

Malone looked the part. He wore the customary black-trimmed circular goggles and the obligatory shiny white scarf double-wrapped about his neck. Nearly a foot and a half of it streamed behind him as he braced himself against the wind. His brown leather flight jacket billowed forth, making him look as if he had the largest chest in the world – he had forgotten to zip it all the way to the top. His wavy black hair and the big grin on his face enhanced a scene that would have made a great movie poster.

Malone, his left hand locked in a death grip around one of the struts, gave McKee a salute with his free hand. McKee was visibly laughing out loud. As he saluted, the big grin suddenly disappeared and the fledgling wing walker's face turned ashen. A huge flame burst forth from the right side of the engine. A millisecond later flames appeared from the left side of the engine. Fire quickly invaded the cockpit. The plane dropped its nose and sped toward earth. McKee desperately fought the controls as he lost altitude fast, plummeting through the sky like a meteor.

He could no longer see through the flames. At around 200 feet, realizing they were doomed, he stood to attention and saluted Malone, then turned to his left and bailed out of the burning plane.

Malone stood frozen and expressionless. He rode the ill-fated craft into the ground at the south end of the airfield. He was killed instantly, burned beyond recognition. McKee, his luck in overdrive, landed violently in a large pile of hay being held for use as ground cover for an airport expansion project. It was not a soft landing. He fractured his skull in two places, was rendered unconscious for the second time in less than two months, and sustained a broken left leg and right arm along with multiple abrasions.

Some well-meaning workman who had witnessed the entire fiasco dragged him unceremoniously into the maintenance building. There he lay unconscious for several minutes until he was finally picked up by an ambulance and taken to the hospital. McKee would spend nine long weeks in that hospital, blowing any chance of flying across the Pacific with Mr Saffell. Worse than that, the plunge into the hay mound would also cause him to miss the 1923 500 Mile Race.

"It wasn't my fault," he would tell whoever would listen.

The press wrote that his career as a driver or mechanic was most certainly over. Betty knew better. After his hospital stay, she took him back to the apartment they had rented where she cared for him day and night. At first he was fairly manageable, being cooperative and thankful that he was alive. It wasn't long, though, before he was his irascible old self. Betty knew that this change of attitude signaled that he would soon be back on the horse. She prepared herself for the inevitable.

Investigation of the crash showed that the exhaust pipes had been inadvertently left off of the manifolds following some hasty repairs. Unprotected, the fabric and wood fuselage was ignited by the hot exhaust. "Lucky Herschel McKee" had survived another one. When asked about Malone, McKee's reply was short and pointed.

"He should have jumped."

Chapter 14

WILL HE EVER LEARN?

McKee was back on his motorcycle by July. He and Betty had remained in California following his latest plane crash and Betty used the time to further her education. McKee's leg was stiffer than it used to be, but he had no trouble jumping his bike over the fires Betty built for him in the evenings. He was still going to the rehabilitation center down the street from where they lived. While there, he spent a lot of time in the pool. He was assigned a therapist who was quite young and very pretty. Her name was Hilda.

Hilda was 17 years old and of German descent. She was assisting at the rehab center on weekends, her goal being to become a nurse. She was tall, slender, and quite shapely with gorgeous eyes. She reminded McKee of a blond Saloua, the French Moroccan he had been with during the war. McKee had a difficult time concentrating when Hilda worked his leg back and forth in the water. "There are just too many good-looking women in the world," he would think to himself.

It has been said that a normal young man thinks about making love to a woman several times an hour. For McKee, it was nearly constant. The occasional and not so accidental underwater contact with Hilda was a lot for McKee to handle. He and his young therapist began spending more and more time in the pool. Betty never questioned the amount of time McKee was spending in therapy, assuming he was working extra hard at his return to competition.

Hilda had one other ambition in life and that was to go up in an airplane. During their frequent encounters she would often ask McKee if he would take her flying some day. For McKee, the question was not if, but when. He was riding his motorcycle reasonably well so there was really no reason he couldn't fly. He told Hilda he would get his airplane out of mothballs and take her for a spin. He still owned Higgins's old barnstormer and kept it in a hangar at Clover Field near Santa Monica. He hadn't flown it for over a year.

It didn't take him long to get it ready to fly again. He completed a minor overhaul of the engine, lubricated the controls, and spent an entire afternoon cleaning and polishing. The plane was old, but McKee felt it was still sound. No problems developed when he test-flew the old bird in late July, and he declared her airworthy. He arranged a flying date with Hilda for August 1.

Hilda's parents never balked. They knew McKee was an accomplished flyer and a well-known Ace during the war. If they had any reservations they didn't show them. McKee picked Hilda up in his Stutz and they headed for Clover Field. Hilda gave McKee a big hug when she jumped in the car and couldn't stop talking all the way to the airport. It was another gloriously sunny California day. Visibility was unhampered by any appreciable smog in those days.

McKee pushed the plane onto the runway himself then helped Hilda get seated. A member of the ground crew gave him a leg up as he climbed into the cockpit. The plane started easily and he taxied to the opposite end of the grassy strip. Lining the aircraft up with a distant landmark, he began his take-off roll. As he applied more throttle, McKee thought he could feel a little misfire from the engine. Gaining speed, they lifted off with Hilda grinning from ear to ear. At around 300 feet, witnesses said, the engine sputtered a few times, then coughed before quitting altogether.

Hilda's flying adventure was over. The old plane headed toward the ground at a very steep angle. With the engine quiet, McKee had no difficulty hearing Hilda's blood-curdling scream. Just before they hit he pulled back on the stick, managing to belly-land the plane with a thud. It slid along the remaining length of runway, shearing off the landing gear in the process. Without the gear the fuselage soon began to disintegrate. It came to a stop in a crumpled mass just past the end of the grassy strip.

Several reserve flyers who had been training at the field all week witnessed the crash and rushed to the scene. By the time they arrived McKee had already climbed out of the cockpit and was doing his customary self-check. Hilda was humped over sobbing in the rear seat. She was gingerly lifted from the wreckage by a couple of the reservists. McKee didn't have a scratch on him. Hilda sustained a few minor cuts and bruises. She was taken to St Catherine's Hospital, where she was released to her parents an hour later. The plane was totaled. Upon hearing the news, Betty went into a rage. "What in the hell were you thinking, you moron? She's not even of age!"

Hilda's parents were just glad she had not been seriously injured. Her mother made sure she got McKee to autograph his picture before they all parted company. It was not a pleasant ride home for McKee. Betty threatened to go back to Indianapolis, telling him she wasn't sure she ever wanted to see him again. McKee sat quietly, letting Betty ventilate. He was thinking about where and how he was going to come up with another airplane. He also had to get cracking on a ride for the 1924 Indianapolis 500. He never saw Hilda again.

Chapter 15

TONG WARS AND THE PARACHUTE PLANE

Two more plane crashes to add to his growing list. Two more narrow escapes. He must indeed be charmed. Betty decided that McKee and the young girl hadn't really done anything wrong so she decided to stick with him. California suited them and they stayed throughout the fall and winter. Betty graduated and received her teaching license.

During the winter of 1923–4 a new track opened its gates in Los Angeles. It was built by the American Legion and was named the Legion Ascot Speedway. Operations began on January 20. The track was a dirt oval, moderately banked, five-eighths of a mile in length. By race day it resembled a paved track more than dirt, after it was repeatedly coated with motor oil to keep the dust down. McKee lurked around the garage area on opening day, talking to every owner he came in contact with. He eventually nailed down a ride in one of the old Frontenac Specials for an event scheduled in April. He and Betty endured the long wait.

McKee saw the car for the first time on the Friday before the race. It was ill-prepared by the owner, appearing to be an afterthought, and McKee was never in contention and failed to finish in the money. However, the race was a one-shot deal for McKee. He and Betty left the next day for Indianapolis to prepare for the 500. Here he was forced to again team up with Elliot, who had asked him to be his mechanic in early March. Sadly it was another lackluster showing. They failed to finish the race, being sidelined by a ruptured fuel tank, but nobody died for the second year in a row and that was a blessing. Saffell, by the way, never made it across the Pacific. The honor of being the first to fly across the world's largest ocean took another four years to achieve and ended up going to the Australian team of Charles Kingsford Smith and Charles Ulm. Flying from Oakland, California, in a Fokker tri-motor by the name of "Southern Cross", they landed in Australia on June 9, 1928.

Following Indy, McKee again let it be known that he was available to drive, but after his crash in California during a practice session, and the poor showing at Ascot, no one called. He continued throughout the summer riding as mechanic for his friend Elliot. They had mediocre success, rarely finishing in the money. As a consequence McKee continued to fly for the postal service and hit what fairs he could with his motorcycle thrill show just to stay financially viable.

In late summer he received a call from Stutz, asking him if he would be willing to test cars for them at the Indianapolis Motor Speedway. He readily accepted the offer and became their primary test driver. Additionally, he would frequently be asked by manufacturers to deliver airplanes to prospective buyers around the country. Owning an airplane was no longer a necessity. He was able to spend nearly as much time in the air as he did on the ground by delivering planes to corporations or wealthy individuals. The year passed quickly.

In the early fall of 1924, McKee, while on a routine airplane delivery, found himself racing a thunderstorm just outside of Indianapolis. He was forced to land at the Mars Hill Airport, a small field south of the city. The landing was tricky, with some wind sheer just prior to touch down. McKee greased the landing. He tied the plane down securely, protecting it as best he could before dodging rain and gusts of rising wind as he ran to a small shelter that served as a hangout for pilots during layovers. The airplane he was delivering was a biplane trainer for the Robertson Aircraft Company of St Louis, the same company that employed Charles Lindberg prior to his famous transatlantic flight.

He had to stoop a bit in order to enter the small shelter. Once inside, he was surprised to see an old war buddy of his, Lieutenant E. D. Alexander. They poured some much-needed coffee and began to chat. They were surprised to learn that they had both been flying the mail for the government during the past three years yet their paths had never crossed. Alexander was married to his high school sweetheart and worked primarily as a mechanic when not flying the mail. He too supplemented his income by delivering airplanes.

McKee had noticed an unusual looking airplane as he was making his dash for the shelter. He asked the Lieutenant if that was the plane he was flying.

"Sure is. Hell of an airplane!"

The plane was a sleek, newly designed experimental monoplane similar to the one Lindberg flew but with more range and horsepower. Alexander was on his way to Chicago, where the plane would be offered for sale.

"Do you ever run into Slim?" Alexander asked excitedly.

"Nope, I haven't seen him since he came to the track [Indy] last year."

Both men referred to the now famous Lindberg as "Slim". They had run into him at different times and each of them thought that had circumstances been a little different, one of *them* might have been the first to cross the Atlantic. The two men consumed a full pot of coffee as they reminisced about their war days and caught up on each other's lives. McKee informed Alexander about his plans to duplicate Lindberg's flight but with a female passenger on board.

"Only you would take on that load," was the immediate reply.

The storm dispersed and the two men shook hands, promising to look each other up before too many months had passed. They departed for their intended destinations with McKee leaving first. The sleek monoplane easily outdistanced him shortly after take-off, and McKee could only watch as Alexander disappeared into the distance. He vowed to get started as soon as he could on his campaign to fly across the Atlantic with a female passenger.

After making the delivery, he hitched a ride home with another pilot friend of his who was on his way back to Indianapolis. Herschel McKee was now 27 years old. Betty remained a mainstay in his life, but he still wasn't ready to commit to marriage. His love of airplanes had not waned nor had his desire to race automobiles. He still dreamed of being a successful racing driver, but so far his attempts were less than stellar. He seemed to lack something the more successful drivers all had. Betty thought he was in too big a hurry most of the time, frequently acting impulsively. For once, McKee had to agree with her.

His immediate problem in life was finding someone with the confidence to give him another chance. 1925 was a complete bust along with 1926. Then, in 1927, he was offered a ride out of the blue in the Thane Duesenberg Special for the 500. He had been helped in his quest by his long-time supporter Frank Elliot. The car was top of the line and very competitive. Sadly, however, he failed to qualify. The press was not kind in its review of his attempts.

Elliot, by this time, had teamed up with a younger riding mechanic by the name of Louis Meyer. This left McKee without a position. Meyer would later become a three-time winner of the 500 and one of America's greatest racing drivers. McKee groused about at home, making life difficult for Betty and others around him. He would take on an occasional mechanics' job when it was presented, but that was not often. He became markedly depressed and that mood dominated his life for the rest of 1927.

He and Betty, more out of habit than because there was anything promising on the horizon, joined the annual migration to California in the fall, with continued poor results. Betty taught elementary school but money remained tight. They were forced to return to Indianapolis before the California season was officially over. McKee was determined to get some type of action going. Automobile racing, for him at least, seemed to have hit a dead end. He sat down at his desk one evening and wrote his first press release. In it he stated: "A round trip flight to Paris and return was the only worthwhile air adventure not yet accomplished."

He also explained in the release that his "long-standing experience as a cross-country pilot, his barnstorming, and his flying the mail through adverse conditions qualified him to make such a trip."

He asked for a contribution of $20,000. His plan was to use an Indiana-built airplane and engine. His passenger was also to be an Indiana product. The plane he intended to use was a Stinson, the engine a Wasp. He suggested a lottery or similar contest to choose his female passenger. He promised a two-day turn-around, staying overnight at a plush hotel in Paris before the return flight to New York.

The press release generated a half-page article in the *Indianapolis Star* printed on January 13, 1928. In spite of the article, a month passed and no sponsors came forward. Few volunteered to be the passenger either. It never entered McKee's mind that the adventure seemed foolhardy to most intelligent humans, and there were a very limited number of girls from Indiana willing to spend two nights in Paris with a strange man. Of those that did make contact, he later told his friend Elliot: "I didn't know women could be that ugly."

McKee was ready to give up on the project when he received a letter from a surety company who said they would sponsor the lottery. The company was based in St Louis with ties to Lindberg. A lottery was held, and a young woman from just outside of St Louis by the name of Green won the contest. McKee was sent a picture and heartily approved the selection. Within hours of the announcement, her father squashed the idea by forbidding her to go, with comments having something to do with "over my dead body".

The second-place winner, Ruth Elder, was then chosen. Plans were progressing well when the company inexplicably had second thoughts and withdrew its sponsorship. McKee later discovered that Lindberg was planning a non-stop flight from Mexico City to St Louis as the swan song for the *Spirit of St Louis* before it was grounded forever at the Smithsonian. McKee's plan had to be abandoned as a consequence.

Perhaps the stock market crash also had something to do with it. The country's mood wasn't up for much. There was talk among most of the track owners that times were going to be really difficult for a while. Most people did not have extra money to spend on entertainment of any kind. Some were barely surviving at all. The chance of McKee finding a suitable ride was made even slimmer because of the Depression. A few of the race teams had closed their doors altogether, and track promoters began to seriously worry.

McKee turned to his usual pursuits. For a time he worked for a commercial aviation concern in Jackson, Michigan, again delivering airplanes to customers. He was lucky to have the job. Betty never abandoned him during these hard times, even though she only saw him on the occasional weekend. Luckily she was able to land a teaching job in Indianapolis, bringing in a steady paycheck. Many of the jobs McKee landed failed to pay as promised. He would deliver a plane, find a ride back home, and then wait in vain to be paid. What used to be free time now had to be spent looking for work.

He soon found Michigan winters to be more miserable than those in Indianapolis, and he moved back to his old home. He was still flying the nation's mail, the Postal Service continuing to pay on time. Mail flights were decreasing in number, however, due to the failing economy. With the flights and deliveries both dwindling McKee was suffering a period of serious inactivity, but just when he was about ready to give up entirely his luck changed abruptly. On a miserable rainy day in early spring 1928, from out of nowhere came what appeared to be a golden opportunity at last.

While in Chicago on one of his mail runs, McKee was approached by a Chinese fellow who told him he wanted to learn to fly. McKee until then had never taught anyone how to fly, but he saw no reason why he couldn't. The man offered him an attractive fee and McKee said yes. The man's name was Lum – he never gave a first name – and the flying lessons began that very day at a local airfield. Lum progressed rapidly, showing a degree of natural ability. He was soon competent enough to make a cross-country flight of substantial distance.

McKee, in spite of his general dislike of most foreigners, took an immediate liking to Mr Lum. He helped the Chinaman map out a course, plugging in spots he was familiar with. One of the airfields McKee frequented while flying the mail was the College Park Airport in Maryland. The field was established in 1909 by Wilbur Wright and was a suitable distance from Chicago to make a challenging flight for Lum. It was one of the places to which McKee most enjoyed flying.

There was a lot of nostalgia associated with College Park and the field was often visited by a number of former World War One pilots. McKee would frequently stay an extra day just to reminisce with whoever might have flown in. The route proposed for Lum's first cross-country attempt was simple. Lum, with McKee on board to observe and help in case of an emergency, would first fly to Cleveland. After staying overnight, they would then fly a second leg in the morning to College Park.

On the day of the intended flight, Lum asked if a friend of his could accompany them. McKee agreed. It would be a tight fit, but the Chinese were small. McKee felt he could squeeze the man in with him in the back seat. The three fliers landed at College Park late on a superbly pleasant Saturday afternoon. Lum did an admirable job flying the plane, allowing McKee to spend most of the flight talking with the passenger. His name was Dr George Chu. Chu was a Chicago physician. McKee learned that both Lum and Chu were jointly promoting aviation among Chinese immigrants in the United States. Lum, he discovered through Dr Chu, was planning to ask McKee at some point to go all the way to China in order to help the good doctor establish a flying school in Hong Kong. McKee had little interest in leaving the States and kept changing the subject whenever the topic of flying to China came up.

After landing, the unlikely threesome spent some time exploring the field and checking out old airplanes. While doing so they ran into a man McKee had met at one of the auto races. His name was James Bradley. He was an inventor from Chicago and wanted McKee's address and phone number. The overly gregarious Chinese explained how they were student pilots and were also from Chicago. Much back-slapping, bowing and hand-shaking ensued.

All of the men planned a return to the Windy City in the morning, but first they would enjoy a sumptuous dinner that evening. Why Bradley wanted McKee's phone number was never discussed during the meal. Most of the talk centered about aviation. After a good night's sleep, McKee and the two Chinese left for Chicago before sunrise.

Lum did an equally good job flying the plane back to Chicago. After repeatedly asking, he succeeded in convincing McKee to remain in town for a few days on the pretense of visiting Chinatown and meeting some more of Lum's colleagues. During the visit it became readily apparent that Lum's main agenda had nothing to do with seeing the sites. He wanted more time to work on McKee regarding going to Hong Kong to create a flying school. McKee agreed to stay in Chicago for three days and no more. He had nothing else to do and was intrigued by the Chinamen.

On his third and final day there, Lum, McKee, the doctor and two other men, unknown to McKee, headed out to lunch before McKee left for Detroit and a scheduled mail run. McKee continued to refuse Lum's offer during the meal, but in spite of his stubbornness Lum remained quite friendly. After lunch, all of them piled into Lum's car and headed toward the Elmhurst Flying Field and McKee's airplane.

The Chinamen insisted on giving McKee a real send-off. On the way to the airport they stopped to pick up some fireworks for the departure, but their tightly packed Chevrolet made it only as far as California and North Avenue. There, they were suddenly overtaken by a speeding police car, its siren blaring. The police vehicle swerved to cut off the odd bunch, forcing them to either stop or risk a major crash. Both cops jumped from the squad car, guns drawn. Within seconds two more squad cars arrived at the scene, surrounding the Chevy. McKee and the four Chinamen were arrested and handcuffed on the spot.

Sergeant William McCarthy, the arresting officer, explained to a gathering press corps that these five men were wanted as part of a large smuggling ring engaged in getting fellow Chinamen into the United States illegally. He went on to say that they were also suspected of instigating some of the recent Tong activities in the city and suggested that these five in particular were the ringleaders.

McKee, speechless, was incarcerated for the second time in his life. He was dumbfounded. Arrested with McKee, the doctor and

Lum were Charley Jin, 26, and Lyee Ho Loe, 24. It turned out that they were the good doctor's bodyguards. McKee demanded to call his lawyer, and then remembered he didn't have one. He sat down on the cot in his cell and stared blankly at the empty wall in front of him.

It was later revealed that Lum, the innocent-appearing student pilot, was really a major Chinese smuggler and the leader of a United States-based Tong gang. The doctor was the boss of the Chicago branch and worked for Lum. The other two men were goons. There was never going to be a legitimate aviation school. McKee would have been in great danger had he agreed to go to China, likely being murdered after all would-be Chinese pilots had been duly trained.

The plot was foiled by the good intelligence work of the Chicago Police Department. McKee was released the following morning when it became obvious that he was not criminally involved. He missed his mail pick-up in Detroit, but otherwise was none the worse for wear. He returned home with a more determined dislike of most foreigners. Betty informed him as soon as he walked in that a Mr James Bradley had contacted her looking for him. He told her he was an inventor, had an idea, and needed an experienced pilot to help in its development.

"Herschel McKee is the man I need," he emphatically informed her.

Betty said she thought the man sounded really important. He was staying at the posh Claypool Hotel downtown, and wanted McKee to look him up as soon as he returned from Chicago. McKee headed straight to the Claypool. Maybe this would lead to something big. At least Bradley was an American.

The somewhat mysterious inventor was an enthusiastic and energetic man. McKee liked him immediately. He was dressed in an expensive double-breasted black suit with a vest that appeared two sizes too small, his face was plethoric and puffy, and he was sweating. The two men sat down in the lobby of the hotel and Bradley began a lengthy description of his invention and project. As he talked, McKee grew more and more excited. Bradley explained how he had developed a way to add parachutes to airplanes in order to ease a crippled plane's return to earth – the same idea as McKee had dreamed up a couple of years earlier. Bradley, unlike McKee, had the engineering know-how and the financial backing to make the idea work.

During the next two hours, Bradley painstakingly described how he would place two small pilot chutes and two larger parachutes into two aluminum canisters fastened to the top wing of a biplane. If the motor stopped, or the pilot sensed that the plane was going to crash, a lever could be pulled that would release compressed air from the canisters. The pilot chutes would be forced from the canisters by the rush of air drawing the larger chutes out behind them. The main chutes would then inflate, and the plane would float safely to the ground. Bradley added that he could do this without significant oscillation occurring during the plane's descent. The potential for oscillation, he explained in an erudite sort of way, would be controlled by having the two canisters placed on the wing equidistant from the midpoint of the airplane. At least, that was his theory.

It made perfect sense to McKee. The two men shook hands on a deal. Bradley agreed to begin the development work immediately and McKee agreed to be the test pilot when the device was deemed ready for trial. He was also guaranteed a small percentage of any profits that might be realized from the endeavor. Whether or not a test of the apparatus was ever undertaken would depend entirely on McKee's approval of the final design. It was also agreed that McKee would move to Villa Park, Illinois, for the last stages of development and the initial testing, an idea that did not sit well with Betty. He did not see or hear from Bradley for more than two years. Finally, in August of 1931, he was told to move to Illinois.

McKee rented a small flat in Villa Park – all he would need, as he planned to spend most weekends in Indianapolis. The day he moved in he met by chance a police sergeant named George Knorr, McKee's new neighborhood being part of Knorr's beat. McKee and Knorr soon developed a friendship. Knorr was a racing fan and knew of McKee's varied history. He was even familiar with the Chinese Tong escapade, as it had been well covered in the local newspapers. With little else to do while he waited for the development of the parachute system, McKee would often accompany Knorr on his daily rounds. They would cruise the normally quiet neighborhood looking for bad guys while discussing racing, airplanes and women.

The parachute device was not ready for testing until November 13, 1931. McKee had given his enthusiastic approval to the design the week before. The initial test was planned for the St Charles flying field in Illinois. Bradley, being part promoter as well as inventor, had planted advance information about the test with the news media. He had also placed leaflets in local stores and eating establishments, and additional seats had to be added to the viewing area in order to accommodate the large press contingent that arrived for the maiden flight. Spectators were allowed to stand along both sides of the runway some distance back. They stood three deep.

The test plane was outfitted with the two large aluminum canisters mounted on the top wing. They looked like the big coffee dispensers found in diners the world over. A military band was in formation at the head of the grassy runway, and a drum roll preceded McKee's take-off. Flash bulbs popped as the plane began to move. People cheered as Lucky Herschel McKee gained speed.

The plane lifted gently into a partly sunny sky. At the pre-arranged altitude of 2,000 feet McKee pulled the lever. The rush of gas from the canisters could be heard by all in attendance. The pilot chutes deployed flawlessly amidst a puff of pale white smoke. Following in tow, the two main chutes blossomed forth and the plane floated gently to earth without significant oscillation. The speed of descent was eight feet per second, much slower than the descent of a man-carrying parachute.

A loud cheer erupted from the audience. Members of the press immediately surrounded Bradley, pumping him for more detailed information on his wonderful new invention. The main bulk of reporters took off toward McKee, who was now climbing from the airplane. He waved to the cheering crowd before being nearly bowled over by the swarm of eager writers and photographers. The semi-circle of flashing bulbs resembled a series of small explosions to Betty, who sat on a nearby fence shaking her head slowly from side to side. *Here we go again*, she thought to herself.

The successful test drew immediate attention from Washington. Bradley was contacted by the Air Force the next day. They wanted more tests done as soon as feasible. All expenses would be picked up by the military. McKee and Bradley carried out a second successful test three weeks later. McKee made some suggestions after the first test in order to smooth out the launching mechanism and these were carried out. The plane again floated safely to earth, this time from an altitude of 4,000 feet. It certainly looked as if Bradley and McKee had hit upon something big. McKee returned to Villa Park to await the third and final test.

On December 18, following his return from the second test, McKee and Officer Knorr were working the neighborhood as usual when they happened upon a suspicious-looking group of four men hanging out at a local gas station. They looked really sleazy to McKee. Two of the men were smoking big cigars, standing dangerously close to the pumps. One of them was filling the car's tank. Knorr didn't like their looks at all. He and McKee watched as the other two, after apparently casing out the station, came running outside and jumped into the front seat of the roadster and started the engine. The two doing the fueling shut the pump down and piled into the rumble seat. They didn't bother to replace the hose.

Knorr and McKee, highly suspicious by this point, followed them from a safe distance as they traveled to another gas station. From there, they went on to a third station. At each stop, the men would get out of their car, pretend to refuel, and appear as if they were searching for something. Their mysterious actions were all Knorr needed. He gunned his police cruiser, squealing the tires in the process. Gaining significant speed, he literally bounced into the station, preferring to scale the curbs rather than to use the driveway. He maneuvered his squad car, blocking the suspect's vehicle against the pumps after almost colliding with it.

As his car came to a stop, Knorr threw the door open and leaped to the pavement. He charged the men with his gun drawn. As he ran toward their car, he found himself staring down the muzzle of an automatic pistol. It was wielded by one of the men in the rumble seat. At that point, McKee, realizing the trouble they were in, grabbed the riot gun from the rack above his head. As he cocked the mechanism, he yelled at the top of his lungs: "Drop that gun or you're a dead man!"

As he did so, a second revolver was seen to fly from within the roadster. It landed harmlessly in an adjacent field. The man in the rumble seat dropped his gun. All four suspects sat trembling in front of Knorr and McKee, who stood on either side of the car. The intrepid lawman and his eager deputy had the situation well in hand. They quickly cuffed the hoodlums, who at this point offered no resistance, and they were taken downtown and booked.

While being driven to police headquarters, all of the men broke down and confessed to robbing several Villa Park filling stations. They blamed their evil ways on low funds for Christmas. A pint of gin was confiscated by McKee as they drove to headquarters, thereby adding a charge of underage drinking to their list of crimes (only one of the men was over 21). McKee now had a new thrill to add to his repertoire, that of armed apprehension. He couldn't stop talking about the experience upon his return to Indianapolis.

The third test of the parachute plane was looming. This test was scheduled for February 14, 1932, at the airfield in Lansing, Illinois. The field there could accommodate a larger crowd, and McKee was to add another 2,000 feet to the altitude. An enormous crowd, estimated by the local newspaper to be more than 1,000 people, was on hand, as Bradley's device by now had garnered worldwide publicity. Several planes equipped with movie cameras were circling above the field in anticipation. The customary drum roll commenced and McKee began his take-off. An altitude of 6,000 feet was quickly achieved. All eyes were on the aircraft. It was a beautiful day for flying, not a cloud in the sky. McKee grabbed the lever to discharge the canisters, but as he raised it the left canister exploded prematurely, causing it to rip clear of the airplane. In doing so it took the main parachute with it. The right chute blossomed fully as intended, and the plane went into a death spiral.

With his rate of descent now more like that of a crash, McKee was caught in the dizzying oscillation of the fall, pinned in the cockpit by centrifugal force. The aircraft's impact with the ground was felt by everyone present. A plume of smoke went up and a hush came over the crowd. Then after a few seconds, as was becoming customary with McKee's exploits, the silence became a deafening cheer as the seemingly indestructible pilot staggered from the twisted wreckage. He waved triumphantly and then collapsed in a heap. The ambulance wisely put in place as a precaution rushed to the scene, the attendants gingerly placing McKee inside and then racing toward the hospital with siren blaring.

"You're a lucky, lucky man," said the emergency doctor.

"No shit," was McKee's only reply.

Miraculously, McKee was only shaken and bruised a little. He was fully awake by the time he arrived in the emergency room, with no broken bones and no internal injuries. By some fluke he had not been seared by the flames. Covered with bandages, he walked through the eager reporters standing outside awaiting his release. He was limping slightly as he made his way to Betty's waiting car. He stopped for a moment.

"Shit happens," he told the crowd.

"Herschel, it just doesn't make any sense. No one man can have that much good luck."

McKee shrugged his shoulders. Betty drove him home without uttering another word. Investigation of the crash found that the left pilot chute had been packed erroneously by one of the technicians, causing the apparatus to deploy non-sequentially. The twisted lines that resulted caused an abrupt and excessive strain on the canister, ripping it from the wing. The project was put on immediate hold. McKee returned undaunted to Indianapolis.

Chapter 16

'DEATH DRIVERS' AND MARRIAGE #2

Life after the parachute plane's failure gradually returned to normal, or as normal as McKee's life had ever been. The Air Force decided to improve individual pilot's chutes as well as the pilot's ability to eject from a disabled plane, rather than to rely on what was now being called a failed invention. The media storm quickly subsided following the crash and McKee went back looking for a ride. He was anxious to resume his racing career even if it meant being the mechanic. He spent the rest of 1932 hanging around race shops in or near Indianapolis. Word throughout various garages had driver Chet Gardner looking for a mechanic to ride with him throughout the entire 1933 season. McKee made contact with Gardner in November, as soon as he heard the news.

Gardner hailed from Missouri and was a popular driver, although not tremendously successful. 1933 would be his second 500 Mile Race. His rookie year had been in 1930, when he lasted only one lap and retired after a spin in Turn 1. He missed the race altogether in 1932 due to a lack of funding. He was not a wealthy man and needed sponsorship to compete. Working hard, he managed to obtain adequate sponsorship for the entire 1933 season from the Sampson Radio Company, a relatively new communications outfit. So far he was doing well in the AAA Sprint Car division, and was optimistic about his chances at Indianapolis. McKee's reputation as a superb riding mechanic was generally known, and Gardner wanted the best man available.

Sampson engineers had recently developed a radio system, the first of its kind, that would allow pit crew members to communicate with the cockpit while a car was competing on the track. The apparatus was a trifle clumsy, but it worked reasonably well. McKee wore a set of large earphones over his leather cap when they were racing, and he would shout to Gardner any messages that came in. They qualified a respectable 15th with a speed of just over 112mph. "Wild" Bill Cummings took pole position with an average speed of 118mph.

There were a whopping 62 entries for the event, even with the Depression still in full swing, though many of the cars were barely drivable due to poor upkeep as a result of the economic situation. They were entered by owners unrealistically hoping for a lucky payout. The Speedway's management, also feeling the effects of the Depression, announced a decrease in the purse for the first time in their history. To appease the disappointed drivers, however, they agreed to a 42-car starting field. This was, and still remains, the largest starting field in 500 Mile Race history.

The smaller purse wasn't the only issue to affect the drivers. On race-day morning Howdy Wilcox II was found by the track's physician to have suffered a diabetic low blood-sugar attack. He was weak, shaky and drenched with sweat when he appeared at the track medical center and was immediately disqualified by the stewards as a potential hazard. Wilcox was in his second year of competition, having astounded everyone in 1932 when he finished second as a rookie. Despite his name, he was not related to the Howdy Wilcox who first introduced McKee to the Speedway after the war.

Wilcox had earned the respect of the other drivers with his outstanding performance the previous year, and was supported as they all threatened to go on strike over his disqualification. A short time after the decision was made, he admitted to his colleagues in a private drivers' meeting that he really was under the weather and that he had even asked the stewards to consider allowing his owner to replace him with another driver. A second meeting was quickly arranged and the stewards unanimously agreed to allow the substitution. This action initially appeased the drivers, but their appeasement did not last for long.

Their confidence was next rocked when they discovered that the driver picked to replace Wilcox had never even been on a racetrack before, let alone in a racing car. They again threatened to strike. Another stewards' meeting was held and it was agreed to have the "rookie" start in last place. The rookie who caused the drivers so much grief was none other than Mauri Rose, subsequently one of the most successful drivers to ever compete at Indianapolis. He would win the famous race three times. McKee stayed out of the controversy, as did most of the other mechanics. He didn't really care who was in the race, wishing only that he was driving one of the cars.

For McKee at least the 1933 race turned out to be a huge success. Louis Meyer won in his Miller with an average speed of nearly 117mph, but Gardner finished fourth, placing McKee in the money at Indianapolis for the first time. For nearly everyone outside the top ten drivers, however, the event was a disaster. Three drivers and two mechanics were killed in the crash-marred race, all pronounced dead at the scene. The traditional victory dinner was cancelled as a result, and a movement was soon initiated by some local do-gooders to discontinue the race altogether. Eddie Rickenbacker, the track's owner, lost money on the race for the first time and began to doubt the wisdom of his 1927 purchase from Carl Fisher.

During a post-race interview in the garage area, McKee was asked the following question by a local newsman:

"In view of the fact that five people lost their lives in this event, have you ever been afraid of losing yours?"

"Sir, I have no fear of death. To me it is no different than falling asleep."

With that comment, he turned to Gardner and they toasted their good fortune with some leftover champagne. The two men planned to continue their apparently successful partnership throughout the remainder of the season. McKee was additionally inspired by the fact that prohibition was over. He grabbed Betty and they headed to their usual downtown haunt.

A few days after the race, McKee was contacted by a representative of a little-known pilots' organization called the Mexican Aero Club. The club was located in Chicago. He was asked if he would become an honorary member and help them organize a flight school for budding Mexican-American pilots.

"You've got to be kidding!" was McKee's reply.

McKee assumed that the Mexicans were another band of slave-traders who must have heard of his Chinese Tong escapade but obviously hadn't heard the end of the story. The Mexicans swore to McKee that they were honest and above-board. A bit suspicious, he confirmed their validity with the Mexican government. The request was legitimate, so McKee accepted the challenge. He worked this new enterprise into his now burgeoning schedule by coordinating his mail flights to Chicago in such a way as to allow ample time to teach the Mexicans. He taught several of them how to fly, and for his efforts received an award of distinction from the Mexican government.

Gardner and McKee finished in the money twice more in 1933. They finished second at Milwaukee, Wisconsin, in July and third at Syracuse, New York, in September. With his share of the prize money from Indy, his monthly check from the government, the money paid by the Mexicans, and his occasional plane deliveries, McKee was now making a fairly good income. Bolstered by a feeling of financial security he decided to go it alone in 1934. He still had the urge to drive, now more than ever, and felt that his time was quickly running out. He certainly wasn't getting any younger.

During the years of the Depression, a gradual change was taking place in American motor sports. The days of the independently wealthy and carefree driver/sportsman were gone. More and more "professional" drivers, men who drove racecars for a living, now dominated the rosters. Mauri Rose, Wilbur Shaw, Rex Mays, Ralph Hepburn and Bill Cummings were a few of the drivers who were fast becoming household names. McKee was also well known in some parts of the country, but mostly because of his daredevil crash history and his World War One exploits, not because of his racing expertise. His success as a racing driver was nil. He enjoyed the notoriety he had, but he wanted in addition to be known as a great racing driver. He began knocking on more doors and making more phone calls.

McKee had no luck finding a willing owner throughout the fall and early winter. 1934 arrived and there were still no offers. He reluctantly placed a call to Gardner, who had yet to hire another mechanic. He graciously took McKee back and they gave Indianapolis another shot. They qualified fifth and were hopeful of a good finish but the engine threw a rod on lap 72 and they finished 21st, the race being won by Bill Cummings. McKee told Gardner afterwards that he was going to give it one more try on his own. He thanked him for giving him another chance, and the two separated for the second time.

Nothing materialized for McKee throughout the summer and he was becoming despondent. He was beginning to think his auto racing days just might be over. In August, with his money again running low, he joined a traveling thrill show out of necessity. The show was aptly named "Death Drivers". Several Fairs around the Midwest scheduled the show. Once finished with their horse-racing events, the Fairs would turn their front straightaways into an arena for the thrill show and the "Death Drivers" would take center stage.

McKee was Act 1. Dressed like an American Flag, he drove his newest Harley-Davidson through his now famous wall of fire. With the torque of this new model, he was capable of jumping nearly 40 feet high before crashing through the flames. To reach this height he had to be going over 60mph when he hit the ramp, the long front stretch providing sufficient room to attain the necessary speed. Advertisements for the show called attention to the fact that he wore no specialized clothing, that his helmet was only leather, and that the fire was really hot. Coating his face with petroleum jelly was said to be the only precaution he ever took. Betty, dressed scantily, played the part of his assistant and hoped for the best. She customarily closed her eyes the second McKee hit the ramp.

Joining McKee in the show was daredevil Harold Stuckey, a local stock car racer who jumped a totally stock Plymouth over a bigger ramp than McKee's for distance. His personal record was stated in the program to be 68ft. At every show, it was pre-announced that he would likely break his record with a truly death-defying leap. At every show, he would fall just short of the record on his first two attempts but would then clear 68ft on his third and final attempt amidst a thunderous roar from the crowd. Stuckey also needed an approach speed of at least 60mph. A mile a minute was considered flying to most highway travelers in those days.

After finishing their separate acts, McKee would jump into a second Plymouth and he and Stuckey would face-off at either end of the straightaway. They would methodically strap themselves into their respective cars amidst an appropriate degree of fanfare and an able assistant would blindfold each man. Betty, of course, took care of McKee. The two "Death Drivers" would then speed toward each other, culminating in a grinding head-on crash at a combined speed of at times more than 60mph. Following the crash, their cars badly crumpled, leaking fluids and smoking, both men would emerge smartly through their respective windows and salute the crowd, who were roaring their approval. Unknown to the audience, both men could see through their specially prepared blindfolds, the deception invariably working. But wait! The show was not yet over.

Following the head-on crash, with the crowd still on its feet and cheering wildly, Wildman Don Stokes, padded and also blindfolded, would leap from the bumper of a third Plymouth driven by Betty at over 70mph. Wildman would do a body slide on his back for the entire length of the front straightaway while giving the crowd a military salute.

"Hell of a way to make a livin'," McKee would say.

The show lasted throughout the Fair season, ending in mid-September. Surprisingly none of the performers was killed or seriously injured. The "Death Drivers" were a big hit in every town they played, being always mindful not to consume too much alcohol before the show. When the tour was finished, McKee and Betty headed west as usual. He notified the postal service and his delivery contractors, said goodbye to his parents and left town, not knowing what might lie in store. The only plan he had was to hang around some of the racetracks and try to procure a ride.

A big race was scheduled for December 20 at the Mines Field racetrack located near the Los Angeles Municipal Airport. McKee began hanging out in the garage area four days before the event. He looked like Jackie Gleason's "Poor Soul" character, and was about to leave at the end of the day when well-known and well-respected driver "Doc" MacKenzie walked up to him. MacKenzie said a quick hello and then pointedly asked McKee if he would be his riding mechanic. MacKenzie was a fairly good "shoe" from Philadelphia and McKee said yes. They signed a deal that gave McKee a generous share of the prize money, if indeed they finished in the money.

MacKenzie had managed to obtain substantial sponsorship from a major oil and gas speculator by the name of Gil Pirrung. Pirrung was a millionaire from California who could buy all of the racecars in the field if he wanted to. He was thrilled to have McKee on board as the mechanic.

Race day saw the largest crowd in Mines Field history with more than 50,000 in attendance. The normally rutted, one-and-a-quarter mile dirt track had been smoothed and graded as never before. High speeds were predicted. All of the top Indianapolis drivers were entered in what was to be a very grueling 200-miler.

MacKenzie and McKee – the newspapers had fun with that combination of names – garnered attention wherever they went. They were described as "a new and formidable team". Both drivers were of Scottish ancestry, but neither of them had ever been to Scotland. A reporter brought their heritage up one day and McKee admitted that he had premonitions about one day being in Scotland. How or why he would get over there remained a mystery.

The race began on schedule with MacKenzie jumping into second place from their fourth place starting position before the end of the first lap. On the 33rd lap, race leader Rex Mays was forced to stop for a tire change and MacKenzie charged into the lead. He drove like "another Barney Oldfield" for the next 40 laps. McKee had never experienced a drive like this one. MacKenzie appeared to be under some sort of magical spell, in the zone so to speak. No one ever got close enough to the pair to launch an attack for the lead. By lap 76, he and McKee had lapped the entire field twice, a feat unheard of in modern racing history.

On lap 77 their bubble suddenly burst when the unthinkable happened. The car inexplicably sputtered to a stop right in the middle of the South Turn. They were out of gas. McKee, frustrated beyond belief, threw his hands into the air and began babbling something in Chinese. Despite repeated warnings from the pit crew, MacKenzie had stupidly refused to make a pit stop. Looking forlorn, he and McKee sat sheepishly in the car, while much of the field passed them by. They were still one lap ahead.

The disgruntled and now anxious crew loaded a few gallons of precious petrol on board their tow car, and sped against race traffic to the stalled racer. They managed to fire the engine, but not until the team was passed for position by three cars. Kelly Pettilo won the race, with Wilbur Shaw second and Ralph Hepburn third. Because of the huge lead they had at the time of the debacle, MacKenzie and McKee still managed to finish fourth. They were awarded a whopping $750 for their effort.

The race did not cover the scheduled distance of 200 miles, being called due to a dense fog that rapidly rolled in from the bay. With visibility at the start of the next to last lap reduced dangerously the officials had no choice but to red flag the event. The press had a field day with the story of MacKenzie's humiliating defeat following such a brilliant drive. Most felt that MacKenzie had become transfixed, transported to some sort of la-la land, seemingly hypnotized by the rhythm he was sustaining lap after lap with no one in close contention.

Mac apologized to McKee after the race and basically kept a low profile throughout the Christmas holiday. Christmas for McKee was spent with Betty. They rented their favorite cottage on Laguna Beach following the Mines Field event, and enjoyed the sand and surf. With nothing scheduled on New Year's Eve, they decided to have a quiet dinner in the cottage. To Betty's surprise, McKee abruptly proposed just before dessert. She was shocked to her toenails. After gazing at the ocean for about five seconds, she looked into McKee's guilty but sparkling blue eyes and said yes.

McKee grabbed her in his arms and took her crashing into the sea. They frolicked in the waves for a time, watching the midnight fireworks launched from shore. As the final flickering pieces of debris settled into the sea, they ran dripping wet into the cottage. McKee had never spent a more passionate night. In the morning, Betty asked if it was for real.

"It is, as long as you don't put no apron strings on me," McKee replied.

The newly engaged couple decided to wait until spring and get married in Indianapolis. McKee continued to run with MacKenzie through the rest of the now abbreviated winter season. The once popular board tracks were rapidly disappearing. Most of them simply deteriorated from decay and infestation, becoming too difficult and expensive to repair. Many were sold to developers. New, permanent dirt track facilities, like the one at Mines Field, were taking their place.

McKee asked and was granted permission to make a practice run on such a track in Mac's car. He discovered immediately that dirt track driving was not his forte. On the boards, a driver could push the throttle to the floor and hang on for dear life provided he was brave enough. On dirt, you had to have a modicum of finesse. It took McKee five attempts before he was able to complete a single lap. He kept spinning out. He lost control on a different part of the racetrack on every lap. Fortunately, he didn't hit anything or anybody.

Riding mechanics, too, were being phased out of the sport. Rumors prevailed that the new car designs would only allow enough room for one man. Aerodynamics began to rule the world of motor sports. In addition, the engines and internal workings of the cars had become more sophisticated, no longer needing an on-board wrench to sort out problems. McKee planned to hang on for as long as he could. He loved the speed, the danger and the small bit of fame that surrounded him.

He reluctantly began to think about finding a steady job. It had been a long time since he had worked at Stutz, and they were not doing all that well financially. The chances of going back there were less than slim. He had no other options on the table. The thoughts he gave to working full time were fleeting. He resumed his search for a car that he could drive.

He and Betty finished out the winter season and headed home to their wedding. McKee, in true McKee fashion, never divulged his first marriage. He hoped he could keep it a secret. If Betty found out, he would tell her that he had simply given in to youthful impulsiveness. Betty never did find out. They were married in April during a quiet ceremony at a small church in their neighborhood. Their parents were the only guests. They honeymooned briefly in New York before returning to Indianapolis, hoping to prepare for the 1935 Race.

The Miller team had a year-old car that was reportedly in fairly good condition. MacKenzie helped convince the team's manager to let McKee attempt to qualify the car for the 500. It would likely be his last chance to drive in what had now become the world's biggest automobile race. He was extremely lucky to have this opportunity and he realized it. McKee practiced doggedly and was up to sufficient speed by the day before qualifying. He drew an early position for the next morning's attempt.

On Saturday, he appeared very relaxed and in control as he headed onto the track for his ten-lap qualifying effort. His first two laps were good, just over 112mph. On lap three, however, he made a costly error, pinching the corner slightly going into Turn 1. He went into a wild spin followed by a long slide. He brushed the wall and came to a stop in the infield grass just inside of Turn 2. The damage to the car was relatively minor and could have been repaired if the team had more time. The damage to McKee's psyche was considerable. His debut as an Indy 500 driver was over before it began.

MacKenzie felt truly sorry for McKee – so much so that he let the young mechanic go that he had recently hired and offered the position to McKee, who humbly accepted. MacKenzie qualified well, in 15th position. He finished ninth. McKee, dealing with a persistent oil leak throughout the race, managed to keep the car running until the end. Kelly Petillo won, with Wilbur Shaw second. McKee stayed in the car following the checkered flag, riding back to the garage area with MacKenzie. He gave him a big hug and returned trackside to enjoy some of the victory celebration that was still going on.

Famed aviatrix Amelia Earhart was in Victory Lane with Captain Eddie Rickenbacker to congratulate the winner. She had worked throughout the month as the first female referee ever assigned to the great race. She was a close friend of the Captain's and he introduced her to McKee. Restraining himself during the introduction was difficult. Earhart was McKee's kind of woman. She was captivating, more cute than she was pretty, and most of all she could fly. Think of the possibilities. McKee and Earhart; Earhart and McKee. The opportunities were endless. Earhart politely declined McKee's not too subtle overtures. She left immediately after the race to continue preparing for her ill-fated flight around the world.

Chapter 17

A REAL JOB

McKee went home to Betty as usual and officially gave up the idea of ever becoming a racing driver. Flying remained his passion – it was what he was really good at. Money was again tight in the McKee household, since he had squandered much of it trying to secure his ride. His share as the riding mechanic, even at Indy, was small in comparison to what the driver made. But now the sport had changed, as had the economy, and there were fewer opportunities for him as a mechanic. To make matters worse, airplane deliveries were down. It took the combined incomes from what deliveries he had, his thrill show and the pay from the government, as well as Betty's salary, for the two of them to live in the manner to which they had become accustomed. The reality of their situation finally hit him. He was going to have to get a real job.

The Allison Engine Company was located directly across from the Speedway on West 16th Street. Started as a small performance company building custom engine parts for race teams in the early '20s, Allison's soon began to refurbish, design and build specialized engines. They had recently started to modernize old Liberty aircraft engines, making them more powerful for use in either boats or airplanes. Gar Wood was a frequent customer. The company, while defining itself, had gone through a couple of different hands before finally being purchased by General Motors in the early '30s. Shortly thereafter they began an ambitious project to develop a V-12 engine for the military.

Allison's was the logical place for McKee to land a job. The business was frequented by familiar racing personalities, former acquaintances of his from the military, and some wealthy aircraft tycoons for whom he had made deliveries. The opportunities working in a place like Allison's during that period were endless. Rumors of renewed unrest in Europe were prevalent, and there was even talk of another world war. Allison's had its hand on the pulse of the world's politics as well as the high-performance engine market.

McKee applied for a job and was hired as a quality control technician. He was also expected to perform as an occasional test pilot for the new engines. As far as his racing was concerned, the contract allowed him to participate in the Indianapolis 500 only. McKee's family was thrilled that he finally appeared to be planting some roots. He did confide to his racing buddies that the position with Allison's was likely to be only temporary. The remainder of 1935 went by in a blur. Between learning his new job and flying the mail he was kept comfortably busy.

Development of the new V-12 consumed most of the winter. Initially turned down by the Army, the 1,000hp engine was being looked at in earnest by the US Navy. They planned to use it in their rigid airship (dirigible) program. The Navy wanted to increase the performance of their two sister ships, the *Macon* and the *Akron*, already in service. These huge airships were unlike today's blimps in that they had rigid skeletons that allowed access to the interior via catwalks. The catwalks led to adjoining rooms or, in the case of these two ships, large hangars.

The *Macon* and *Akron* could store, launch and retrieve up to five fighter planes at a time through T-shaped openings in the floors of their two hangars. A welded metal hook, called a "skyhook", would latch onto the top of a fighter plane's upper wing, being guided in place by the pilot. The plane would then be pulled into the bowels of the dirigible. The apparatus resembled a large trapeze.

Using the skyhook, planes could be raised or lowered from the mother ship. When docking, the pilot was required to delicately guide the plane into contact with the trapeze. To do this successfully he had to match the speed of the dirigible exactly. It was a hazardous maneuver, with any slip-up a potential disaster for both plane and airship.

The purpose of the Navy's airship service was to give more range to scouting missions and to improve observational capabilities. Dirigibles would climb several thousand feet into the air and remain stationary while the fighters used them as a base for operations. The dirigibles essentially functioned as aircraft carriers in the sky. The idea was felt by many in Congress, and most of the military's top brass, to be promising in the event of a war in the Pacific. The potential for danger was unacceptable to most.

McKee, of course, jumped at the offer to pilot a fighter into, and out of, the dirigible. He chose the *Macon*. This was 785ft long, nearly as long as the *Titanic*. It held accommodations for 100 individuals. Rooms, in addition to the hangars, included sleeping berths with toilet facilities, a mess hall and a galley. The *Macon* could cruise at nearly 80mph, propelled by two German-built engines, each of 560hp.

It took McKee only two tries to connect with the trapeze. Few had learned the maneuver so quickly. Once inside the enormous airship, he was given the grand tour. He informed the Captain that with two of the new 1,000hp Allison engines installed, the speed of the *Macon* would increase by 10–15mph. The idea of using dirigibles for their intended purpose appeared sound to him.

McKee returned to Indianapolis from the *Macon*'s home base at Moffett Field very keen on the project. He actually became the project's biggest cheerleader, instilling new vigor into the engine team. Development was revved up, and the V-12 engines were made ready. Installation was scheduled to begin within two months.

On February 12, three weeks after McKee's visit, the *Macon* was returning home from an offshore exercise in marginal conditions. Without suitable radar, it flew directly into a massive storm off Point Sur, California. The extreme turbulence and wind shear tossed the *Macon* around like a small boat in a hurricane. Significant structural damage occurred. The huge airship foundered and was swallowed by the sea. Miraculously, only two men died in the incident. The *Macon* sank into deep water, taking its airplanes with it. All equipment and supplies were lost. The Navy elected to abandon the controversial program shortly after the crash. In turn, they abandoned the Allison V-12 engine program.

McKee, along with the rest of the Allison employees, was disappointed to say the least. He grumbled around for days trying to gain interest in one of the company's other projects. After about three weeks, the Army, who had initially turned down the engine, suddenly developed renewed interest and signed a development contract. It would be another two years before the final design was approved and put into use.

In the spring of 1937 the huge engine was finally approved and certified at 1,000hp – the first aircraft engine that powerful. It was quickly installed into America's new generation of fighter planes, the P-38 Lightning, the P-39 Airacobra and the P-40 Warhawk. "Lucky" McKee was allowed to test fly them all.

Chapter 18

VIOLA, A MISTAKE, AND MARRIAGE #3

The 1936 Indianapolis 500 Mile Race found McKee with yet another new driver. Cliff Bergere was born in Ohio and started his automotive career as a stunt driver. He was a regular on the AAA circuit with several top-five finishes to his credit. He was fast, capable and very confident about his chances to win. He convinced McKee that he had a good car with excellent financial backing. What he needed, he said, was a proven mechanic. He asked McKee to accept that responsibility. McKee agreed.

Bergere qualified fifth and was a pre-race favorite to win. McKee had been with a successfully qualified driver before and knew not to get his hopes up too high. Good thing. They finished 22nd due to a failed engine mount. In spite of the disappointing finish, McKee still experienced an exhilarating May, although his exhilaration was only marginally related to the sport of automobile racing.

Early in the month he was informed of his admittance into the International League of Aviators. At the time this was the highest honor a pilot could receive. The induction ceremonies would not be held until July, but McKee could not keep the secret and told almost everyone he knew. The story broke in the Indianapolis papers, with a number of articles touting McKee's deeds both in and out of the military. McKee used the story to introduce himself to a Miss Viola Cain.

McKee met Miss Cain while judging a beauty contest the weekend the track opened for practice. Miss Cain was one of the contestants. She was, in fact, the prettiest contestant and won the contest. McKee could not take his eyes off of her. After the trophy presentation, he introduced himself. His charm unsettled her a bit, causing her to whisper her words as her face turned almost crimson. Miss Cain had entered the contest mostly because she loved auto racing. She grew up near the track, and was enamored with its sights, sounds and smells. She admired the men in the machines, considering them to be heroes. McKee, with his devilish smile working overtime, took her arm in his and they headed toward the parking lot.

Betty was not at the track that day, having remained at home for most of the month. In fact she did not hang out at the track at all. She was planning to attend the race, but that was it. Her teaching job was keeping her busy and tired – she had taken the job in order to help out with their finances. It wasn't that McKee's income was all that bad, it was the fact that his tastes, and subsequently her tastes, had increased so substantially. They were occasionally hobnobbing with some of the country's elite.

Money was pouring into motor sports from every corner of the globe. The Depression was nearly over and the rich were getting richer. Auto racing had evolved into one of the favorite pastimes of the privileged, along with other less traditional sports such as yachting and powerboat racing. Oilmen, auto magnates and industrialists enjoyed the danger-laden competition. McKee, in fact, had just dined with famous yachtsman Sir Thomas Lipton the day before he met Viola. The pomp and circumstance seemed to attract them all.

As they entered the parking lot, Viola gasped, clutching her throat. She had just laid her eyes on McKee's new car. He was driving a baby blue Cadillac convertible, top of the line. It was to become his signature automobile for many years to come. He deftly guided Viola into the driver's seat and invited her to go for a ride in the country. She was still in her bathing suit as she slid alluringly and without protest into the soft, dark blue leather passenger seat. It was the beginning of what would become a long and bizarre relationship.

Viola was a brunette, trim, and usually very proper in her appearance and demeanor. That is, unless she had just won a beauty contest at the racetrack. She was 23 years old and had no idea that McKee was married. All she knew about McKee was that he was a riding mechanic and war hero; that was enough. He wasn't about to acknowledge Betty's existence, nor was he going to tell her much more about himself.

"The less a woman knows about you the better," he would often tell his driver friends.

McKee had a formidable task ahead of him. Juggling two women at the racetrack is not easy. To survive, you need the help of a trusted friend. MacKenzie fit that bill. Mac agreed to summon McKee, either by phone or in person, at prescribed times to get him safely from one encounter to another. While McKee sat around bored at home in the evening, Mac would call announcing a card game in the garage area. McKee would jump into the Cadillac and meet Viola for a drink downtown. Their nights were short by necessity, as overnight stays were out of the question, at least while in Indianapolis. Betty, being forever naïve, never questioned his late-night returns home. She would simply admonish him not to lose their house in a game of chance.

Viola and Herschel grew quite fond of each other as the month progressed. Their encounters became more and more intimate. McKee would often think to himself that what he was doing might not sit well with most people, but he didn't want to stop doing it. It wasn't that he was tired of Betty, in fact he truly loved her. He just could not believe that a man should be limited to only one woman at a time.

"They all have something different to offer and I don't mean just in bed either," he told Mac one day.

"You may just end up dead," was the quick reply.

McKee wasn't sure how he was going to handle both women on race day. He and Betty had developed a well-defined ritual over the years. She would always travel to the track with him early in the morning, and then help him with his gear prior to the cars being placed on the grid. After the race, she was the first one to the car with a big smile and a hug regardless of how the team finished. Later, following the team's debriefing in the garage area, she and McKee would hit a tavern somewhere and get smashed. This routine had been going on uninterrupted for quite some time.

McKee formulated the following plan. He would tell Viola that it was bad luck to be with a woman on race day. Women were not allowed in the garage area in the 1930s and wouldn't be until many years later. Viola thought this a reasonable practice. After the race, he would announce that he had to go straight to the airport for an emergency mail run to Chicago. He would tell Viola he would not be able to see her until he returned on Wednesday. He would let Betty know that he would come right home after delivering the mail. *Piece of cake*, he thought.

Viola and Betty were none the wiser. McKee left in a borrowed plane for Chicago immediately after the race. He arranged for a special friend from Granite City to meet him when he landed. She was an add-on to the plan following a quick post-race phone call. She would make the short stay in Chicago infinitely more pleasant. On inspection, McKee was not thrilled with the condition of the airplane he had borrowed. He found oil visible, oozing from beneath one of the valve covers, and the tires looked to be well worn. He cranked her up anyway and took off into a clear sky for Chicago.

A cold front had passed through Indiana the day before, leaving a brisk north wind and a crystal blue sky in its wake. McKee arrived in the Chicago area toward dusk and he began his descent. The plane had performed well. But as he approached the runway on final, the engine suddenly made a disturbing noise and burst into flames. Thick black smoke obscured his vision as he came in to land with the aircraft fully ablaze, but he was able to get it down safely by using the visual image he had stored of the runway before the flames had erupted. He bounced a few times on landing and one wheel came off as he rolled to a stop. Otherwise the plane stayed intact. McKee hastily climbed out of yet another smoldering wreck unscathed.

A newspaper reporter, at the airport to cover another story, watched the entire episode in amazement. Sadly there was no photographer present to record the crash, but an article in the *Tribune* the next morning would tell the tale. In essence, it stated that "Lucky Herschel McKee, having just finished the grueling Indianapolis 500, is lucky to be alive (again) after bringing in the mail aboard his flaming aircraft just as the sun set over Lake Michigan."

McKee talked to the guy for more than an hour after the episode while the special friend from Granite City, whose name was Grace, waited patiently in the car.

"Hell of an entrance, McKee," she said.

"Yep, I guess I lucked out again. Let's get out of here."

McKee spent a lovely night with Grace at her home on the near Westside. He had met the dark-haired beauty two years earlier while drinking the night away with the Chinese Tong members. In the morning he awoke early, said his goodbyes, and left to inspect the burned airplane. It was a goner. He informed his friend back in Indianapolis that he should be more careful about his maintenance. He then began to search for a ride back home. As luck would have it, his friend Bill Alexander landed just as McKee finished his inspection. Alexander was on a mail run with a return trip planned to Indianapolis that afternoon. McKee was sitting in the pilots' lounge when Alexander walked in.

"What in the hell are you doing up here, you crazy son of a bitch?"

"Got one in every port, you know," McKee snickered.

The two men hadn't seen each other since their Mars Hill encounter several years earlier. They reminisced a bit, both men still miffed that Lindbergh managed to make the flight across the Atlantic and not one of them. They each downed several cups of coffee and left for Indianapolis with the sky still clear. When they arrived, McKee took Alexander to St Elmo's for dinner. It was a beautiful night so he put the top down.

"I didn't know racing paid so well."

"It don't."

McKee had been keeping his job at Allison's a secret. He did not want his racing friends sniffing around job-hunting – he was afraid they might get hired, diluting his position in the process. He told Alexander the job was only part-time and he would be racing full-time again soon. They said their goodbyes at the airport, promising not to take ten years before seeing each other again.

McKee returned home to Betty. Viola didn't expect him for another day. He told Betty about seeing Alexander again but kept the flaming plane story to himself. No reason to make things more complicated than they already were. He was due at Allison's by 8:00 in the morning. Betty received him with open arms.

Luckily, no one had seen the article in the Chicago paper and the wire services hadn't picked up the story. For all anyone knew McKee had been on a routine mail run. He and Viola got together by the end of the week, extending his juggling act. He manipulated the two women unabated for the next several weeks. The relationship with Viola accelerated. In mid-July, McKee phoned Viola during his lunch break to say he would pick her up around 6:00pm. He told her he had big plans for the evening.

Betty bought the story that he would be playing cards with the boys until the sun came up. So far, he had only met with Viola in places away from her home and for brief encounters. Tonight he was going to pick her up at her house. He had not yet had the pleasure of meeting her mother. McKee parked the Caddy next to the curb in front of the small home. He leaped from the car, not bothering to open the door, and jogged up the short walkway. Taking the porch steps two at a time, he nearly ran into the door. He rang the bell in eager anticipation.

"Who the hell are you?" came an unknown voice from behind the locked door.

"I'm Herschel McKee. Are you Viola's mom?"

"You just get right on out of here, fella. Viola's not home."

While deciding whether or not to leave, McKee caught a glimpse of a small, lithe figure, hunched over, tip-toeing from the back of the house. The person, if that is indeed what it was, was shrouded in a gauze-like material looking for all the world like an apparition. It moved to his car with increasing rapidity and jumped in. The hooded top slipped back once the figure had settled, exposing a giggling Viola.

"Hurry up, McKee, let's get the hell outa here."

McKee bolted for the car with Viola's mother in hot pursuit. He jumped in, starting the engine before his butt hit the seat. With tires smoking he sped away from the scene, Mom and broom filling the rear view mirror. Viola, her head on his shoulder, was laughing hysterically.

"I forgot to warn you about Mom."

Viola's mother treated all potential lovers with the same initial kindness. It was very likely the reason Viola was still single. *This will certainly be a new and imposing challenge*, thought McKee. He turned the corner and headed for the Circle downtown. A whisky about now would sure hit the spot.

Dinner, accompanied by a fine bottle of Cabernet, was consumed at the Claypool Hotel. McKee had already booked a room upstairs and the couple retired there after dessert. The room he chose for their pleasure was the palatial presidential suite. A bottle of brandy sat invitingly before the fire. McKee had thought of everything. It was to be the perfect night.

In the midst of their passion, Viola, with some apprehension in her voice, whispered into his ear "Herschel, didn't you bring any protection?"

Whoops! He hadn't thought of everything. There was nothing he could do about it now. Viola announced her pregnancy six weeks later. Her doctor said she was due sometime in the early spring. McKee took the news as he always did.

"Well I'll be damned. Guess we'll just have to get married."

"Oh Herschel, you're the sweetest, kindest man there is!"

Herschel married Viola in October. He negotiated for and, after a long and somewhat heated exchange, received a change of venue. They married quietly in Las Vegas rather than Indianapolis. He simply told Betty he needed to go out West to put a deal together for Indy. After the marriage, McKee decided he would be much safer in California. He sent Viola back to Indy and headed to Laguna Beach. He summoned Betty to join him in November, leaving Viola pining away at home. He got a leave of absence from Allison's on the pretense that he needed to revamp his racing career.

I'm not sure I need all this trouble, he thought to himself, *but it certainly makes life more challenging.* McKee worked at several odd jobs along the California coast, even considering a movie career at one point. He had met a bit actor by the name of L.H. Hooper and through him landed a couple of stunt gigs. In one, he drove a getaway car, and in the other he flew a biplane in a World War One re-enactment. Becoming an actor was curtailed by Howard Hughes, who told him that he didn't have the voice for it, though Hughes did acknowledge his flying expertise.

McKee wrote to both wives regularly, keeping them informed of his whereabouts and adventures. Neither one had an inkling about the other. For the previous 20 years McKee had repeatedly faced almost unimaginable dangers. Every time he crashed he managed to escape death, having suffered only a few serious injuries in the process. During all those years he had never once shown an ounce of fear or developed any symptoms of what is now called "post traumatic stress disorder". Whether he was dogfighting over Germany, flying the mail while dodging snow and thunderstorms in and around Indiana, upside down in a burning racecar, or racing on the infamous splinter tracks of California, he was unafraid. Being married to two women at the same time was a different deal. He was terrified!

Sympathy was scarce. Even his racing buddies failed to bolster his confidence. They were all happy it was him and not them. McKee wasn't sure when he would return to the potentially life-threatening situation in Indianapolis, but he did want to compete in the race one last time. Word was out that 1937 would be the last year for riding mechanics. He began searching for a new driver, one he thought he could finally win with. He accepted plane deliveries that would take him to cities with racing venues in order to get close to more potential drivers.

In February 1937 he agreed to deliver a plane to Chicago. It was destined for a General Motors' executive who frequented California during the winter months. It was a new monoplane built by Lockheed called the Vega, designed by Jack Northrop, a flying colleague of McKee's in WW1. It was a newer version of the plane flown by Miss Earhart on her successful solo flight across the Atlantic in 1932. McKee's flight to Chicago was, for once, uneventful.

When he landed he went straight to the old greyhound dog track to take in an indoor midget race. Midget auto racing had been introduced in California in 1933 and was becoming very popular in the Midwest as well as along the eastern seaboard. The cars were scaled-down versions of Indianapolis-type racers, with small block engines. Some of the cars used motorcycle engines. Tracks were oval in shape and as short as one-fifth of a mile. The racing was extremely exciting, dangerous and hotly competitive. Midgets soon became the most popular form of entry-level racing in America.

McKee was introduced to driver Herb Ardinger that evening. Ardinger told McKee that he had a good car and sponsorship for the 500 and did indeed need a mechanic. McKee agreed to a deal and they shook hands. Ardinger was from Pennsylvania and a fairly quick driver. He was 27 years old when he met McKee. The car was sponsored by the Chicago Rawhide Company and was called the "Oil Seal Special". McKee had never heard of the company, but he had a ride. He and Ardinger agreed to get together in April to plan for the race in May. *How many times have I done this?* he thought.

Viola was doing well with her pregnancy, the only issue being her mother. Mom wanted to know when the father was coming home, when they would get a house of their own, and was there any real hope of him ever being a responsible husband and father? There was no let-up in her questioning. Viola tried to ease her mind, even to the point of letting her read the letters that arrived weekly. McKee's letters offered little comfort to the smoldering soon-to-be grandmother. Most of the subject matter dealt with racing and airplanes, there was no mention of the coming child.

Betty, who lived on the opposite side of town, also received a weekly update from McKee. She very much wanted to be in California with him as they so often were at this time of year. She wasn't sure she should buy his excuse. Rather unconvincingly, he blamed their current separation on his need for extensive travel. Being the good sport that she was, she went along with it regardless of the fact she remained doubtful.

McKee kept busy trying not to give too much thought to being a father. He had always been good at repressing the uncomfortable events of his life. At times his repressive skills worked extremely well, like when he was in the German prison. However, he was having more difficulty with this one. Viola reminded him relentlessly of the impending birth of their child in her return letters. This made the situation that much harder to ignore.

The inevitable reality of it all hit him square in the gut on April 10. McKee, like it or not, was the father of an 8½lb baby girl. Viola and her mother named the child Linda in his absence. The two parents had never discussed names, let alone anything else. Viola promised pictures. McKee went straight to the bar. Avoidance was another of his familiar defense strategies. He left the bar at closing time, barely able to navigate his way home. Once home, he became good and drunk, not seeing the light of day for nearly 72 hours.

McKee and Ardinger arrived in Indianapolis with the weather change. It had been mainly cold throughout most of March and early April and the citizens of Indianapolis were ready for winter's end. McKee – and this was no surprise to anyone who knew him – went to see Betty first. Viola did not expect him for another three days. At Betty's, he lamented on how tough the winter had been in California, "what with all that traveling and stuff".

He did tell her that he was thrilled to have the ride with Ardinger and that he thought they had a fair chance to do well.

Betty yawned, having heard all of that pre-race confidence before. She welcomed him back with a big hug.

In the morning, they headed to Brown County on the motorcycle, but not before McKee had to spend two hours getting it to run properly. Their trip was uneventful. It was unseasonably warm, with a lengthy wet period having preceded their ride. Consequently the leaves were out in abundance and the early blossoms were in spectacular bloom. They stayed with Celia and Tom in the old boarding house, talking well into the night. Stark had died and many of the impressionists had left the area seeking new locations. McKee and Betty stayed the night, leaving shortly after a big country breakfast. McKee again promised young Tom a position on the race team in May. His mother again said no.

McKee could avoid the issue no longer. He had to see Viola and the child. When he and Betty returned home, he phoned Viola and then informed Betty that he had to go to Chicago for a couple of days. She frowned, then smiled, and made him promise to be careful. He kissed her goodbye and went straight to Viola's. He rang the doorbell and stood patiently waiting for someone to answer. The outside screen door was standing slightly ajar while the main wooden door was tightly closed. He wasn't prepared for what happened next.

From out of nowhere came Viola's mother. McKee slammed the screen door the rest of the way shut in self-defense. She jerked the main door open, charging right through the screen with broom in hand. A hole, the shape of a grandmother with broom, was all that remained of the door. She beat McKee mercilessly about the head. He tried to ward the blows off with his arms, but they kept coming. Hunching into a ball, he managed to half run, half stumble off the porch. Mom was again in hot pursuit. The enraged woman kept swinging all the way to the car, managing to whack two dings in the Cadillac before

McKee was able to drive away. Viola was nowhere to be seen. He cursed himself as he sped down the narrow street.

On a hunch, McKee headed to the Claypool Hotel. Realizing he was driving way over the limit, he slowed his pace. He parked and entered the hotel. There she was, sitting in the lobby, baby basket in hand. McKee felt his heart skip a beat or two. He peered into the basket. The little girl had red hair, was asleep, and looked to him like a store-bought doll. He was deathly afraid to pick her up.

"Pick her up, Herschel. She's your daughter."

He slowly placed his two big hands, still with an abundance of grease under his fingernails, beneath her head and tiny body. As he gently lifted the child from the basket little Linda opened her eyes, took one look at her father and screamed. McKee held the baby out at arms' length and began turning in ill-defined circles.

"What the hell did I do?" he yelled.

Viola laughed and took the child from her now pale father. The screaming ceased. It was to be the last time McKee ever held Linda. With the initial encounter behind them, they sat down to a quiet dinner with conversation held to a minimum. Skipping dessert, McKee stood to leave. As he did so, Viola informed him that she had moved into a small house near her mother's and that he was welcome any time. She wasn't sure why she hadn't told him during dinner. She guessed she had been smitten with whatever she had been smitten with in the first place. His charm was still irresistible. They kissed and he walked out the door. He did not look back. He would not see his child again for nine long years.

With avoidance in high gear, McKee met Ardinger at the racetrack to go over the new car. She was a beauty. Ardinger was confident he could make her run up front. McKee spent nearly every waking hour at the track, effectively ignoring his domestic catastrophe. Most of the month had been miserably hot and he was growing impatient for the race to be run. Many of the teams were bickering internally among themselves. This race would be the last for all of the riding mechanics. Improved mechanization and aerodynamics made them obsolete. Much of their time was spent massaging the drivers' arms or shoulders anyway. McKee was quoted as saying: "I feel more like a masseuse than I do a mechanic."

The first part of the month went extremely well. There were few crashes, and those that did happen were of a minor nature with no injuries. This tranquil beginning was to end sadly on the first day of qualifying. Riding mechanic Albert Opalko was tragically killed when his driver, Frank McGurk, crashed during his qualification attempt and flipped several times. Opalko was tossed from the car and died on impact with the ground. The car ended up upside down in the infield with McGurk still inside. He was uninjured. McKee did not know the dead man at all. He was waiting impatiently to qualify.

When the time came, Ardinger qualified a very respectable third. The race itself was won by Wilbur Shaw and was marred by the additional deaths of two track workers. One was a fireman, the other a crewmember. It was the hottest 500 on record. Ardinger and McKee ended up 22nd after a variety of mechanical problems plagued them throughout the day. With the waving of the checkered flag, Herschel McKee's auto racing days were over for good.

PART
III
WORLD WAR TWO

Chapter 19

THE ANNULMENT

Herschel McKee, for the first time in his life, had no idea what he was going to do with himself. He sucked as a racecar driver, his personal life was in turmoil, and money was again scarce. He regularly sent what he could to Viola and the baby, but managed to stay away from them. Viola left him alone. He and Betty were still getting along reasonably well and she was bringing home a regular paycheck. Most of his riding mechanic friends were busy trying to become racing drivers. Some did well, most failed miserably. When they failed, they would hang around their former teams as crewmembers. McKee wanted none of that. "Much too boring," he would say.

He was drinking too much and so was Betty. By fall, most everyone they knew had left for the annual migration to the West Coast. He couldn't afford to keep an airplane any longer and his thrill show was now old hat. Well-organized traveling shows had replaced the freelancers like McKee. To make matters worse, barnstorming had lost its initial appeal to the point that generating a crowd was nearly impossible. Back in 1925 he had been asked to join the Army Air Reserves and as a result was still able to fly on selected weekends, allowing him to keep up his skills. He flew out of Wright Field in Ohio. However, because they were routine the flights held little in the way of excitement and failed to satisfy his thrill-seeking addiction. By the end of the year he was fit to be tied.

Not good at taking advice, he turned to his father largely because he had no one else to turn to.

"Pop, I don't know what in the hell to do any more."

It was the first inkling of weakness or indecision that McKee ever revealed to his father, or to anyone else for that matter. He and his Dad had spent little time together following the war because McKee was rarely in one place for more than a day or two. Even when he was in Indianapolis for the race, or for a car test, he would still find himself too busy for any type of extended visit. When time allowed he would occasionally pop into his parents' home, rarely staying for more than a couple of hours. As always, the talk during those meetings was centered on his own exploits.

"Son, you're 40 years old now. It's past time for you to grow up and settle down."

McKee hated those words, "grow up". As far as he was concerned that was a fate worse than death. But he did agree with his father about the settling down part. He reluctantly agreed to apply for his old job at Allison's.

Allison's rehired him without hesitation and at a higher salary than before. He was assigned the position of Technical Advisor to Engine Development – a lofty-sounding title that basically required him to come to work every day and throw in his two cents regarding the performance and design of the company's new aircraft engines. The position was not at all bad considering that this was a man who had failed to graduate from high school. He hoped that opportunities to fly experimental aircraft would eventually present themselves, allowing him to eventually become a test pilot perhaps.

Back at work, McKee's drinking subsided substantially. An occasional weekend binge would still occur, but during the week he abstained. He and Betty had fallen into a routine not unlike other married 40-year-olds. Shortly after New Year's they drove downtown to do some after-Christmas shopping. With the drop in physical activity, his waistline had increased, necessitating a new wardrobe. They were having lunch in a small cafe when in walked Viola and her mother.

"Oh shit!"

"What's wrong, Herschel?"

Before another word was spoken Viola's mother yelled from several feet away: "You mangy son of a bitch!"

Betty jumped in front of McKee just as the crazed woman started raining blows on his head with her umbrella. McKee managed to grab the flailing weapon, tossing it aside. It nearly hit an old man sitting stooped and alone by the window.

"Leave us be, you old battleaxe," he yelled.

"Hell of a father you are, you bastard!"

"Com' on Betty, let's get out of here."

"Who the hell are *you*?" shouted the harridan.

"I'm his wife. Who are you?"

"Just a goddamn minute, *I'm* his wife," piped Viola, her face now a brilliant crimson.

McKee beat feet for the door. What transpired after his escape is not recorded. Betty awoke the next morning with a black eye and markedly swollen jaw. There were several painful knots in her hair. Viola reportedly lost a tooth. Grandmother was unharmed. Viola succeeded in getting her marriage to McKee annulled by a judge the following week. Miraculously, McKee was never charged with bigamy. No one bothered to press charges and the judge looked the other way. After all, McKee was a local hero.

Betty didn't allow him back home for a month. He was forced to live with his closest ally, Frank Elliot in St Louis. During much of that time he was fortuitously on assignment from Allison's. He was having a series of meetings with Howard Hughes's people regarding an engine deal for his rapidly enlarging airline. While in the famous aviator's office, McKee charmed one of Hughes's secretaries into helping him draft a peace offering letter to Betty. It was a sincere tear jerker. Betty took him back on Valentine's Day.

The fact that Betty took him back at all is truly remarkable. Whether or not McKee realized his good fortune is unknown. He and Betty resumed their lives as if the other marriage had never existed. Betty continued teaching without interruption, considering herself to be a responsible adult. For her at least their daredevil days were over. She was, not surprisingly, unaware of McKee's daughter growing up on the other side of town. What concerned both Betty and McKee in spite of their domestic unraveling was the growing talk around town of increasing tensions abroad, and the threat of another world war.

At Allison's, the engineers were hinting that a German-designed, jet-propelled aircraft was in the works. Although a plane of that type was thought to be at least a year away from its inaugural flight, research and development had been accelerated in McKee's own department. The British were also said to be experimenting with jet engines. In the meantime, McKee was working hard with a team to develop more efficient superchargers for the current line of American fighter planes. The device he was developing was actually referred to as a turbo-supercharger.

McKee was able to maintain his flying skills with monthly visits to Wright Field. He was no longer flying the mail, having quit that job in 1937. No longer barnstorming or sailing motorcycles over ramps, he had to admit he was slowing down. With a potential war looming, his work at the plant was becoming much more intense and time-consuming. Even though he had no formal education, his knowledge of things mechanical was considerable. His flying career had essentially begun at the dawn of aviation, and McKee had learned to put together and take apart every engine of every plane he had ever flown.

Fellow employees marveled at his knowledge and far-reaching

ideas on engine design. He was unexpectedly commissioned by the Army to liaise with Allison's in the provision of technical assistance and design development on behalf of the military. He was essentially the middle-man. He fashioned himself as an executive of sorts. Wearing a coat and tie was not his style by nature, but he could appear very dashing. Speaking engagements were becoming more frequent too, in and around Indianapolis and as far away as Illinois and Ohio. During those talks he would both charm and terrify his audiences.

McKee would begin the talks with a vivid description of his World War One experience and what it took for America to win the war. He would then follow with a discussion of the hazards inherent in racing automobiles and flying barnstormers. His talks would invariably end with a warning about the impending war in Europe and the specter of a German conquest of Britain and France. His description of the Boche as treacherous, determined, ruthless and evil would often leave his audience terribly frightened. Following his talks, a few members of his audience could be seen peering expectantly behind every bush and tree as they walked to the parking area. He was paid handsomely for some of his talks, but many were given free to service or military organizations. McKee was in no way an organization man. He left Betty to do all of his scheduling. She became his assistant and publicist.

McKee was awakened on September 4, 1938, with the news that his good friend and former driver Chet Gardner was dead. Betty delivered the terrible news. The *Indianapolis Star* reported that Gardner was killed instantly when his car spun and then flipped during a race at the Flemington, New Jersey, fairground. He crashed while trying to avoid a small child who had strolled onto the track through an unmanned hole in the fence. McKee looked up at Betty and said in a rare, somber tone: "It's never going to stop, is it Betty? We want it to, but it never will."

It was Sunday morning when he got the news. He left for work on Monday deeply saddened. Gardner wasn't the only one killed that year; in fact, on average a driver died nearly every two weeks. Yet men of a different nature than most were still more than willing to risk a violent death racing cars or motorcycles, in spite of the overwhelming odds against their long-term survival. Still being asked the familiar questions, McKee had difficulty finding suitable answers. Rather than attempt a philosophical and profound explanation of man's quest for thrill-seeking adventure, McKee settled on the trite response he gave most often:

"We simply do it because we can."

The following weekend McKee drove the Cadillac to Wright Field. The day was one of those freakishly warm days that occasionally teases people in the Midwest during the fall, just before winter sets in. The Army was still undecided about the fate of its recently developed B-17 bomber. The original B-17, designated Model 299, had been showcased at Wright Field in 1935 following a very successful flight from its home at the Boeing factory in Seattle, Washington. The flight took only nine hours and three minutes, handily beating out the competition. The plane also performed well in a subsequent fly-off against two other manufacturers and was tentatively picked as America's new long-range bomber. The final decision required a few more tests.

One of these mandatory tests took place on December 30, 1935. Prior to take-off, the two very experienced pilots neglected to unlock the "gust locks", which were devices used to lock the wing's control surfaces in place to avoid them being damaged by sudden gusts of wind while the plane was on the ground. After taking off smoothly, the B-17 entered a steep climb. The routine nature of the flight took a drastic turn when the captain started to change directions. The plane became uncontrollable, went into a stall and crashed, killing both the pilot and co-pilot. Some of the Army's brass already thought the plane too expensive, and following the crash they wanted the program scrapped.

In spite of the mishap, interest remained high among most military officials. Dubbed "The Flying Fortress" by a Seattle reporter, the B-17 was a considerably superior long-range weapon to most of the then current planes of that category. Its speed, bomb-carrying capacity and on-board defenses were second to none. It was finally chosen over both of its rivals when it was determined that the crash had been human error. Further development continued through several model changes over the ensuing two years. Included in these changes was the addition of turbocharged engines.

Throughout the winter of 1937 and the spring of 1938 McKee had been engaged in the development of a new Allison turbo-supercharger destined for the latest version of the B-17. He was traveling back to Ohio to meet with representatives from the Army along with a couple of Boeing engineers to discuss the enhanced performance that could be expected if the new turbo-superchargers were installed. The latest model of the bomber was dubbed the B-17C, the third version produced by the company.

Even though McKee had seen multiple diagrams and photos, it was a long time before he saw a B-17 up close. When he finally did get on board he was overwhelmed by the defensive firepower and bomb load it carried. He could not help but compare it to his 1918 SPAD with its single unreliable Lewis gun for both attack and defense. The B-17 had five strategically placed .30 caliber machine guns to ward off attacking enemy fighters as well as 4,800lb of lethal bombs stored in its bays.

At this stage only a few of the planes were planned for construction. A couple of them were destined for Britain, one for Australia, and the rest were to stay in the United States to be used for reconnaissance and air defense should that ever become necessary. McKee, of course, wanted to fly one of them. He asked, and was granted permission to captain one of the planes on a training mission. The proper arrangements were made and he took off on what looked to be a decent day. The plane had a full crew on board. They left Wright Field headed for an undisclosed location over the Great Lakes.

McKee commented: "It's like flying a giant bus!"

There was plenty of power, but the plane did not quite handle like the nimble fighters he was used to. They departed the Dayton area at daybreak. At a cruising speed of 225mph, they arrived over the waters of Lake Michigan well before noon. Their exact destination was not revealed to them until they were a few minutes into the flight. The mission called for a rendezvous with three P-38 Lightnings at a predetermined point off the coast near Ludington. The Lightnings were to meet up with the bomber and act as escorts in a simulated bombing raid over Milwaukee. *Much more sophisticated than what we did over Verdun*, McKee thought to himself. With the rendezvous completed successfully, he turned for home.

Unusually warm days in April would normally portend the advance of a significant cold front. This day was no exception. The crew of one of the only two B-17Cs in existence was met with an uneasy black sky around two o'clock in the afternoon. The fringe layer of the rapidly approaching cloudbank was darkly serrated. Developing turbulence could be seen within the oncoming storm as volatile cloud layers boiled, darkened and expanded ominously as the plane pressed on.

"Hold onto your seats, boys," said McKee. "This one's going to be a lu-lu!"

They were still two hours from Dayton. McKee pulled back some on the throttle as he drove the Fortress headlong into the maelstrom. The plane lurched and bounced uncontrollably. At times, it seemed to lose all support and would drop into a stomach-wrenching freefall before it hit some invisible floor several hundred feet down.

Black remnants of fragmented clouds zoomed by the observation ports. The two waist gunners were tossed about violently, repeatedly bouncing off of each other and everything else as they wrestled to secure their heavy weapons. For them, it was like flying inside a soccer ball during the World Cup. The youngest crewman, one of the waist gunners, tossed his cookies in the direction of his hapless partner. Both men began to vomit uncontrollably.

The crew in the cockpit was not faring much better. McKee hunched further forward in his seat, eyes trying to pierce through the storm. He held the wheel as steady as he could.

"This thing's built like a brick shit house," he remarked, just as a bolt of lightning dazzled the interior.

Hail the size of tennis balls pelted the fuselage. Some of the men prayed out loud. The rest sat in frozen silence. To the relief of all, the bouncing finally began to subside, and a thin rim of light could be seen directly ahead.

"We've got her made now!" yelled McKee.

Those who were able cheered. The Flying Fortress poked her nose into a clear sky ten minutes later.

The subsequent review of what transpired revealed that they had entered a severe thunderstorm from behind after leaving the rendezvous. Fuel was low and they had no choice but to fly into the storm. Going faster than the storm itself, they broke out from its leading edge into the clear as it menacingly approached the Dayton area. The remainder of the flight, with the storm behind them, was a piece of cake.

McKee set the big plane down amidst a group of onlookers who realized the danger the crew had been in. An earlier call to the base had reported a funnel cloud just northeast of Dayton. A warning of the storm's imminent arrival was issued simultaneously by the Weather Service. While the crew of the B-17 was battling the elements, those on the ground were securing all of the remaining aircraft. As McKee looked up, he could see the fast approaching storm moving in.

With the exception of some minor cuts and bruises all on board were safe, although three of the crew were somewhat dehydrated. The plane was pockmarked from the hail, with several indentations noted along the fuselage and wing. Otherwise it was intact. The ground crew hurriedly secured the B-17, finishing the job just before the full force of the storm hit.

"This bird can handle anything," pronounced McKee.

With that said, they all bolted for the canteen to do some serious damage to the base's whisky supply. The crew, hoisting McKee onto their shoulders, marched him into the pub. In a rather melancholy way, the men began singing the old World War One ballad *Over There*. McKee thought he might have choked up just a little.

Chapter 20

WAR LOOMS; McKEE WAITS

M cKee jumped in his Cadillac and set off for Indianapolis following the excitement in Dayton. While there, he had been successful in convincing Boeing to trial Allison's new turbo-supercharger in the B-17. He also learned that a new, bigger bomber was in the works from Boeing. He was eager to see what they would come up with next. As he drove due west back to Indianapolis, past the sprawling farms that dotted the lush green countryside, McKee reflected on his life, something he had rarely done before.

He was now over 40 years old, a few grey hairs were beginning to show, but he still felt like a young man. Sure, he had some rheumatism and his leg still troubled him when he walked, but that seemed a small price to pay for the life he had led. What bothered him was the fact that his having no real goal or purpose to his life *didn't* bother him. Various headlines referred to him as a thrill seeker, a daredevil, or an adventurer. Occasionally, but not often, an article would appear that made him out to be something of a nutcase. "What am I really?" he would ask himself.

These things were certainly not avocations, not like being a teacher, farmer, lawyer, doctor or businessman. He was none of those things. He was an entertainer of sorts, but not in the sense that an actor or musician is an entertainer. People had been in the stands, but they were there for the most part to watch the spectacle, not him. Where would it all lead? He realized that he had no truly defined purpose to his life. Only one thing did seem to stand out: he was a damn good pilot.

"Yep, that's what I am. A damn good pilot!"

He knew he had been exceptionally lucky on numerous occasions, but that didn't really affect him either; the thought of luck rarely entered his mind. He just assumed he *would* be lucky, since he always had been. Up until today, he had not given any serious thought to his future. After the conversation with his father, he realized that he needed to come up with something sustaining if he was going to continue enjoying the things he liked. Whatever it was, it had to involve flying. That he was sure of. He shifted his focus to the road ahead, stomped on the accelerator, and saw the speedometer needle climb well past 100.

Speeding into Indiana, McKee suddenly realized what it was he wanted to do. With the war looming in Europe, why not plan a return to the action? He knew pilots would be needed by the Allies. Only the British and the French had the resources necessary to fight a full-scale war against the Germans, and both countries had made it clear that they needed pilots. Surely he would not be considered too old?

For McKee, it was like World War One all over again. Going abroad in uniform would allow him to escape the very difficult situation he faced at home. It would also give him the needed time to sort out what he wanted to do with the rest of his life. He made the decision to look into a European move as soon as he got home. As he entered the city limits he smiled to himself, realizing that he had likely made the 90-mile trip from Dayton to Indianapolis in record time.

For the remainder of the year McKee worked diligently at Allison's. He developed a reputation as an individual who could quickly assess a problem, then come up with a simple, logical solution in a reasonably short period of time. He was reassigned to the engine division to help with the further development of the V-1710, the 1,000hp 12-cylinder in-line engine now used successfully in most of the nation's fighter planes. The year went by quickly, with talk of a war continuing to heat up throughout the world.

Like the proverbial bolt out of the blue, tragedy struck McKee in late November when his beloved mother, Laura, died unexpectedly. He had never spent much time with his mother, his traveling had seen to that, but she was often in his thoughts. He remembered the concern she always had for his safety and the fact that he persistently challenged that concern. Most of all he remembered her comfort when he had needed it and her encouragement for him to succeed. He attended the funeral with Betty, spending most of the time comforting his bereaved father. His desire to leave Indianapolis was now even greater than ever. His father was a strong man and McKee felt that he would handle the situation reasonably well. He had a number of friends in the Brotherhood of Locomotive Engineers, and McKee's own rationalization of things had them looking after him. McKee began to plan his move in earnest.

Unrest ruled Asia following Japan's invasion of China in 1937. At the same time Hitler was rearming Germany, creating marked anxiety throughout Europe, especially in Britain and France, still reeling from World War One. 1939 was promising to be a very upsetting, if not a potentially devastating year for much of the world. McKee kept his eyes and ears open, looking for just the right opportunity to enter the burgeoning conflict.

If it were not for the constant fear of running into Viola and her child, his domestic situation would have been reasonably tolerable. Betty was happy teaching school and he was pleasantly up to his elbows at work. *What a difference a pack of rubbers would have made*, he often thought to himself.

By summer, activity at Allison's had revved up considerably. Rumors were rife that Germany was going to invade Poland. Japan and the Soviet Union were already fighting with each other in an ever-intensifying border war, and Germany had recently made a pact with Italy that caused more unrest throughout Europe. Additionally, Russia was threatening to take over Finland for fear of Germany's potential encroachment into their territory. The Germans had already occupied Czechoslovakia.

Anticipating an increase in the war business, Allison's were continually designing new and better engines. At the same time they were stepping up the manufacture of existing models. The company was in high gear. Their turbo-superchargers were being installed in the majority of B-17s, and the new B-24 was now being tested in Michigan, with contracts to several nations going up for bid soon. McKee was right in the mix. He wanted to be in the war.

At this stage Americans in general felt safe from any direct involvement in the coming conflict. Businessmen looked at the war as an opportunity to make money. Even though German submarines were everywhere, the US felt secure, separated from European and Asian unrest by the two great oceans. President Roosevelt continually assured the nation that America would remain neutral. Behind the scenes, however, preparations for war had been well under way for some time.

On September 1, 1939, Germany's long anticipated invasion of Poland marked the official start of World War Two. Three days later McKee took Betty to see the latest Hollywood blockbuster, *Gone with the Wind*. After the show, Betty, feeling comfortable and with a reassuring voice remarked: "Oh Herschel, I'm so glad you're too old now to go off to war."

"That Scarlet was sure some kind of bitch," was his only reply.

By November, Russia was waging an undeclared war on Finland, hoping to obtain that small country as a buffer against Germany. McKee heard the news, and on that very day devised a plan he hoped would get him into the war. He fired a telegram off to the Finnish authorities volunteering his skills as a civilian aeronautical instructor. The Russo-Finnish war ended before he heard back from them. Disappointed, he remained at Allison's, continually thinking up new ways to escape the country. None of them proved fruitful. Then, on March 25, 1940, McKee was surprised to receive a letter from an old friend of his, Colonel William Bishop, an honorary Air Marshal in the Royal Canadian Air Force.

Bishop was a fellow member of the International League of Aviators and knew that McKee had logged a record number of air hours in the United States. His total of 4,229 hours did not even include any of those he had racked up over Germany in the previous war, when reportedly he had flown more than a thousand. Bishop was also impressed with McKee's number of "kills", especially considering the short time he had been a fighting pilot, taking into account the time he spent in hospital and captivity. McKee really hadn't flown combat missions for very long. Bishop therefore extended an invitation for McKee to join the Royal Air Force in Britain.

McKee was ecstatic at first. *Another stroke of amazing luck*, he thought. Then he read the fine print. If he accepted the invitation to join the Royal Air Force he would have to pledge allegiance to the Crown and therefore lose his American citizenship. He did not show the letter to Betty. He did tell a friend of his at work, and found out that after volunteering, Kermit Roosevelt had been granted special dispensation from the British government through his diplomatic connections (he was a friend of Winston Churchill). The chance to join the Allied fighters was certainly tempting to McKee, and he set about trying to get a similar release.

Meanwhile, Viola continued bringing up their child and had recently started working as a fashion artist for the *Indianapolis*

Star on behalf of the L. S. Ayres department store. It was a talent she did not realize she had until one of the executives saw her doodling at her desk. She had been slowly working her way up the secretarial ladder at Ayres, and was in line to become the Executive Secretary for Management, but now Viola was reassigned to become the company's fashion designer instead. She was still single, and continued to harbor thoughts of McKee's eventual return to his family, even though she was no longer married to him. At least, she thought, he should pay some attention to the child.

McKee's dispensation never materialized. He was not willing to give up his citizenship and therefore would have to wait another two years for his chance to enter the escalating conflict. For those two years he miraculously managed to avoid Viola and the child, his charmed life continuing to work in mysterious ways.

Chapter 21

OFF TO WAR AGAIN

America's call to war sounded loud and clear the morning of December 7, 1941, when the Japanese surprised the American fleet at Pearl Harbor. Like the rest of the country, Indianapolis was taken aback. Anger filled the streets, the phone lines and the airwaves. No one was more pissed off than McKee. On hearing the news, he shouted at Betty: "Goddamn Japs! Now we have to fight assholes on both sides of the world."

On May 31, 1942, McKee received the news he had been hoping for. Shortly after arriving for work that morning he was handed a telegram that had come in during the night. He opened it on the spot. It stated that he was being removed from reserve status and was to report immediately to Wright Field as a Technical Consultant and Engineer to the Army Air Corps representing the Allison Division of General Motors. It was not quite the assignment he had in mind, but it did get his foot in the war. He left Betty and the Cadillac behind, and hopped the bus to Dayton, Ohio.

McKee was assigned to the 77th Aeronautical Systems Wing, where he was to train reconnaissance personnel for overseas duty. In addition he was to diagnose any problems that occurred with Allison's engines and report them back to the factory. He was assigned a desk in a small office that he was to share with six other engineers and technical support people – not quite the setting he had pictured for himself. Soon bored, he began to badger his commanding officer daily, asking to be transferred to active flying status. He was politely informed that he had done his part already, and that he was too old to be considered for active flying status at this time. On one occasion, McKee went so far as to slam his fist on the CO's desk as he exclaimed: "Sir, I'm no good behind a desk. I'm a pilot. I need to fly!"

Major Hubert Bullock understood McKee's frustration. Not promising anything, he told him he would see what he could do to get him transferred to a more active unit. McKee was smart enough to do what was expected of him in the interim. He buckled down and did his job as well as he could. He was given a commendation for his efforts and promoted to the rank of Captain. His affability and carefree attitude quickly won friends and influence in the right places. An additional stroke of luck befell McKee when his wartime friend Captain Eddie Rickenbacker visited the base. Rickenbacker put in a good word for McKee and this helped his cause immensely.

"Why Major, a man like McKee should be over there killing Germans. He's a waste of talent back here."

After tolerating two months of boring office work, McKee was summoned into Bullock's office on one grey, drizzly Monday morning.

What'd I do wrong? he thought to himself.

He had never been disciplined before, but he did push the envelope when it came to proper protocol around the base, especially when it involved interaction with the base's female employees. He gave a crisp rap on the Major's door and waited to be acknowledged.

"Come in, McKee. Got some news you might like to hear. Have a seat."

McKee sat down on an austere government-issue wooden chair, still at attention.

Reminds me of grade school, he thought to himself.

Bullock told him to relax.

"McKee, you're going to Alabama. You are to report to Brookley Field on September 1. You're assigned to the 44th Bomb Group and will be working with the new B-24s. They're considering you as a potential back-up pilot – God help us all."

McKee leapt from the chair, an ear shattering war whoop erupting from him as he did so.

"Son of a bitch! I could hug you, Colonel."

"You're dismissed, Captain McKee."

McKee left for Indianapolis early the next morning. He was given the month of August to spend at home before leaving for his assignment in Alabama. He hoped, of course, that this transfer would prove to be a stepping-stone to Europe. The bus trip home took an agonizing five hours. He had given Betty the news the night before. He was so excited about the possibility of returning to combat that he realized, as he bumped over the highway, that Betty must think he's crazy.

Poor thing, he thought, *she just doesn't get it*.

It had been after ten o'clock when Betty hung up after speaking with McKee. She had gone into the bedroom and cried herself to sleep.

"Forty-five, and they may let him fly in combat!"

She couldn't believe they would allow it, and she couldn't believe he wanted to do it.

What was it she wasn't giving him? Their recent weekends together had been great fun.

"Why can't he be like the other men around here?"

She fell asleep holding the only picture they had kept of each other from the wedding.

McKee arrived home late in the afternoon. He and Betty went straight to his father's house. The man now appeared decrepit and old. The news put him into a state of shock and he shook his head slowly, unable to speak. He was trembling. Herschel hastily toned down his obvious enthusiasm, but his attempt to look sad failed miserably. His father, looking off into the distance as if he were trying to visualize the future, remarked shakily: "Son, you are what you are I guess. All I can do is wish you luck, and may God be with you."

By the time Herschel and Betty left the house his Dad appeared more relaxed. He was no longer in tears and could smile a little, a testament to McKee's bullshit. McKee told him that he thought the war would be over quickly and that he would be back home in less than a year. He kissed his father on both cheeks and emphatically shook his hand. He promised to write. He and Betty left after another round of vigorous hugs. McKee wasn't sure what he was going to do for the next 29 days, but he would think of something.

The next morning Betty heard him rummaging about in the garage. He had uncovered the old Harley and was changing the oil. Following the oil change, he replaced what was left of the stale fuel still clinging to the bottom of the tank. He practically wore himself out kicking the starter but the engine finally fired. He yelled for Betty and the two of them headed for Indiana's northern lake district.

After riding for more than three hours, they came upon a quaint little bed and breakfast outside of Syracuse, a small farming town barely large enough to have a traffic signal. Betty was enamored with the place so they decided to spend a week enjoying Lake Wawasee and the surrounding countryside. McKee parked the motorcycle and they checked into the B&B, tossing what little baggage they had onto the bed. Betty threw on a halter-top and a pair of short shorts while McKee changed into a pair of wrinkled old Bermudas and a partially torn T-shirt. The water's edge was just a short walk from the front door.

Mock's Boat Rental had some small outboards available. Betty picked out an orange and green one and they rented a fishing pole and bought a can of worms for bait. The hunt for monstrous perch and bluegill commenced. Betty sat proudly in the bow, a big round hat blocking the sun's rays. She watched as McKee deftly cast his line into the thick expanse of bright green lily pads. After making one particularly long cast, the line suddenly grew taut, bending the rod into a defined U-shape. Betty's eyes widened as McKee managed to flip a good-sized catfish into the bottom of the boat. It was dark brown and ugly as sin. Betty cried out in horror.

"Get that hideous slimy thing out of here, Herschel!"

"Hey, those things are good eatin'."

"I ain't eating anything that ugly, get it out of here."

With that, McKee picked the fish up, being careful to avoid its dangerous dorsal spine, and tossed it at a surprised Betty. She rolled backwards right off the bow and into the warm August water. McKee jumped in after her and they frolicked for nearly an hour, jumping into and out of the little boat. Betty forgot the war entirely that warm and sunny afternoon. Dinner was consumed at the Sleepy Owl tavern, with the tired couple stumbling into bed shortly after sunset and a few too many gin and tonics.

They ended up staying at the lake for ten days. It was the best ten days they had ever spent together. Tanned and relaxed, they jumped on the bike and headed for home. Reality struck when they hit the city limit sign. Betty began to cry as McKee turned onto their street. She was thankful that he was not aware of her sobbing. The bike was vibrating so much he couldn't feel her shaking behind him. She quickly dried her tears with her jacket sleeve as they pulled into the driveway.

The next several days were spent visiting with old friends. They saw his father once more, and, at Betty's insistence, made some necessary arrangements for the unexpected. Until then McKee had paid no attention to any serious planning for the future. He had no life insurance, no will, and had never discussed any of these things with his wife. Betty's family knew a good attorney and he drew up the necessary documents for them to sign.

August 28 was McKee's last full day at home. That night he took Betty to see Tommy Dorsey at the Circle Theater following a scrumptious dinner at the Claypool hotel. McKee was to leave for Alabama in the morning. At the end of the performance, the band's young vocalist made the announcement that he was leaving the orchestra to set out on his own. The audience applauded with a standing ovation. The singer and the bandleader shook hands and the skinny young man turned and walked slowly off the stage.

"That Sinatra kid's gonna make something of himself one day, you watch," said Betty.

"Too skinny," McKee replied.

He left on the bus the next morning, just as the rising sun poured a grey, pink light over the city. Betty did not go to the bus station with him. She cried alone in the small bungalow on West Washington Street.

Chapter 22

WELCOME TO THE 44TH

McKee hopped off the bus in downtown Mobile. He had received his Captain's gear while still in Dayton, and looked handsome in his newly starched uniform. After a short search of the area, he located his driver and Jeep around the corner from the bus stop. The man was smoking a big cigar while displaying a cardboard sign with McKee's name on it.

"Welcome to the 44th, Captain McKee."

"Happy to be here, Sergeant."

McKee, still feeling a bit awkward with his new rank, reluctantly climbed into the back seat of the Jeep and the driver set off toward the airfield and McKee's new war. Brookley Field was located three miles south of Mobile. Originally called Bates Field, the Army had changed the name when they took over the facility in 1938. It was now the Army's major supply base for the southeastern part of the United States as well as the Caribbean, and also functioned as a repair and modification center for the Army's various aircraft. At the time of McKee's call-up, a squadron of the 44th Bomb Group had been detached from the main force that traveled on to England. The planes were detained at Brookley for some repairs to their navigational systems. While stationed there, those crews that remained operational were assigned patrols over the Gulf of Mexico and along the Mexican border. As he neared the field McKee could just make out a line of the hulking B-24 bombers.

"They sure aren't very sexy looking."

"No they ain't, Captain, no they ain't."

McKee had been briefed on the B-24 while at Wright Field. He ran the specs through in his head during the short ride to the base. Built by Consolidated Aircraft, the B-24 was faster and had greater range than the B-17. Even so, it was not favored by the Army's pilots, nor by many of the pilots flying it in other countries. The B-24 had a tendency to catch fire easily due to the location of its fuel tanks and there were some subtle structural issues. It was more difficult to fly than the B-17, and it was more vulnerable to battle damage. Pilots referred to the unappealing-looking plane as "The Flying Boxcar". Nevertheless, it was produced in greater numbers than any other aircraft in US military history, and its combat role in World War Two is highly acclaimed. It was flown throughout the conflict by the air forces of several Allied countries in both the European and Pacific theaters.

McKee was taken straight to squadron headquarters, where he was introduced to the other pilots and their crews. Most of the men had heard of him from his racing exploits and he was welcomed into the fold immediately. The squadron's commander was Tim O'Reily, a young man from Boston, Massachusetts. He told McKee up front that he would be his co-pilot while in Alabama, and that they would be doing daily patrols over the Gulf.

"Have you seen any U-boats so far?" McKee asked.

"Nothing but private yachts and fishing boats," was the reply. "Oh, and not to scare you or anything, we've seen some big schools of sharks swimming just offshore."

"Awesome!"

McKee unpacked his things and with O'Reily headed for the local bar. With the rest of the 44th already in England, it was apparent the lone squadron was not happy stuck in Alabama. O'Reily wasn't sure they were serving much of a purpose flying over the Gulf. He told McKee his men felt like traitors. Their buddies overseas were busily readying themselves for involvement in the real war and they were stuck in the States flying watch over a bunch of rich yachtsmen. Flying from a base in England, the 44th Bomb Group was expected to eventually join forces with the Royal Air Force to deliver bombs throughout Europe. O'Reily's men felt left out.

"When do you think we'll get over there?"

"It won't be long, McKee, not if I have anything to say about it. Not long at all."

But on his second day in Alabama, McKee learned the disappointing news that he was not going to fly as a captain of his own airplane; in fact he was not expected to fly at all. He was to oversee his squadron's maintenance operations and manage the repair of damaged aircraft instead. He had not yet read the full content of his papers, and the bad news was in the fine print. He had been so consumed with learning all he could about the B-24, expecting to fly it, that it never occurred to him he would actually be assigned to do maintenance only. O'Reily told him it was likely due to his age. Age to McKee meant little. He finished reading all of his papers that morning. There it was, his official job title: Aircraft Maintenance Officer.

O'Reily, it turned out, was only taking him flying because his usual co-pilot was ill with the flu. McKee took the news in his stride, realizing that he was still miles away from his domestic entanglements, and for that he was forever grateful. He enjoyed the company of every man in the squadron. They were a fun-loving, boisterous bunch, itching to get to England and into the fray.

O'Reily, McKee and the rest of the crew took off one morning for a routine patrol over the Gulf of Mexico. Nothing suspicious had been sighted the previous 30 days, but there had been an incident in early May when one of the other planes actually did spot a U-boat. They set their sights, dropped a charge, and noticed the development of a confirming oil slick a short time later. There was no question the Germans were patrolling the area.

O'Reily's crew had been flying for nearly four hours. They had seen nothing but a large expanse of turquoise, bejeweled water. At altitude, the sun made the waves sparkle like small diamonds. Then just after one o'clock, the bombardier shouted: "Over there, 11 o'clock, Nazi mother-fuckers."

Sure enough, there was a distinct spindle-shaped patch of dark water visible just off the port side of the airplane. It didn't take much imagination to envision a German U-boat lurking just beneath the surface. The command to fire was given. A 300lb bomb was released from its bay. The crewmen with a view watched in eager anticipation. No oil slick appeared. There was no U-boat after all. Instead, several Atlantic dolphins met their untimely death that day, just off the coast of southern Alabama.

The men had a good laugh and returned to base before the bar opened. When he arrived at his room, McKee faced a message scrawled on a piece of notepaper tacked to his door. He was to go to the main office immediately to receive new orders.

Maybe I'm out of here, he thought.

Practically running to the office, McKee, nearly out of breath, tore open the envelope he was handed. Hot dog, he was being transferred to England on September 6 – just three days away.

"I told you you wouldn't be here long," O'Reily grumbled at the bar later that evening.

McKee was being sent overseas alone. The remainder of the squadron, O'Reily included, would, by necessity, be stuck in Mobile. They would, in fact, remain there until March of 1943. The government felt that the patrols over the Gulf were necessary for the Nation's defense. McKee, on the other hand, was desperately needed in England to prepare for and manage the anticipated maintenance burden that would occur as soon as the bombing raids over Europe and Africa began. The 44th was destined to be the first American bomb group equipped exclusively with B-24s, and the planes were high-maintenance. McKee was expected to memorize the manual on his trip over the pond. Next stop: Liverpool, England.

McKee couldn't sleep he was so excited. He left Brookley Field on August 5 bound for New York in an Army transport plane. He was accompanied by 11 other airmen, all with different destinations. In New York he was transferred to a troop-carrying ship for the passage to England. Being a Captain, he was assigned his own stateroom on the converted passenger liner, recently christened the *West Point*. The ship had just returned from the Pacific, where it had been engaged in similar duties. It was due to arrive in England on September 11. McKee spent his waking hours circling the deck, learning everything there was to know about the B-24. The salt air agreed with him, causing him to realize that the sea was what he missed most when he was stuck in Indianapolis.

The *West Point* left New York City on time, scheduled to join a convoy of five other ships in Nova Scotia for the remaining voyage to Liverpool. In Nova Scotia a destroyer escort would also join the fleet, providing much-needed security in the event of a U-boat attack. McKee considered the stopover an unnecessary delay.

Like most troop ships, the *West Point* was a converted commercial vessel, formerly called the SS *America*, operated by the United States Line. She was 723ft long and could carry more than 8,000 troops plus a crew of 512. The ship was disguised for the war effort, painted white and grey with the portholes covered from the inside with black crepe. No lights were allowed on deck in the hope of thwarting attacks by the Luftwaffe, a real danger once the ship reached Irish waters. As they approached Ireland the ships would also begin a zigzag course for the rest of the passage in an attempt to avoid prowling U-boats.

Food and drink was plentiful aboard the *West Point*, and one of the Army's bands played nightly in the subdued lounge. While others were writing home to their loved ones, McKee was painstakingly reviewing his manuals. Life on board the *West Point* was not as luxurious as it was for the lucky ones who crossed on the *Queen Mary*, but it was a far cry from the SS *Santa Barbara* that took McKee to Europe for World War One. No one else on board the ship belonged to the 44th Bomb Group. Most of the other officers were younger than McKee, seeming to be more interested in poker and looking at each other's favorite pin-ups than they were in any meaningful conversation. McKee kept to himself.

The ship arrived at Liverpool on schedule and unharmed. McKee, as he disembarked, was surprised at how much English weather resembled Indiana in August. What he did not know was that all of Britain was having an unusual heat-wave at the time, with temperatures much higher than customary. Practically no one in Britain had air conditioning, and the entire country was sweating profusely. McKee took it all in stride, grabbed the train for Norfolk, laid his head back on the rest, and promptly went to sleep.

It was a relatively short trip to Norfolk. McKee woke up refreshed, having missed the beautiful English countryside. The bus ride on to Shipdham and the airfield was even shorter. No time for any more sleep. When the bus reached the airbase, McKee was surprised to see a number of peculiar piles of thick, brown, clay-like mud scattered about. He later learned that the airfield had not been designed for heavy bombers and, as a consequence, the runways needed shoring up.

Construction was in progress everywhere on the base. Add in the usual amount of British rain and you had a major quagmire.

McKee was also surprised to learn that walking boots had not been made available to the American Army Air Corps. Suitable boots had been issued in France during WW1, so why not WW2? He made a mental note for his next shopping trip after spending over an hour of his first evening trying to pry the thick mud from his shoes and socks.

McKee endured the initial admissions process and settled into his meager quarters. He knew little of British customs but was introduced to Irish Guinness shortly after his arrival. The 44th was not actively involved in combat at this point and the men were making the most of the situation. McKee was quick to note, however, that women were scarce. Some locally purchased magazines filled the void. He set about overseeing the arrival of new planes and organizing the massive array of parts and supplies he found stockpiled in the well-used hangar assigned to him.

As fall set in the men suffered more, due to a lack of basic amenities like gloves, suitable jackets and reliable heat. Staying warm involved fending for yourself and a lot of midnight acquisition. Blankets, if you could find any, were kept under lock and key. Immediate warmth could only be had by stomping one's feet and generally thrashing about, flailing the arms and shouting, but the situation gradually improved over the next two months as more supplies rolled in. The 44th Bomb Group began combat operations as scheduled on November 6.

McKee, with his assigned ground crews, had ample time to get all of the aircraft he was responsible for up and airworthy. He was an immediate hit on the base, quite easy to work with, and was a nightly treat at the local pub where he told stories of his experiences during World War One, as well as exaggerated stories of his racing career. He reluctantly accepted his non-combat role, realizing that he was indeed a vital member of the team. Deep down, however, he hoped a situation would arise that would allow him to fly.

While working in the supply hangar one afternoon, a young lad approached and asked if he could meet with McKee for a short time.

"Sure son. What's your name and what's on your mind? We can use my office."

"My name's Dennis. I'm from Iowa."

McKee cleared the only other chair he had and the young fellow sat down. He looked a little sheepish and appeared a bit anxious. He began:

"Captain, I'm scared."

"Nothing wrong with that, son, most of the men here are a little scared."

"I'm real scared, sir."

"If you're real scared, that's bad. It's the ones that are real scared that get themselves killed. You just aren't keeping yourself busy enough, young man. If you're busy you don't have time to be scared. What is it that you do, boy?"

"I'm a tail gunner."

Oh shit, McKee thought to himself.

"Son, you're in this war whether you want to be or not. Your job is to make your gun work without a miss. You need to treat it as if it was your favorite huntin' dog. You need to massage every single part, make sure the bullets'll run true. Then you need to have a brandy every night before you go to bed, take each day as it comes. That's all you can do son, the rest'll take care of itself, one way or the other."

The gunner thanked McKee, shaking his hand vigorously. He appeared much more relaxed as he left the office. McKee caught a glimpse of the lad the next afternoon. On his station, he was dismantling his weapon, polishing and oiling each separate part.

The gun shined. McKee ran into Dennis three weeks later. The lad informed him that he had been on two bombing raids already, shot down one German fighter and he wasn't afraid any more. McKee saluted the young man, smiled, turned, and walked away.

Now that boy's in control of something, he thought to himself, *he's going to be all right*.

Chapter 23

ADVERSITY FORGES A STRANGE RELATIONSHIP

Indianapolis was dark and cold for the better part of the day by the beginning of December. Betty was teaching fourth grade in a small public school nestled in a section of the city known as Irvington. She had not heard from McKee since he left for the war four months earlier. She had no idea where he was or how he was doing. There had been no word from the government so she assumed he must still be alive. News of the war was difficult to interpret for the citizens at home. One day great progress was announced, the next the news was all gloom and doom. With the war taking place throughout much of Asia and the Pacific, as well as all of Europe, there was a claustrophobic feel to it for most Americans. They imagined the country being devoured in the middle.

At a time when Christmas spirit was normally in high gear there was not much to be happy about in Indianapolis. Six inches of wet snow covered the ground and it was extremely difficult to get anywhere. Betty spent what time she could with McKee's father, but he was growing more infirm and was not very sociable. He had not heard from his son, and didn't believe Betty when she told him she hadn't heard from him either.

Needing to feel somehow involved with the war and to do her patriotic duty, Betty volunteered at the local Red Cross facility. There, she prepared Christmas packages for the soldiers overseas. She laughed to herself a little, unable to picture McKee using some of the stuff they were sending out. Chocolate Santas would seem childish to him she was sure.

On the second Saturday of the month, she was seated at a large table with some other lonely women in the Red Cross headquarters filling the last of the boxes scheduled to go to Europe the following day. Some of the women would sob occasionally, but most packed their boxes deliberately, looking grim and determined. As Betty packed, an unfamiliar voice cried out from behind her: "I'll be goddamned!"

Betty turned to look and was shocked to see the woman she had hit, and who had hit her, in the restaurant four years earlier. She had a small child in tow and was fulfilling her patriotic duty the same way Betty was.

The woman asked: "How is the old son of a bitch?"

"If you mean Herschel, I don't have a clue. He's been off to the war for four months now."

"He hasn't written?"

"No. You haven't heard from him either?"

"God no! I have his child, and I haven't heard a thing from him since that day in the restaurant."

She sat down in an empty spot next to Betty and introduced herself.

"I'm Viola and this is Linda. She's five. McKee sends her money every month, nothing else."

"He never mentioned her to me, never. He never mentions you either for that matter."

Betty was dumbfounded upon seeing the child and didn't know quite what to think. She felt numb for the most part.

That bastard, she thought.

The two women wrapped a couple of the remaining boxes and then left the building together with the child half-walking, half-skipping behind them. Viola suggested they go to the same restaurant they fought in and have a chat. Betty agreed, deciding that Viola didn't seem to be all that bad a person. She was

Above: After a period of seeing each other only every four to ten years, the two World War One fliers ended up in the Army Air Force Reserve. Lieutenants Herschel McKee (left) and E. D. Alexander are seen together at Wright Field in 1928.

Below: McKee sitting in Bob McDonogh's FWD Special during a practice day at the Indianapolis Speedway in 1932. Behind the car are boat racer and designer Gar Wood, along with famed racer Barney Oldfield, who is smoking his ever-present cigar. Wood and McKee's friendship developed in the early 1920s when they discovered how much they had in common.

Above: James Bradley's famous parachute plane. Tested successfully twice, the parachute apparatus failed on the third test. Test pilot Herschel McKee spiraled to the ground from an altitude of 6,000 feet, suffering only minor injuries to the amazement of the assembled throng. Initially interested, the military abandoned the project and the system was never developed further.

Left: Article dated March 6, 1932 depicting the ill-fated third flight of the parachute plane. McKee, wrongly given the forename 'Hugh' in the caption of the top articles, was credited with a superb landing under the circumstances, saving both him and much of the airplane.

202

Above: McKee with driver Chester Gardner after qualifying for the 1934 Indy 500. They finished fourth in the race, the highest finish at Indianapolis for McKee. The car, sponsored by the Sampson Radio Company, was the first to be equipped with radio communication with the crew in the pits. Wearing large earphones, McKee would relay messages to his driver as the race progressed.

Right: Poster depicting the "Death Drivers". During difficult financial times, McKee would resort to thrill shows of one kind or another to make ends meet. The "Death Drivers" lasted for one season, thankfully without killing anybody. Joining McKee in the show was his wife Betty and daredevil stock car racer Harold Stuckey.

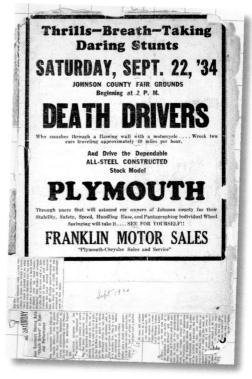

Left: Miss Viola Cain, mother of McKee's only child, conceived out of wedlock following a heated romance triggered by Miss Cain's winning of a beauty contest held at the Speedway in 1936. He married Viola when he learned she was pregnant, thus becoming a bigamist for a short time. He somehow managed, through charm, deception, and luck, to remain on good terms with both his wife Betty and the lovely Viola.

Below: Driver Herb Ardinger and McKee in the Chicago Rawhide Company's "Oil Seal Special" after qualifying for the 1937 Indianapolis 500 Mile Race. They ended up 22nd in the big race after mechanical problems plagued them all day. The race would be the last for all riding mechanics – aerodynamics and improved engine reliability made their presence unnecessary. It was also the end of Herschel McKee's auto racing career.

Above left: Promoted to Captain soon after his transfer to active status at the beginning of World War Two, McKee was given a desk job at Wright Field. He was assigned as Technical Consultant and Engineer to the Army Air Corps, representing the Allison Division of General Motors. He was to oversee any issues with Allison's engines and report them back to the factory. Additionally, he was to train reconnaissance personnel for overseas duty.

Above right: Captain Eddie Rickenbacker, the "Ace of Aces", who helped get McKee into the real war with his eventual transfer to the 44th Bomb Group in England.

Below: The B24 Liberator shared the American bombing offensive with the better-known B17 Flying Fortress, and was famous for the Ploesti low level raid on 1 August 1943 in which the 44th Bomb Group took part. Liberators are shown taxiing from their dispersals at Shipdham, Norfolk, where McKee spent most of the war. (Martin Bowman Collection)

Left: Captain McKee in full Scottish attire having just learned of his heritage in the Highlands. The original family name was McKay. He and his girlfriend Penny discovered his ancestry in a gentlemen's shop in Inverness during a lull in the activity at Shipdham.

Below: McKee with a group of test pilots at Wright Field after the war, including the legendary P-51 Mustang fighter ace Don Gentile. The jet age had begun and McKee was very jealous. He still had a lot in store, however.

Right: Monument Circle, Indianapolis, Indiana. Picture McKee flying his B-24 around the circle at rooftop level. The famous Circle was the hub of activity in downtown Indianapolis and remains so to this day. This picture was taken in the late 1950s.

Right: Captain McKee advising Allison engineers on the new V-12 engine. His technical knowledge regarding engine development was phenomenal considering he never graduated from high school.

Below: In civilian clothes, McKee describes the intricacies of an experimental engine to Army brass. His connection with Allison's continued in both civilian as well as his military life.

Above left: Lieutenant Colonel Herschel McKee toward the end of his career. He was promoted at the end of the war, prior to becoming involved in covert activities with the CIG, forerunner to the CIA.

Above right: In civilian dress, admiring a new United States Air Force jet, a supersonic F-102 Delta Dagger interceptor, the engine of which he helped design. This picture was likely taken following his first stroke. The inscription reads "To Linda from your Dad, Lt. Col. H.J. McKee".

Below: The last picture known to have been taken of H.J. McKee. He is shown at his home with his wife Betty and his only child Linda, daughter of Viola Cain. He was home on leave from hospital following his second stroke. He died peacefully shortly thereafter.

obviously a good mother as Linda looked lovingly upon her, seemed happy, and was very polite and obedient in the short time Betty had observed her.

Good thing Herschel's not been involved with her upbringing.

The one-time adversaries followed each other through town, struggling through the snow and ice as they drove to the Circle. They picked a table by the window, partially obscured by an icy frost, and ordered lunch for themselves and a chocolate sundae for Linda. The sundae was gone long before the conversation ended. Viola and Betty talked well into the afternoon while Linda slept in a nearby booth. The discussion was never heated. What sparks did fly flew in McKee's general direction. Both women felt scorned and vented their fury on McKee, who had rapidly become their common enemy.

Betty admitted to Viola that she knew McKee fooled around, like with the young girl Hilda he'd crashed with in California. She had mostly let it go, dismissing it as something he couldn't help because of the dangers he perpetually faced.

"Bull!" was Viola's reply.

She felt just the opposite; that his occupation, or diversion, or whatever it was, should have made him all the more faithful. Neither could believe they had not heard from the wretched man since he bailed out on both of them. They agreed that he had left town just to escape the mess he had created. The conversation eventually ended with the two women traveling full circle to agree that he was a personable bastard with an irresistible grin. They vowed to see each other on a regular basis. History will show that they became life-long friends.

With time, each one merged somewhat into the other's family. Betty would occasionally sit with Linda to allow Viola some free time, and Viola was included in all of the McKee family gatherings. Wherever Herschel was, they were sorry he was missing it. Discussing what would happen if he ever returned was left unsaid. Their growing friendship carried and consoled them through the entire miserable war. Linda grew up to be a happy and well-adjusted child, never lacking for family support. To this day she remains all about the family.

Chapter 24

LIFE AT SHIPDHAM

The situation at Shipdham remained difficult. Some improvements were finally made in the quantity and quality of the needed supplies, but the men still lacked many of the basics. They were constantly cold, still without suitable gloves to wear, and there was no place to really warm up. On several occasions the maintenance crews were forced to tend to airplanes that were encased in ice. The pilots fared no better. At altitude, the B-24 was sparsely heated, with the gunners having to suffer the most. It was not unusual for the crews to border on significant hypothermia for the duration of a flight. Several men had to be treated for frostbite to their nose and fingers when they returned from a mission. On a positive note, the ground crews were no longer required to work by flashlight during the night, and some meager warmth was finally finding its way into the barracks.

As was customary for a newly-arrived group, early missions for the 44th were mostly short diversionary flights. These were considered to be less risky and less technical than the major bombing raids, allowing the crews to become acclimated. "Diversionary flights" were meant to confuse the Luftwaffe by keeping the German fighters away from the more strategic and longer bombing runs being carried out by the more experienced groups. In spite of the many hardships, McKee and his ground crews managed to have all nine of the B-24s under his supervision ready for their first actual mission. That mission left Shipdham on November 7, 1942.

It was to be an uncomplicated venture. The men were to fly a diversionary route off the coast of France while the 1st Wing flew 68 B-17s to the U-boat pens at Brest. U-boats were constantly wreaking havoc in the Atlantic and were a regular target for the Army Air Corps. McKee waited nervously for the return of his planes.

After a little over four hours, he strolled outside and watched apprehensively for the familiar shapes to appear on the horizon. Straining his eyes, he could make out seven of the B-24s as they crept into view. They appeared to have suffered little if any significant damage. One of the planes, he knew, had been forced back early because of some malfunctioning weaponry. The only missing plane, he would learn later that night, had been forced to divert to another airfield as a result of a mechanical malfunction after the mission had been completed. McKee was genuinely happy that all of the men were safe and sound, and that no planes had been lost to combat. He knew that soon, every night would be like this one, a constant worry over the safe return of his airplanes.

During the post-mission debriefing the pilots reported that they had dropped no ordnance and that they did not encounter a single German fighter. Of great concern to the pilots, however, was the fact that the scheduled RAF fighters never arrived to escort them through the areas known to be dangerous. Had they encountered German resistance, the 44th might have been history before it truly got into the war. This dangerous omission was the result of poor communications between the British and the Americans during the early part of the war. Their equipment was rarely compatible, and there was considerable jealousy and even some genuine animosity among the pilots of both countries.

McKee and his men were allotted very little time to service the planes upon their return from that first mission. Just 48 hours later the 44th Bomb Group took off again. This time they were to bomb an actual target: the U-boat sanctuary at St Nazaire. The crews faced heavy flak for the first time as they neared the target area. Puffs of black smoke with burning red centers dotted the sky above, below and all around them. Miraculously, no planes were lost. The number of U-boats destroyed or damaged was never recorded, but the mission was considered a success.

The RAF fighters arrived on schedule this time and they were a welcome sight to the crews. The men in each of the bombers began to gel, developing a team-like spirit. The mood on the base early in the war was generally good. McKee was handling his maintenance position with aplomb, actually enjoying the intricacies of the big bombers. He fancied himself as a kind of "father goose", painstakingly watching over his young flock.

The B-24 was one of the most versatile aircraft of World War Two. It was used for photographic reconnaissance, anti-submarine work, as a tanker and troop carrier, and most of all as a long-range strategic bomber. The high aspect Davis Wing allowed for the extra mileage. By the end of the war 18,000 of these planes would be made, more than any other United States combat aircraft. Once the bombing raids started the moniker of "Flying Boxcar" was dropped and it became the "Liberator". It could cruise at 250mph, climb to more than 25,000ft, and had a range of up to 3,000 miles. It was not a pretty aircraft, nor was it very maneuverable, but it was functional. McKee knew the plane like the back of his hand.

The often marginal weather in late fall took a sudden turn for the worse on the first day of December. Dense fog and drizzle plagued the area and would often linger for days at a time. The pea-soup-like conditions caused the majority of scheduled missions to be scrubbed, but one important mission did manage to get off the ground at least.

Planes from the 44th, 66th and 68th Bomb Groups left Shipdham on the evening of December 6. All of the planes took off safely. However, what looked to be a perfect night for a bombing run soon turned into a flop as this mission too had to be scrubbed shortly after the planes had lumbered into the mostly cloudy sky. Late intelligence information reported that the weather at the target site had deteriorated markedly and would not be suitable for a drop. The bombers were instructed to return to base.

Unfortunately not all of the squadrons heard the news. The planes from McKee's group were flying at mid-altitude and for some unknown reason never got the message. They failed to see the other planes turn back due to the heavy clouds, and subsequently were left to go it alone. The intended target was an airfield in France called Abbeville/Drucat. They pressed on aided by navigator Erwin L. Adler from Vermont. Adler, using dead reckoning, somehow found the way.

When they arrived inside the target area, the lone squadron was able to penetrate the heavy flak batteries and made a successful drop on the field. They then immediately turned for home. As they approached the shore of the English Channel the crews began to relax, but as they did so more than 25 German fighters came at them from every angle. One of the B-24s, that piloted by Lieutenant Dubard, took a direct hit into its No 4 engine. The fire spread to the No 3 engine and the plane faltered.

The gunners on Dubard's crew fought back valiantly and were able to down three of the German fighters before the fatally damaged plane plunged into the icy Channel. At the mission debriefing it was reported by a pilot who had seen Dubard's plane attacked that it was hit simultaneously, both from above and below. The ill-fated B-24 quickly sank and its entire crew was lost. The 44th had been tragically bloodied on its first month of operation.

When he heard the news, McKee sadly remembered that young Dennis was the doomed plane's tail gunner. Dennis and his pals were the first of many American airmen who would never return home from the war. The incident was all too familiar to McKee. He told the men who did return from the mission that he had seen it all before.

"It is what it is. You've got to let it go."

He left the debriefing early, going out to inspect the damaged landing gear of one of the returning planes. As he did so, it started to pour. It was an icy cold rain. The man he was working with was an independently contracted local technician, hired to assist the Americans with hydraulic repairs. McKee turned his head skyward and remarked sarcastically:

"Is the weather going to be this crappy all winter long?"

"Mate, this is a glorious winter's day – the rain's falling straight down!"

The extended periods of bad weather did offer one advantage: there was more leave time granted to visit the town of Norwich and the surrounding countryside – that is, if the frequent dense fog didn't make the narrow, curvy and treacherous road to town virtually impassable.

When the Americans first arrived in England, they had some difficulty with the Brits understanding them. The Americans wanted ice in practically everything they drank, a very difficult habit for the British to comprehend. On the other hand, the beer served by the British seemed flat to the Yanks and was normally served at room temperature. This was an equally disturbing habit as far as the Americans were concerned. The men of the Army Air Corps still drank the stuff, requiring something with alcohol in it to settle their often shattered nerves. The American bomber crews and RAF pilots had by now developed a mutual respect for each other and a true spirit of cooperation developed. At least, they cooperated when it came to matters concerning the defeat of Germany; it was another story when it came to matters concerning the conquest of one of the local "birds".

McKee, as was his habit, went after the prettiest girl in the Horse and Hound pub the first night he was there. Not a good move. The local lads took immediate offense and a fight soon broke out. The RAF pilots who were in the pub at the time stayed put, but the Americans and a small clan of local toughs ended up having a decent scrum. Beer mugs were shattered, tables were overturned, and many threats were made. One of the Americans was hit by an errant dart thrown by a woman. It pierced his left upper arm, sticking out grotesquely. Blood oozed from the wound and he fainted.

Just as one of the RAF pilots moved to join the fray, the fight was stopped by the local constable, whose name was McKnight. He arrived for a whisky before anyone had become too severely bloodied. McKnight frequently stopped by the pub to have a drink while making his neighborhood rounds. "To ward off the cold," he would say.

The evening was salvaged by someone on the British side of the room, who called for a round. Within minutes the previously vicious combatants looked more like a victorious rugby team. All of the men had joined together, placing their arms around each other's shoulders, and had begun to sway to and fro to the swing music being played on the jukebox. Any casual observer would have sworn that the men had been well acquainted for quite some time.

McKee did eventually meet the girl he had gone after, and the inevitable encounter followed. Her name was Penelope, but everyone called her Penny. She lived only a short distance from the pub, allowing for frequent rendezvous. The house was a small brownstone nestled in among several others on a road designed for two-way traffic when the traffic was exclusively four-legged.

Largely because of these frequent trysts, some being accompanied by an inkling of guilt, McKee realized that he had not written home since his arrival in England. He subsequently spent one entire evening writing his father, Betty and Viola, in that order. It was to be the last letter his father ever received. James Marion McKee died after a short illness on December 12, 1942. His obituary mentioned that he had a son named Herschel J. McKee, thought to be somewhere in England, but said nothing more about him. Herschel did not find out about his father's death for nearly a month.

McKee's letters home had a very different tone this time around. During World War One he and the other American pilots were fighting more for the adventure than to defend their own freedom. In his letters now, McKee described how this war was entirely different. He described a sense of urgency and a hatred for both the Germans and the Japanese. He didn't really hate the Germans in WW1, they were looked upon as chivalrous adversaries and his job was to shoot them down. Now he hated their guts and wanted to kill them.

Back home, Betty and Viola read their letters to each other. They were a bit surprised by the patriotism and the love for freedom expressed by McKee. Of course, in typical McKee manner he wrote mostly about himself and the airplanes, offering little of substance about England and her people. He did mention that he was looking for a pet, probably a dog of some kind to keep him company during the long spells of bad weather. Betty and Viola felt only partly sorry for him.

With that chore out of the way, McKee took up again with Penny when circumstances permitted. Over the next several months the 44th Bomb Group did their job and took their licks. Many of the correspondents covering the war remarked that the 44th seemed to have more than their share of tragedy. By January 1943 they had lost more than half of their original planes and the majority of their original combat crews. Planes returned from missions with unimaginable damage – landing gears that could not be lowered, gaping holes blown out of the fuselage, usually the result of flak damage, and parts of their wings either missing entirely or severely damaged. McKee was amazed at how some of them managed to land. His relaxation came with Penny.

Gruesome sights were forever embedded in the young minds of those men who did manage to return uninjured. Casualties would be carried from the planes minus one or more of their extremities. They would be soaked with blood and often unconscious. Many would later die, having lost too much blood trying to get home. Some who did make it back would be left crippled or paralyzed for the remainder of their lives. For some, their injuries were more to their psyche, making a normal existence after the war impossible. The uninjured were asked to fly again, usually after only a few hours' rest. They were haunted by the thought that each night might be their last.

Planes that failed to return were not all lost in combat. Many of them crashed shortly after take-off without ever managing to reach their target. Others ran into each other while en route to the target because of the lack of reliable positioning equipment. But the majority of the planes lost were either shot down by German fighters or overwhelmed by the lethal flak. It became readily apparent to all that the influx of new airmen was not sufficient to keep up with the mounting losses. Volunteers from the available and qualified ground crews were sure to be needed at some point. McKee waited patiently, knowing he would soon get his chance to fly.

He was working on one of the damaged planes late on a Thursday afternoon when a letter was hand-delivered. It was marked urgent. The return address was the familiar one on West Washington Street in Indianapolis. It was from Betty. It read:

"Herschel, your father passed quietly on December 12th. Your brother, sister, and I were there when he died. He talked often of his son the pilot and racing driver. He loved you, Herschel, and even though you were gone much of the time he felt close to you. We all do. We're proud of what you are doing and miss you very much. I love you my dear. Take care and as always God speed, Betty."

McKee sat down on one of the plane's wheels and cried real tears for the first time since he was a child. It began to rain. His hands trembled as he hurriedly folded the letter, trying to keep the ink from smearing as he placed it in his jacket pocket. He left his tools under the plane, walked to his Jeep, started the engine, and turned onto the road leading to Penny's.

Chapter 25

DISCOVERING SCOTTISH ROOTS AND OFF TO AFRICA

M orale at Shipdham hit rock bottom following a debacle that occurred over Kiel, Germany, on May 14, 1943. The weather had improved dramatically during the preceding two weeks, making for good flying, and missions were being mounted daily. The mission over Kiel was planned to inflict as much damage as possible to the U-boat facilities there, as well as to destroy the Krupps submarine-construction yard if enough ammunition and planes to do the job were left intact after attacking the primary targets.

The war over the Atlantic was at a stalemate, making the destruction of German sea power a top priority. For the first time in the war, powerful incendiary bombs would be carried in the bays of all B-24s assigned to the mission. The decision to carry these hideously destructive bombs had been made by High Command only minutes before the mission was to begin.

The assigned planes took off for Kiel into clear skies. The plan was to fly very low until well over the North Sea where, at a prescribed time, a bombing altitude of 19,000ft would be attained. Problems soon developed. A not-so-rare navigational error caused the entire Group to fly off course over the Frisian Islands. As they did so, they encountered a heavy barrage of flak from the defending batteries. To the crews it looked as if they were flying through a Fourth of July fireworks display. Amazingly, only one plane – the *Rugged Buggy* – was damaged. It suffered hits on two of its engines, resulting in a severe loss of manifold pressure. The pilot, ignoring the potential catastrophe, nevertheless flew his severely wounded plane into the target area undeterred.

A second problem encountered by the Group was created by the unexpected trajectory of the new incendiary bombs. They did not drop straight down. This realization required the bombers to fly over the target for at least two miles further than was generally customary. As a result, the planes were exposed to heavy flak for a much longer time. Hampering the mission as well was the fact that when the incendiaries were dropped, they quickly scattered in an unpredictable fashion, unlike conventional bombs that normally held a tight pattern. This scattering effect required the pilots at lower altitudes in the formation to dodge their own bombs or be blown to smithereens. Having to separate from each other also increased the amount of available air space for the German fighters, allowing the Luftwaffe to infiltrate and attack at will. The American bombers became sitting ducks.

As the Group turned for home following the drop, three of its planes were suffering from serious damage and struggling to stay aloft. Two of them had been severely damaged by the German fighters, while *Rugged Buggy*, still hanging in there, was now faced with a dangerously low manifold pressure. To make the situation worse, their fuel tank had ruptured, causing lethal vapors to seep into the fuselage.

Nobody moved. Any spark and the plane would explode. Minutes after turning for England, their worst nightmare occurred. A rogue fighter appeared from out of nowhere and hit them from behind. Flames surrounded the bomb bay doors. With great difficulty, one of the crewmembers managed to pry the doors apart and the crew was successfully able to bale out of the stricken plane just before the inevitable explosion. The ensuing fireball added to the existing incendiary display, giving the night sky a hellish quality. Eight of the ten airmen who made the jump from *Rugged Buggy* survived and were taken prisoner for the duration of the war. Those still aloft and headed back to England were glad it wasn't them.

On the trip home a number of other planes were lost for one reason or another. By the time they reached Shipdham, the entire Group had been decimated. As the stragglers stumbled in two planes crashed into each other while attempting to land. They were extensively damaged, but no one died. Damage assessment, once all of the planes were on the ground, revealed that several of the gunners had been injured by penetrating flak, two of them fatally. The mission had been a disaster.

McKee, who had waited expectantly at the base, had his work cut out for him. Most of his returning planes required significant repairs. Some had to be scrapped. His men worked around the clock for the next three days. In spite of the deaths and the massive amount of damage inflicted, McKee still wanted a chance to fly.

His wish was finally granted on the second day after the Kiel disaster. For their valor over Kiel, the men of the 44th Bomb Group were awarded a Distinguished Unit Citation, the first awarded to any unit of the Eighth Air Force. The 44th, however, was now in a predicament. There were more seats available than there were men to fill them. An order was issued from High Command to obtain replacements from any trained, available ground crew. Some of the men were like McKee and had initially been judged too old to be active combat pilots. They were volunteers who had entered the war in spite of their age. Most of them were content with the less dangerous jobs, especially those who had repeatedly risked their lives in the previous world war. But McKee was unusual: he couldn't wait to fly a mission.

On the afternoon the decision was made to use available men, McKee was inspecting one of the bombers that had returned from Kiel. He was approached by the Group's commander and asked if he would co-pilot one of the planes on the next mission. The commander apologized for the short notice. The mission was to go the very next day. Bordeaux was the target, with the goal being to destroy the U-boat repair depot there along with the Matford aero-engine factory.

McKee acted so excited when he was given the news that it caused genuine concern in his commanding officer, Colonel Leon Johnson. Johnson never expected such an eager response from an individual working a job that was relatively safe from harm. He was especially surprised because McKee knew full well of the extensive losses suffered at Kiel just two days before. He told McKee to get some sleep.

They were to leave for Bordeaux shortly after midnight the morning of the mission. Hoping to avoid German fighters, their route of travel would not take them directly into France. Instead, they would take a much longer route directed out over the Atlantic and would return to shore by way of the Bay of Biscay. Because of the increased distance fuel would be an issue, so they would first have to fly to Davidstow Moor in the extreme south of England to top off their tanks.

McKee was up before anyone else, on-board, and buckled in well ahead of schedule. He was to fly with Captain Lou Kendall, also a substitute. They were assigned a plane that had not yet seen combat. It had just arrived on the base, and McKee himself had overseen its preparation for battle. On May 16, 39 planes left for Bordeaux, their fuel tanks full to the brim. Remnants of at least two other bomb Groups were also involved in the raid. The 44th was chosen to lead. Kendall and McKee were placed in the middle of the squadron. The ancient navigational technique of "dead reckoning" would be necessary to find their way since there were absolutely no fixed markers to allow the use of conventional navigation located anywhere along the entire route.

Navigating by best guess was the responsibility of Lieutenant Mikolowski. He performed admirably and the target came up precisely as expected. The bombardiers dropped their explosives with precision, the bombs falling in tightly bunched patterns. The result was a near total destruction of the aero-engine factory and a total demolition of the harbor gates to the submarine base. Many of the buildings surrounding the base were also destroyed. Reportedly only light flak was encountered, and just one of the planes failed to make it back to England – it had mechanical problems and was forced to land in Spain. The unfortunate crew was detained in Spain until August, when they were finally repatriated.

Even though the rest of the planes returned safely to England, there was, sadly, one bizarre fatality. Technical Sergeant Light was standing by an open waist gun window as the planes turned to head for home. Somehow, his parachute opened mysteriously, allowing the slipstream to drag the chute and Sergeant Light from the plane. He dropped into the icy waters of the Bay of Biscay. He was never found and was presumed to have drowned.

Kendall and McKee were both ecstatic upon their return to the base. The entire Group was granted a short leave to get some rest and relaxation and to carry out some much-needed maintenance on the planes. New men were now arriving daily to fill in the gaps of those departed. With this new influx, McKee was unsure whether he would be called upon for any further missions. He set about organizing the ground crews to get the work done as efficiently as possible. He was planning a short trip himself during leave time and wanted everything to run smoothly in his absence.

On May 22 McKee borrowed a Jeep from the motor pool and picked Penny up at her home just as the sun was rising. They headed north toward Scotland to satisfy one of McKee's lifelong dreams. They planned to visit the Borders area first. Penny made all the arrangements, designing a trip that would showcase the points of interest that most typified Scotland's historical troubles with England. While researching the trip, she was surprised to find that McKee's ancestors were Highlanders, originally bearing the name McKay. The two explorers hoped to make it all the way to Inverness to look up his ancestry during the short ten days they had available to play.

Driving for the better part of the first day, they made it as far as Berwick at the very tip of the east coast of England. The second day they arrived in the little town of Coldstream around noon. They downed a quick lunch, and then made the short drive to Kelso, where they checked into the Keys Gate Hotel for the night. McKee tried unsuccessfully to hire a guide for a day of salmon fishing at the junction pool formed by the Tweed and Travois rivers. He was disappointed at not having been able to fish his entire time in England. He could not be called an avid fisherman, but it was something he enjoyed doing from time to time. Instead of fishing, he and Penny visited the home of Sir Walter Scott before taking a long and romantic stroll along the riverbank across from the estate belonging to the Duke of Roxburgh. Thoughts of Betty and Viola never entered his mind.

Deciding to skip Edinburgh and Glasgow, they made it to Inverness by the afternoon of the fourth day. Penny dragged McKee into a small men's store where he found out about his heritage. Douglas McCloud, the slightly bent and graying proprietor, was a history buff who had become quite adept at heraldry. By the time he was finished with McKee, the man from Indiana had purchased the full regalia of the Clan McKee (McKay). Penny took several pictures of him in full dress.

The couple's return route took them through Perthshire, where they visited Stirling Castle and a cave supposedly used by Robert the Bruce. They also managed to hit every distillery along the way, requiring Penny to do most of the driving. McKee proclaimed as if fact that in a former life he had fought valiantly beside William Wallace in the battle of Stirling Bridge. Penny told him to have another dram.

While skirting Edinburgh on their way home, they had a flat tire. They were fortunately able to fix it with the help of a shepherd who befriended them while they were stopped in front of his property, pondering their next move. He brought his entire family out to see the curious American airman. After a lunch of potatoes, haggis and a curious-looking vegetable he couldn't identify, they headed on towards England. The shepherd's boy was still beaming after McKee had presented him with a small lapel pin in the shape of an Indianapolis racing car.

In a reflective moment during the drive, McKee asked himself what he was doing with yet another woman. The thought was fleeting as he and Penny settled down for the night, her cheeks a rosy pink after the day's ride in the open Jeep. Her reddish-blond hair, perfect smile and shapely body eliminated any thoughts of atonement. I might die next week, he thought as they held each other tightly beneath the covers. They returned to Norfolk the next day.

Back at the base everything was status quo. Missions were scheduled to begin again the next evening, and the men continued to die in record numbers. Scuttlebutt on the base spoke of a possible move to North Africa before the summer was over. The buzz claimed that there was a special mission being planned for a target, or group of targets, somewhere in southern Germany, possibly in conjunction with a large-scale land invasion of France. What the men did not know, and probably where most of the rumors originated, was that a major conference had been held in Morocco in January attended by both President Roosevelt and Prime Minister Churchill, as well as other Allied commanders.

McKee listened intently to the gossip but largely paid it no heed. Rumors always popped up during a war, just like they did in WW1. He continued to service the planes and to see Penny when he could get away with it. No missions came his way, actually causing him to feel a bit melancholy. Most of the other pilots thought he was crazy.

Quite unexpectedly, during the third week in June word came down from High Command that the entire 44th Bomb Group was indeed being moved to North Africa. There was little warning given. They were to leave in less than 24 hours, and there was no time to say a proper goodbye to Penny. McKee got hold of her on the phone. The conversation was short and to the point – McKee's always were.

"We're off to Africa, Penny. I've never been there, you know. See you somewhere sometime. Stay pretty."

"But Herschel..."

He hung up.

The only information the men were given was that they were to join part of the Ninth Air Force for some specialized training. Whatever it was they were in store for, it was obviously going to be big. McKee had a sudden memory flash when he learned they were going to join part of the Ninth Air Force. He remembered seeing something that puzzled him greatly at the time. On an unusually beautiful afternoon one day during the past month he had seen an unfamiliar squadron of B-24s sweep over the base at an extremely low altitude, going full speed. They were not part of the 44th. The planes flew so low that it looked dangerous even to McKee. At the time of the fly-over, if it could be called that, no matter how much of his fingers he stuck in his ears the noise of the many Pratt & Whitney engines was so loud he thought his head was going to explode.

Slowly, more of what he had been doing lately began to make sense. He had just finished replacing all of the bomb-sights on his squadron of B-24s. The replacement sights were a very basic gun-type of fabrication, much like you would see on a deer rifle only much larger. Modifications had also been made to the nose guns that allowed them to fire at a much steeper angle.

Holy shit, we're going to be shooting from the hip, he thought to himself.

The entire Group left for Africa that evening. After refueling in the south of England, they headed for Morocco, and then on to an unnamed airfield close to Benghazi, in Libya. They landed and quickly discovered they were going to be living in extreme isolation for at least the foreseeable future. They touched down on a patch of nondescript desert sand, nothing to see but sand in every direction. Sand would suddenly become part of their lives.

Carried by the ever-present wind, it abraded the skin of the airplanes, infiltrated the engines and other working parts, permeated their food and was forever in their hair, ears and mouths. The men hastily erected a tent village, which provided little protection from either the heat of day or the cold of night. England at its worst suddenly looked pretty damn good. The only one who seemed relatively happy was McKee, who had just learned that he was going to fly again. Lou Kendall gave him the news the night of their arrival. The two of them were assigned to be tent-mates and Lou waited until they were ready to turn in to give him the news. It was all McKee could talk about at breakfast the next morning.

Low-level flying practice became the order of the day. To keep the men sharp, these practices were interrupted on occasion by short bombing missions into Sicily and Italy. On one of these, following a stopover in Malta, one of the crews returned with a plane-load of excellent red wine. None of these missions was very intense, no planes were lost and little in the way of defense was ever encountered. Their purpose was to keep the men battle-ready. The final raid into Italy was completed at the end of July. Low-level flying exercises were immediately intensified, filling the daylight hours of each and every day.

Both Kendall and McKee were already accomplished at low-level flying, having been barnstormers in the '20s and early '30s. The B-24 was more of a handful than were their much smaller biplanes, but they were able to quickly adapt to the plane's characteristics. All of the pilots were still in the dark as to what this training was ultimately to be used for. Each day, the crews were awakened early, donned their gear after a quick breakfast, and then took off for a simulated bombing run over the desert. They would descend to less than 20ft at times, dropping wooden bombs on makeshift targets scrawled in the sand.

A massive grid had been traced in the dessert with the targets laid out in a peculiar fashion. Whatever it was they were planning to destroy, it was certainly different from anything else they'd previously bombed. There was no time allowed for relaxation. Darkness brought on a definite feeling of extreme tiredness, more mental than it was physical. McKee and his tent-mate survived by managing to commandeer a substantial amount of the confiscated wine. They were having quite a good time of it, flying all day then getting half in the bag at night.

On the last day of July the crews were finally told what their intended mission was to be. Colonel Jacob Smart, a member of "Hap" Arnold's advisory council, was chosen as the messenger. General Henry H. Arnold was the US Army Air Force commander for the entire European theater. His orders had come directly from Allied Supreme Command, and resulted from the big conference in Morocco.

Smart revealed the target to be the massive Ploesti oil refineries. Ploesti, he informed the men, was a Romanian city of over 100,000 inhabitants. The city itself was not the target, only the oil refineries. The main refinery was located just outside of the city, with at least eight other refineries scattered in close proximity. The mission was to be called "Operation Tidal Wave". It was part of a much larger plan formulated at what was now being referred to as the "Casablanca Conference".

The raid on the refineries would begin at some yet to be determined point, sometime after the North African Campaign ended but before a planned land invasion of Sicily began. Smart went on to say that 40 per cent of the Romanian oil production at Ploesti went straight to the Nazi war effort, so eliminating the refinery would seriously cripple the German military. He also explained how a normal, high-level bombing operation would risk dangerous intervention by German fighters. It was additionally felt by Supreme Command that a high level approach would allow too much lead time for the mobilization of other defense capabilities such as flak batteries and balloon installations. By coming in low, it was felt that the element of surprise could be counted on.

McKee listened intently as the briefing progressed. The only other operation he was familiar with that had used low-level bombing was when the RAF attacked the dams in Germany's Ruhr valley using bombs shaped like large bowling balls, designed by a scientist by the name of Barnes Wallis. When dropped from a precise altitude, these bombs would skip along the water at intervals of several hundred yards before exploding on contact with the dam. The raid had been declared an overwhelming success, although eight of the 19 aircraft involved were lost along with 53 airmen. The planes on that raid had flown at an altitude of 50ft. In Operation Tidal Wave the bombers would be asked to fly as low as 8ft.

McKee told Kendall that it sounded exhilarating. Kendall wasn't so sure. Smart went on to say that a mixture of incendiaries and delayed-action bombs would be used. He explained that there were actually nine separate refineries placed at three different locations. The main one was very near the city of Ploesti, a second group of refineries was near Braze, and the third group was near Campina.

McKee and Kendall left the briefing with mixed feelings. They were going to be involved in one of the most dangerous and significant raids of the war, but there was no doubt in anyone's mind that the mission was going to be somewhere beyond dangerous. They returned to their tent and finished what was left of the wine.

"It's going to be one tough son of a bitch, Lou!"

"That it is, McKee. That it is."

Chapter 26

OPERATION TIDAL WAVE

Kendall and McKee finished putting on their flying gear. First they donned a suit of silk long johns, then a layer of heavy wool was added before they put on their leather flight jackets. Most airmen wore two pair of woolen socks but their feet still occasionally froze to the point of frostbite, especially on the longer missions – Ploesti was going to be one of the long ones. Finally they put on their Mae West life jackets and their parachute harness. Each man was given a thermos of hot coffee, a few candy bars and several sticks of chewing gum. Additionally, each was supplied with an escape kit containing maps of the countries they would be flying over, some local currency, and fake passports. They were told to leave behind anything that might positively identify their unit or its location. Selected personal items were placed in a different container to be sent to their next of kin if necessary. The last thing they grabbed as they boarded the plane were their actual parachutes. Each man carefully packed his own.

It was 2:45 in the morning, August 1, 1943. Operation Tidal Wave was to begin at some point during the next three hours. Most of the men were still suffering from the late stages of a severe bout of dysentery, thought to have been caused by some bad dates. The men ate what they could of their breakfasts, most of them simply picking at what was in front of them. The beginning of the day was not blessed with much in the way of optimism. The simulated raids over the desert had been successful, with most of the targets destroyed within two minutes

232

of arrival, but even so the commanders remained pessimistic. The pessimism trickled down to the crews.

A loss of 50 per cent of the airplanes and a similar percentage of crewmen was predicted. General Eisenhower had approved the plan knowing these terrible predictions. The top brass deemed the mission absolutely necessary to win the war in Europe. If the Ploesti raid was successful, Hitler's oil supply would be cut by one third and the war could be shortened by as much as six months. One of the commanding officers was overheard to remark: "If nobody comes back, the results will be worth the cost."

It was the first time anyone could remember that Supreme Command handed a task to a Theater Commander without first asking if the task was feasible. As McKee and Kendall surveyed the scene in the early morning, they were struck by how young nearly all of the men were. The average age could not be more than 22.

"Do you think we're too old for this shit?"

"Probably," replied McKee.

The 44th Bomb Group, or "Flying Eight-Balls" – a nickname conjured up over drinks by adding together the fours of "44th" – would play a principle role in the raid under the able command of Colonel Leon Johnson. Born in Missouri in 1904, Johnson had been accepted by the US Military Academy at West Point at the age of 18, and following his graduation in 1926 he became an infantry officer. He soon tired of being miserable on the ground, however, and wisely transferred to the Army Air Corps, where he spent five years flying observational aircraft. For a brief period he studied meteorology and served as a weather officer. In June of 1942, when the Eighth Air Force was activated, he began training to become a bomber pilot and was one of the first to land in England. By the time of Operation Tidal Wave he had already won the Distinguished Flying Cross twice, and a Silver Star.

The 44th was assigned Target White #1, the industrial complex at Columbia Aquila on the near southwest side of Ploesti. Any planes that survived the initial attack would then fly on to Target Blue, the refinery at Brazi, five miles south of the city. The targets selected for the massive raid were designated White #1 through #5, all of which were located in and around Ploesti; Target Red, the refinery at Campina; and finally Target Blue at Brazi – a daunting undertaking if ever there was one. A total of 178 airplanes were poised and ready, anxiously awaiting the signal to go, take-off time being kept secret from all but the individual Group Commanders.

Most of the men were sitting or lying around the mess tent waiting for the signal. They were either drinking coffee or smoking or both. McKee was smoking a big cigar. Kendall was pacing, first one way then another, his cigarette dangling precariously from his lips. There was little conversation. At last, the signal was given.

At precisely 5:00am on August 1, 1943 the first of the Liberators took off. Operation Tidal Wave was under way. Many historians would later comment that it was probably the most intricately planned mission in history, led by the most accomplished flyers. Several "rookies" were also included in the mix, along with a few older, experienced volunteers like McKee and Kendall. Some of the men were already referring to the day as "Black Sunday". The sky around Benghazi was soon darkened by airplanes.

As the last group of bombers began to taxi, one of the Liberators was forced to turn back because of mechanical trouble. Flying very low, it made a slow turn and hit a pole. It exploded on impact, all but two of its crewmen being killed outright. Many of the men who witnessed the incident became convinced the mission was ill-fated.

The remaining 177 planes disappeared into the early morning sky.

The attack force was organized into five separate waves, flying at an altitude of 500 to 1,000ft as they crossed the Mediterranean. A strong emphasis had been placed on the necessity of the five waves sticking as close together as possible all the way to Ploesti. The planes of the 44th were in the fourth wave as they headed across the sea on a direct path towards the enemy-held island of Corfu.

By the time the first two waves made landfall the remaining three waves were nowhere in sight, having become widely separated during the crossing. The gap between waves was later blamed on the different choices of altitude made by the various pilots. Seeking to penetrate the intervening thick clouds most advantageously, each pilot selected his preferred altitude based on the information he had at hand. Radio silence was mandated during the crossing so no one knew for sure who was at what altitude. The winds that day varied widely at each level, resulting in the separations. Poor visibility added to the problem. Not only did the waves become separated, but individual groups within waves also drifted far apart. The 44th became separated early on, and was forced to go it alone to its first target, White #1.

Adding to these early problems was the fact that the first two waves, still flying ahead of the remaining planes, made a wrong turn at their first checkpoint. This mistake set them on a course directly toward the city of Bucharest, which was not on the list of potential targets. When they realized their mistake they completely lost their bearings, having no idea how to reach their intended targets by the most direct route. They essentially became freelance bombers over Romania. Some of these planes actually ended up heading to Ploesti from the opposite direction to the oncoming waves of the main force, setting the stage for possible head-on collisions.

One plane, *Wongo-Wongo*, foundered during the crossing. Witnesses said that it suddenly pitched upward for no apparent reason and crashed into the sea. Before *Wongo-Wongo*'s demise, another plane was forced to turn back to North Africa after having flown for only three hours. A total of 175 bombers therefore successfully made it across the sea. For the short time they were all flying together, the mass of airplanes resembled a giant horde of prehistoric locusts. The foreboding shadow they cast over the landscape signaled a wide swath of potential death and destruction.

The plane flown by Kendall and McKee was performing flawlessly as they entered Rumania. The success of the mission was almost totally dependent on the element of surprise. What the bombers did not know as they neared the refineries was that they had been tracked by the Germans since they left Benghazi. Over 200 German fighters were in the vicinity of Ploesti on the day of the raid, and all of the German pilots had been placed on alert status soon after the operation got under way.

The city of Ploesti was well defended, with more than 200 strategically placed anti-aircraft guns. These included 88mm flak guns as well as 37mm rapid-fire cannons. Stretching across the city as an additional line of defense was a large number of barrage balloons, their cables loaded with high explosives. The cables, made of hardened steel, were lying in wait to snare or sheer off the wings of any approaching bombers.

Mid-afternoon. The massive force of invading bombers was still more than 150 miles from its targets. McKee looked down and was surprised to see several friendly Romanians standing unafraid in their fields, waving to the Americans as they flew over at an altitude of only 50ft. Kendall was using railroad tracks to guide them to their first target. Columbia Aquila – White #1 – was fast approaching.

McKee calmly read the numbers to his pilot: "Altitude, 50 feet, speed, 220 knots, no bogies in sight."

As soon as he uttered the last word, blazing ground fire erupted. The plane shook violently. When the artillery battery opened up, the 44th Bomb Group still had all of its 37 planes flying in a loose formation. The gunners below must certainly have been awestruck by the sight of this many planes flying wing-tip to wing-tip only 50ft off the ground at over 240mph. The noise was deafening. The ground shook, resembling a major earthquake to the gunners below. Kendall decided to go lower.

"Keep your eyes on the horizon and don't look down whatever you do," shouted McKee.

When McKee looked down what he saw amazed and frightened him at the same time. There was a train racing along the tracks just beneath them and slightly to the right. Suddenly, all of the boxcars' doors opened to reveal several small-bore flak guns substantially manned by German troops. The B-24s' gunners opened fire in response, taking advantage of the low-level revisions made to their weaponry. The train exploded, splitting in half. The resulting smoke and flames blinded the planes bringing up the rear. Two of the Liberators crashed into the train, adding to the inferno. The few remaining flak gunners managed to down two more before they themselves were consumed in the mass of flames.

Kendall doggedly continued toward the city, now at an altitude of only 20ft.

"Thank God we were toward the front!" yelled McKee.

Kendall maintained this altitude even though confronted by the city's tall chimneys and utility poles. As they neared their first target, bursts of flak again increased. A jagged piece of metal tore into the left front of the fuselage just below the windscreen. McKee saw it hit. Kendall slumped lifelessly onto the controls, blood spewing over the instrument panel. McKee saw him go and grabbed his own controls instinctively. Ten or more feet of altitude was lost before McKee could steady the plane. Kendall remained motionless, twisted slightly to his left side. McKee concentrated on the task at hand. As the plane brushed over tall weeds, his eyes tried to see through the debris exploding in front of him.

Looking very much like an erupting volcano, the target area lay just ahead. McKee gained a few feet of altitude and steadied the plane. Earlier bombers had done their job well. Much of the area was in ruin, with large plumes of smoke and flame rising from several burning buildings and associated structures. As he entered the target zone, McKee glanced at a plane flying just to the left of him. It was full of holes with smoke trailing from the right-hand outboard engine. He knew it wouldn't make it much further. He risked a quick glance toward the ground. Almost within arms' length he flew over a string of mangled, still smoldering B-24 carcasses. He grabbed the intercom for a quick roll call.

The rest of his crew was still alive: the tail gunner reported a wound to his left shoulder but said he could still fight. The plane was still largely intact. The instruments were reporting acceptable levels and McKee was able to hold altitude without difficulty. He pressed on. His course took him directly toward the twin smoke stacks of Columbia Aquila, which rose undamaged from the ashes of the city.

As he drew closer to the target, two badly-damaged B-24s came straight at him, flying at full speed at a slightly higher altitude. On their tail were two German fighters, guns blazing. McKee watched as one of the planes suddenly caught fire. It twisted abruptly, now heading on a direct course toward McKee. With a collision imminent, the doomed plane fortunately dipped further down just before impact. It nosedived into a field, having missed McKee's plane by less than 15ft. It disintegrated as several small parts pelted his windscreen.

Just ahead, McKee could barely discern what appeared to be a chain reaction of large explosions running nearly the entire length of the city's refinery. The bombers flying ahead of him were certainly doing their job. Now flying at only 15ft, McKee heard one of the other pilots in their group ask the Commander if they should all turn back because, as he nervously stated: "To go on is certainly suicidal."

Colonel Johnson was heard to reply something to the effect that "You're right on target, son. Give 'em hell!"

The planes were taken off radio silence when the bombing began but the action held conversation to a minimum. What remained of the Flying Eight-Balls struggled onward, into the mountain of smoke and fire that lay ahead. Explosions were still occurring. With his windscreen almost totally occluded, McKee had no idea where he was going. He could barely make anything out at all. By now it was all he could do to keep the plane in the air. They were jostled about mercilessly. Flak continued unabated, even at this very low altitude. At times McKee sensed they were no more than a couple of feet off the ground.

Much to the amazement of everyone on the plane they soon emerged from the carnage. Even McKee had doubted their ability to survive this one. Getting his bearings as the windscreen cleared somewhat, he was able to join what remained of the Group. They were headed towards their second assigned target, the refinery at Brazi.

McKee flew south for a short time, managing to escape the heaviest ground fire. Once near Brazi, however, machine-gun fire became heavy again and the artillery batteries opened up. Flying at an altitude of 25ft, McKee's crew hit the refinery with 1,000lb bombs while his gunners destroyed several of the artillery batteries. Delayed action fuses kept the bombs from taking the B-24 with them. Nearing the end of their run McKee's plane took multiple hits to the fuselage, but it remained in the air. As they emerged into what appeared to be clear sky, he could hear the men cheering loudly over the noise of the engines. They were now several miles from the city. As he looked about, McKee could make out a few other B-24s still flying.

Several planes had been lost in the early bombing, but amazingly not a single one was lost over Target Blue. The refinery was totally destroyed. The 44th still had 21 of its planes in the air. The daunting task of getting them all home now lay ahead. German fighters were still swarming about the area; most of the bombers had sustained significant damage, all were low on fuel, and many were out of ammunition. Some had all three issues to deal with plus injured personnel on board. McKee refrained from looking at his dead friend; he climbed to an altitude of 12,000ft and limped toward home.

Most of the planes around him were trailing smoke from one or more of their engines. Some could not keep up and quickly fell behind. They appeared to be struggling just to stay aloft. McKee opened his first candy bar as he reached the water's edge off Cyprus. He finished the rest of the meager provisions as they crossed the Mediterranean. He landed the plane in Benghazi later that night.

Seven planes from the 44th were known to have been lost in combat during Operation Tidal Wave, their hulks and crews left in the fields or along the roads around Ploesti. Another two of the Group's planes had been forced down in neutral Turkey, where their crews were interned for the duration of the war. Twenty-one planes landed in Benghazi. Of the 169 planes involved in the actual bombing, only 89 made it home, and of these just 33 were judged capable of safe flight following inspection the next day. In all, 1,726 men flew in the raid. More than 300 died and 140 were captured. Of those who returned,

440 suffered wounds of one kind or another; some were disabled for life. The Allied Supreme Command declared the raid an unequivocal success.

Once the bombing started, the entire mission took just over half an hour. Germany lost over 40 per cent of its oil-producing capability. Colonel Leon Johnson was awarded the Medal of Honor along with the four other Group Commanders, and every man on the mission received the Distinguished Flying Cross.

Interviewed by the *Indianapolis Star* after the war, McKee was quoted as saying: "After we landed, I picked corn stalks from the bomb bay doors."

The 44th remained in Africa for a short time following the Ploesti raid. They continued to bomb Italy and Sicily and even went as far as Austria on one occasion, before the Group returned to England for good late in August. All of the men were given a brief but welcome respite from the war. McKee hooked up with Penny as soon as he was able to leave the base.

"McKee, you truly are one lucky son of a bitch."

"Charmed," he replied. "I truly am charmed."

Chapter 27

"Lucky"

There was very little news regarding the Ploesti raid back in the States. All Betty and Viola knew was that McKee was in England doing something in the war. The two women were busy working and jointly taking care of little Linda. On one particularly gorgeous afternoon in the early fall, they took her to the Indiana State Fair. A thrill show of sorts was under way along the front straightaway of the harness racing track. It reminded both women of their former daredevil.

"Remember those days?" Viola said to Betty.

"Sure do. The crazy bozo would to try to commit suicide on a daily basis."

"I only saw him perform once. You were gone someplace. He told me to come and watch him. I went to the Vigo County Fair in Terre Haute. It was the longest 60 miles I had ever driven. The crazy loon jumped his motorcycle over a bunch of old jalopies they had set on fire. The turkey made it, of course."

"Of course. I'd sure like to hear from the bastard some day. I expect the son-of-a-bitch is still alive."

McKee had no intention of writing to the two women. He had all but forgotten Indianapolis and the mess back home. Penny was keeping him entertained in every way imaginable given the circumstances of the war. They had taken a number of historical side-trips and on one occasion even visited London. In early September they had seen the famous Glen Miller orchestra at a concert held on the base. As the band played the beautiful

Moonlight Serenade, Penny whispered to McKee that she loved him very much.

Here we go again, he thought to himself. *Oh well, England's a hell of a long way from Indiana.*

The day after the concert he and Penny went shopping for the dog he had been wanting since he arrived in England. Penny knew of a family that was trying to place three dogs from an unwanted litter. She dragged McKee to a small farmhouse early one misty English morning. One of the dogs took to McKee right off. A male, he was mostly Labrador, black as coal. The rest of his heritage was questionable. He was already four months old, house-trained and full of energy. He could not stop licking McKee's hand or whatever else he could get his tongue on. McKee named the dog – you guessed it – Lucky.

They purchased the necessary dog items. No girly stuff for Lucky – his collar was ringed with giant chrome spikes, and his name was emblazoned in big black letters on the dark brown leather. Late that afternoon they took the newly adorned Lucky for a stroll to the Horse and Hound. He was an immediate hit with the assembled airmen. They proclaimed him base mascot on the spot. Several rounds were consumed in celebration.

McKee wanted Lucky to live with him. He was unsure whether or not he could have a dog around the barracks. Needing to return to the base, he left Lucky with Penny. Lucky didn't seem to mind. As soon as McKee arrived on the base, he located the Colonel and was surprisingly given permission to keep Lucky with him as long as he remained outside in some type of enclosure.

"In this weather?"

"Yes Captain, in all weather. I don't ever want to see that dog inside."

McKee spent the better part of the day building a small house for Lucky and a wire-fence enclosure for him to romp in. With

Kendall gone, he had no one he felt close to. It was not that he was aloof: it was simply because of the age difference of most of the men he worked with. He was more suitable as a father figure than a buddy. The men enjoyed his company at night and often accepted his occasional advice, but it was difficult for a 45-year-old man to be on the same wavelength as a 21-year-old. The result was that he and Lucky became nearly inseparable.

Lucky had the run of the base in a very short time. McKee continued to do his job as maintenance chief, being allowed to fly on occasion. He had performed so well under the very difficult circumstances at Ploesti that his commander felt it advantageous to keep him sharp. The missions he piloted were for the most part diversionary. These carried less risk and were not nearly as intense as a real bombing raid. For McKee, life had become fairly decent. He was happy to be out of Indianapolis, he could fly occasionally, he had grown quite fond of England and her people, and there was his dog and Penny. He was often heard to say: "If the weather weren't so damn miserable this would be a great place to live."

On September 2, 1943, Colonel Leon Johnson left the 44th Bomb Group and moved up the ladder to the larger responsibility of Commanding Officer of the 14th Combat Bomb Wing. He was succeeded by Lieutenant-Colonel James Posey. Life on the base changed little with the change in leadership. Diversionary missions continued unabated. Some of the planes had recently been sent back to Africa for some needed touch-up work in southern Italy. With these planes away, large-scale bombing missions were out of the question.

During this relatively quiet period, life on the base became as close to routine as it possibly could. However, McKee's relatively contented mood was rocked violently one day when Penny began to talk about marriage. The two were sitting on the couch at the time. She still had no idea that Betty or Viola existed. McKee countered by placing Lucky between the two of them. As he did so, Lucky did what male dogs do all too frequently. The aroma that subsequently permeated the room spoiled the mood. Penny bailed to the kitchen. McKee jumped from the couch, taking Lucky with him. They went for a walk to ponder his situation.

Not good, he thought. *Why do they always want to get married?*

He reached for a large stick lying on the ground in front of him, tossing it as far as he could throw it. Lucky, ears up and tail wagging, took off in the opposite direction. Penny's next-door neighbor's dog just happened to be in heat. Lucky was unable to scale the fence surrounding the neighbor's yard but his barking brought everyone in the neighborhood outside.

"Mornin'," they all said.

McKee refused to say "Mornin'," having a sudden disdain for the English. He grabbed Lucky, and as he did so he slipped and fell into a large muddy puddle. He landed flat on his back, legs and arms outstretched. He splashed around a bit then rose like some creature emerging from beneath the sea. He mumbled, fortunately to himself: "Kill everybody, burn everything."

Penny, hearing the commotion, was also outside by this time and remarked: "What a sight you are, Captain McKee!"

He grabbed her in his arms as Lucky tried to lick both of their faces at once. Hugging each other tightly, they walked to the house and sat down to a full English breakfast. Penny did not mention marriage again and McKee renewed his love for England.

All of the planes were back from Africa by October 5. The diversionary missions stopped, and regular bombing raids began anew. Many new recruits were now flying the planes. In addition to his maintenance responsibilities, McKee was sought out nightly to help calm the lads down following their return from a particularly harrowing mission or near miss. He was not expecting to fly again until the projected invasion of Western Europe, reportedly being planned for early in January, 1944.

By now the RAF and the USAAF had become essentially one united air force. The men had long-since ceased their animosity toward one another and were working together closely. Their mission had two purposes. One was to incapacitate the industrial potential of Germany, and the other was to permanently cripple the Luftwaffe. McKee was counting the days.

Chapter 28

BOMBS OVER NORMANDY AND MARRIAGE #4

G eneral Eisenhower was the man in charge of planning the invasion of Western Europe. Beneath him were assembled all of the other Allied commanders. To help accomplish the mission, he asked the Ninth Air Force to move to England in early October. There they would train, expand, and join forces with the Eighth Air Force and the RAF. Operation Point Blank was the first mission planned to use this combined force. It was to be a prelude to the big invasion.

In addition to planes, a large ground contingent was also assembled. In all, over 200,000 military personnel were massed in England in preparation. The Ninth Air Force was given the responsibility of tactical support for the ground operations as well as to try and render the German Luftwaffe ineffective. The Eighth Air Force continued its strategic bombing role, weakening Germany's infrastructure. A squadron from the 44th Bomb Group was transferred to the Ninth Air Force to bolster its strength. Several fighter planes were also added. McKee was temporarily transferred from Shipdham to help sort out the maintenance logistics.

During the winter and into spring, the Ninth Air Force expanded exponentially. Its eventual strength reached 45 flying groups with more than 5,000 aircraft. McKee organized the maintenance operations for the transferred bombers along with the added responsibility of maintaining three squadrons of fighter planes that included P-51 Mustangs, P-47 Thunderbolts and P-38 Lightnings – manuals he would have to brush up on. The drive to Penny's was longer, but he didn't really mind the change of location for a time, especially after getting the OK to take Lucky with him.

"Operation Point Blank" was intended to severely weaken the Luftwaffe. Bit by bit, the German air force was rendered less effective as the Allies attacked it in the air and on the ground. Included among the targets were rail yards, industrial plants, airfields and other military installations. Missions were carried out over Germany as well as France, Belgium and the Netherlands. The defenses along the wall on the French coast of the English Channel were also targeted. All of these efforts were in preparation for what was now being called D-Day.

Strategic bombing missions began on January 4, 1944. Several were planned, but most had to be scrubbed due to the ever-present problem of inclement weather. During this period of heightened activity, the first B-24J appeared at Shipdham. McKee was still on the base when it arrived. Improved over previous models, it contained an electrically operated turbo-supercharger, an idea that was being developed while McKee was still at Allison's.

I'll be damned, he thought.

The previous superchargers were operated hydraulically and would occasionally malfunction when the fluids became too cold – not an unlikely occurrence when flying over the North Atlantic in winter. When a malfunction such as this did happen, catastrophic engine failure would usually result. A crash often followed.

McKee lobbied for, and got, a chance to fly one of the new planes on an actual mission. He replaced one of the regular pilots who had become ill with some form of stomach virus. The mission was a massive raid not unlike the one over Ploesti. Instead of an oil refinery, the target this time was the city of

Berlin. Two previous attempts had been made to bomb Germany's principle city but each had failed due to the weather. This time the weather was cooperating. Seven hundred B-24s and a group of smaller B-17s left England at dawn, flying over the North Sea. They resembled a massive flock of prehistoric birds.

McKee was flying with a young co-pilot by the name of Hank Mummery. Mummery had been at the base for only two weeks following his accelerated training program in the States. McKee noticed that the young man was not just a little bit nervous, he was extremely nervous. He turned his head continually from side to side as if he was frantically looking for something. He actually looked to be battery operated. He couldn't stop jabbering.

Just as young Mummery asked McKee when they could expect some flak, the sky in front of them lit up like a giant array of fireflies. The way ahead looked to be totally impassable. To make matters worse, German fighters suddenly approached from every direction, their guns blazing. Mummery's head no longer moved. His eyes were focused dead ahead in a blank stare.

Sixty-nine Allied bombers were destroyed by the Luftwaffe and German flak batteries that day, but remarkably the 44th Bomb Group didn't lose a single plane. McKee and his crew successfully destroyed a large industrial and rail complex outside the city. After their last bomb was dropped, they made the turn for home. McKee glanced at the now more relaxed Mummery and said in a triumphant sort of way: "You had nothing to fear, lad – you're flying with Lucky Herschel McKee."

Other than sighting an occasional lone fighter, the trip home was peaceful. Mummery, it turned out, was from Ohio. McKee was reminded of his earlier traveling pal, Will Hennessy, who had finally made it into the Lafayette Flying Corps only to be shot down three days later while dogfighting over the same country McKee was again fighting.

"This is a scary business, son."

"That it is, Captain, but there sure is a hell of a rush to it!"

Bet he ends up driving racecars if he ever makes it back home, McKee thought to himself.

As they began their approach into Shipdham, both men witnessed something they were not at all prepared to see. Likely due to the angle of the setting sun, they watched in amazement as a lone P-47, approaching rapidly from the east, ran smack into the side of a returning B-24. The right wing of the big bomber was ripped from its fuselage. The plane wobbled slightly then plummeted to earth. All on board perished, as did the pilot of the fighter plane, whose wreckage wasn't found until several hours later.

Mummery was visibly shaken. McKee consoled him with his usual speech about it being what it was. They headed straight for the Horse and Hound, where they tied into the universal remedy men have used since time and wars began.

It was now March, but you would never have known it by the weather. One day merged into the next with no noticeable change in the density of the fog. Lucky didn't seem to mind one way or the other, accompanying McKee wherever he was allowed to go. When the weather was good, missions to "soften up" the Germans went on around the clock. McKee and his ground crews were kept eternally busy. Penny, ever faithful, was a constant comfort to McKee, who still shied away from becoming too friendly with any of the flight crews. He was actually beginning to entertain the idea that he just might be able to tolerate England forever. In a surprise move, he asked Penny to marry him on March 6.

Their vows were spoken two weeks later during a lull in the missions. Any honeymoon was out of the question as McKee continued to work diligently at the base. Preparations for the big invasion were now in full swing. In the world according to

McKee, the Atlantic Ocean divided one distinct civilization from another; being married in both England and the United States made perfectly good sense to him. He never planned to remain in any one place for very long at a time anyway, and he greatly enjoyed the company of a woman.

Theirs was not an unusual occurrence. Several airmen, becoming aware of their exceedingly short life expectancy, wanted the experience, security and pleasure of being married. Romances were kindled overnight in many cases, with a hurried marriage occurring within days. Personal effects in boxes of downed aviators would often contain a brand new wedding band, the symbol of a marriage unknown to all but their closest pals. Some men would be found to have two or more of these next-of-kin boxes prepared for shipment if the unthinkable happened.

Living arrangements for married couples were determined by individual base commanders. Most did not allow cohabitation on the base, but would allow couples to live in close proximity. One old British commander allegedly banned all women within a radius of 40 miles. Children from such marriages have been a problem since wars have been fought, often overwhelming social service agencies once a conflict ends.

For Herschel and Penny, nothing about their lives really changed following their wedding. When on duty, he remained on the base with Lucky; off duty, he and Lucky lived at Penny's. They enjoyed each other's company immensely and frequently discussed their future once the fighting was over. After the war, they thought Scotland a good place to settle in. Herschel preferred the Western Isles, while Penny liked the Borders area.

"Too populated," he would say, preferring the fewest number of neighbors possible.

In January, General Dwight Eisenhower had been officially named Allied Supreme Commander. At roughly the same time, a

P-51 fighter plane with a much longer range entered service, resulting in a change of tactics for the Americans. Until then, fighter planes were primarily used defensively, to protect bombers during their raids. Under Eisenhower, fighter pilots were placed on the offensive. During the early part of the war the main thrust of the Allied forces was to kill the German air force on the ground by blowing up airplane factories, support structures and oil refineries. With the improved capabilities of the new P-51, the Allies began to entice the Germans to fly and engage. A noted increase in the number of air battles occurred. The tide of battle swung toward the Allied forces. Coupled with this increase in dogfights was a concomitant increase in bombing raids against Germany's synthetic oil production facilities.

The winter weather through January had been rotten. February had finally seen some improvement, and the P-51s went to work. They downed over 2,100 German airplanes before the month had ended; March added another 2,000 or more, depending on who was counting. German air power never completely recovered, and the sizable dent made in the Luftwaffe allowed the planned invasion of Normandy to proceed as scheduled.

For McKee, this was both good news and bad. He felt the invasion would surely require his services as a pilot, but it more than doubled his workload on the ground. Instead of being responsible for a squadron of nine planes he now cared for 12, and had been informed that soon it would be 20. No equivalent increase in ground personnel was anticipated. During this period of heightened activity, flight crews were surprisingly allowed a choice of either going home to the United States for a leave of 30 days, or remaining in England. McKee chose to stay.

He, Penny and Lucky went to the Isle of Skye. Managing to hit a streak of really good weather, they were able to spend much of the time outdoors. They fished, hiked and consumed large quantities of whisky. The beaches were actually warm enough to lie on. McKee, not wishing to repeat his past mistake, brought with him an ample supply of prophylactics. Penny marveled at his unbridled optimism.

When they returned to Shipdham the base was abuzz with rumors as well as activity. McKee's squadron was now up to 15 planes. He was to expect five more within a week. The Allies' preliminary raids seemed to be working: the combined efforts of the Eighth and Ninth Air Forces were beginning to isolate the planned battlefield at Normandy. By severely damaging the railroads and highways leading into and out of the area, they made the likelihood of German reinforcements after the invasion nearly impossible. Bombing missions continued nightly, weather permitting, and were comprised of planes from the RAF as well as the Eighth and Ninth Air Forces. The raids lasted for more than two months and cost the Allies over 2,000 aircraft. McKee flew several of these raids, filling in for sick and/or disabled pilots. He remained uninjured. He was advanced to Major, and made squadron commander before D-Day commenced.

There was no time to celebrate his promotion. Raids went on non-stop. Unknown to all but the Supreme Command, the massive Allied invasion of Europe was planned for June 5, 1944. McKee was summoned back to the base the day before, leaving Penny's much sooner than he wanted. As he drove back a queasy feeling grew in the pit of his stomach. He found that his squadron had been placed on alert status, but the rest of that night and the following day passed without anything happening. He went to bed early. Then at about ten o'clock on the night of the 5th he was awakened. This is it, he thought. He quickly dressed, grabbed his gear, pistol, maps and escape-kit and headed to the briefing room.

He sat down next to one of the younger pilots. The kid appeared barely old enough to shave; he was obviously quite nervous and kept tapping his knee with the fingers of his left hand. The room was hazy with smoke as the men filed in one by one. When it was announced that D-Day was on, some of the men gave a muted cheer, others could be heard to groan; most sat expressionless. Few drank their coffee.

McKee was to fly in the first group out of Shipdham. He hoped that the months spent softening up the Germans had been successful. If the job was done properly, perhaps the invasion might not be as tough as expected. There should be little in the way of air resistance from the once mighty Luftwaffe, compliments of the new P-51.

As the young pilot continued to tap his knee, it was explained to all present what a previous, seemingly pointless mission had been for. Three days earlier they had bombed the daylights out of a large expanse of empty beach in Normandy. They were now informed that a huge landing was to be made there. Previously, no mention of a defined land invasion had been made to the pilots.

The weather data was announced; it was not as hoped. There would be thick cloud cover for the better part of the day.

The 44th Bomb Group was picked to lead the air invasion, with Colonel Leon Johnson flying as Command Pilot. McKee would be towards the rear. The Chaplain made a few remarks, but McKee left the building before he was finished. He placed a hasty call to Penny; she slept through the ringing. He met his crew at the plane, said a few words of encouragement and settled into his seat. He recognized his co-pilot from the brief time he had spent in Alabama – it was a name that was hard to forget. St Julien Hornaday III was smiling at him as he buckled in.

"Can you believe it? I just got over here. We've been patrolling that damn Gulf for almost three years now."

"Better there than here, my boy."

Their bomb bay full, they rose laboriously into a leaden sky. As they passed London, there was a small separation of the cloud layers and they could just make out the darkened form of the sprawling city below. Over the Channel the air grew turbulent. They had only their compass and airspeed indicator to guide them to the target. They were to bomb those German defenses still functional along the Atlantic Wall. A few clear spots allowed a glimpse of the two columns of ships streaming endlessly in both directions. Resembling ants going to and from their home, one column headed to France the other to England. Every size and type of ship imaginable was on its way to or from the invasion site. McKee and Hornaday were comforted by the fact that so far they had encountered no German fighters.

Two-thirds of the way across the channel both men watched helplessly as two planes suddenly banged into each other. One of the planes, caught in a sudden updraft, smashed into the underbelly of the plane flying directly overhead. Pieces from both planes broke off, narrowly missing another bomber flying nearby.

"Too many planes; too little space. Reminds me of Indianapolis at the start of the race," McKee remarked.

Time and direction finally told them they were over their target. The bombardier released his load and they circled back toward England. Visibility remained poor. They hoped the pilots coming at them remembered the flight plan. They made it back to the base in time for breakfast. After a quick debriefing, McKee and his co-pilot went to the mess hall. They enjoyed the usual fare, steering clear of everyone's favorite, "shit on a shingle" (chipped beef on toast). The men yet to fly wanted to know all about their mission, what the conditions were like, was there any resistance, and could they locate the target? One young pilot kept asking McKee how dangerous it was.

"It's really scary, kid," said McKee lightheartedly, winking at Hornaday.

Hornaday took a deep breath to curb his rising anger after McKee's flippant remark. He couldn't help but visualize the violent struggle taking place on the beaches they had just so easily flown over. He was sure he had friends down there – men who would be there for weeks, men who were being killed by the thousand as he and McKee safely ate their breakfast. Many would never make it to shore, being killed the second they stepped from their landing craft. More would die before they ran 20 yards. Thousands more would die in the weeks to follow. He put a hand on McKee's shoulder and said softly: "We don't know how good we have it, McKee."

In all, over 7,000 bombers participated in the missions to prevent the enemy bringing reinforcements into Normandy. Eisenhower had promised his troops prior to the invasion: "When you look up and see aircraft, they will be ours."

His prophecy was fairly accurate. The Luftwaffe was rendered ineffective during the weeks leading up to the invasion. Bombing raids would continue over Normandy for many weeks to come, being interrupted only by the weather. It was during these weathered-in periods that McKee was busiest. Keeping the planes flying was a major challenge. He did it with aplomb and was given his second letter of commendation. He flew only a few more missions, always coming back intact. Hornaday didn't fare as well, succumbing to a crash that occurred shortly after taking off with another pilot. McKee spent what free time he had with Lucky and his British bride.

Chapter 29

THE WAR ENDS

T he invasion of Normandy marked the turning point of the
War in Europe. The extended operation took the better part of
the summer. Following a second large invasion into southern
France in August, Paris was liberated on the 25th. In September,
McKee was reassigned to France and appointed liaison officer to
the French Air Force. His main task was to coordinate logistics
between the French and American air forces. The job though was
multifaceted: he helped organize their maintenance operations,
established a training center for new pilots and helped familiarize
the French with the operation of the newer American planes,
especially the P-51.

He, Penny and Lucky moved to Avord in France in late
September, where they found themselves a small flat, located
roughly three miles south of the base. Avord housed the central
maintenance facility for the Free French Air Force and was the
strategic command center due to its central location. McKee was
happy to be back in France after such a long absence and spent
his free time showing Penny some of his old haunts. He even
proudly showed her a couple of his crash sites. He made a meager
attempt to locate Saloua to no avail. If she was still alive she
could be anywhere, even Africa, as a result of wartime chaos.

Life at Avord was a far cry from his more hectic, danger-filled
existence at Shipdham. Other than short test flights, McKee
stayed on the ground. He enjoyed immediate credibility among
the young French pilots as a result of his Lafayette Flying Corps

experience, and was remembered by some of the area's older inhabitants who had so far survived the war. As a result of his notoriety, he and Penny enjoyed a much more active social life than they did in England. They dined out three to four nights a week, either in a small pub or at someone's home. The area around the base was secure. Life was good.

The war continued to swing in the Allies' favor. By spring 1945 it was basically over in Europe. Hitler committed suicide in April, with Germany surrendering on May 7.

The war in the Pacific dragged on a bit longer. In summer, Japan, continuing to ignore the Allied demands made at Potsdam in July, suffered the first nuclear attack in history when America dropped atomic bombs on the cities of Hiroshima and Nagasaki. Following the total destruction of both, Japan surrendered on August 15.

World War Two had cost the lives of over 60 million people. More civilians were killed than soldiers by a ratio of almost two to one. Germany eliminated between nine and eleven million people in the holocaust while Japan murdered three to ten million Chinese. Large-scale bombing on both sides caused an enormous amount of damage to cities like London and Dresden, while single bombers had leveled Hiroshima and Nagasaki. The war was the costliest in history, both in lives and dollars. The United Nations grew from the ashes and several treaties tied to human rights and values were signed.

During a ceremony at Avord, McKee was presented with a Distinguished Service Medal by General Charles de Gaulle himself. He agreed to remain in France for a few more months to finish training some of the pilots, but was then faced with a monumental decision: should he stay in Europe or return to the United States? On the practical side, he was still an American citizen and job prospects were not good if he stayed in Europe. He could remain as part of the US Military, but how long he would be needed was uncertain. On the other hand, he had no idea what the situation might be in Indianapolis. He had not written the two women and they had not found him. And then there was the child. He assumed that Viola was receiving the money he occasionally sent to her.

Penny hadn't earned a dime since he had met her. She had no specialized skills. If the military wanted him to continue as a reserve officer back in the States he could carry on with his already successful career and might even be allowed to fly. He vacillated daily trying to decide what he should do. A pauper's life with Penny, even though he adored her, was becoming less and less attractive. Then, his decision was suddenly made for him. He was promoted to Lieutenant-Colonel and asked by the Army to return to his old job at Allison's. There was a hint of something on the horizon in the letter he received from Washington, but no details were provided.

It was early fall, 1945. His work in France was finished. How was he going to break the news to Penny? After pondering the situation, he did what he always did. He discretely arranged for Lucky to be shipped to Indianapolis, made his own arrangements with the Army, took Penny out to dinner one evening and left for the States the following morning, supposedly on a covert mission for the government. She even kissed him goodbye.

Penny watched him go. In her heart she knew he would not be back – not a man like McKee. She had sensed an uneasiness about him over the last few weeks. As he walked toward the waiting car, she wiped the few tears from her eyes and went to find Lucky, who hadn't been around that morning to eat his breakfast.

"Must be off chasing something," she thought to herself.

On her own again, she began looking for a job the following morning. McKee had left her enough money to get by for at least a month. A good friend had told her that a big airport outside London was going to begin commercial service shortly after the first of the year and that they were hiring unskilled workers in several departments.

"I must look into that," she said.

PART

IV

AFTER THE WAR

Chapter 30

DOES THE CHILD EVER LEAVE THE MAN?

McKee arrived back in Indianapolis on the morning of September 15, 1945. Before leaving France he mailed a letter to Betty – he sent it to the old address, anticipating that she would still be there. He provided few details of his nearly three years in Europe, saying only that he was heavily involved in the war and lucky to be alive. He informed her of his rank and that he was coming back to Allison's and his old job. He gave her the date and time of his expected arrival and told her about Lucky and the fact he was being delivered to her address.

Betty and her newly acquired pet met McKee at the bus station. He looked stellar in his uniform, a big grin on his face. She kissed him for a full three minutes. Lucky licked him profusely while exuberantly whipping both of them with his tail. All three rode to the house in his old Cadillac. On the way, McKee remarked that the "old girl" needed a tune up as smoke billowed profusely from the exhaust.

The house was as he remembered, the exception being a few added female accoutrements. The bedspread was now a shocking pink, as were the towels in the bathroom. *Those have to go*, he thought to himself.

He and Betty were in bed before lunch, with Lucky making frequent visits to check out the proceedings. The following morning found McKee in the garage digging out his old Harley. He had it running within a couple of hours, having to jump-start it in the driveway. He summoned Betty and off they rode in the direction of the Speedway. The track had been purchased from Eddie Rickenbacker the previous year by a wealthy Terre Haute businessman by the name of Tony Hulman. Hulman bought the track in a state of horrible disrepair. Acres and acres of sprawling neglect faced the new owner. Grass and weeds were growing between the bricks, the wooden stands were on the verge of collapse, and the garages were in a shambles. A massive and expensive campaign was under way to restore the Speedway in time to stage the big race in May.

Herschel and Betty bumped into a few of their old friends shortly after arriving at the track. Drivers Rex Mays and Mauri Rose were checking out the progress being made with the renovations. At the end of the day they and their wives accompanied the returning hero and his wife to St Elmo's for some whisky, steak and stories. Mays and Rose described life at home during the war, saying it was really tough. Blackouts, rationing, shortages and uncertainty made life fairly miserable even for those not involved in the fighting. Few sporting events were held and everyone's finances were markedly strained.

McKee told them what he could about the war and what he did. He described some of the action, managing to leave out the more gruesome details. He talked about England, the base and Scotland. They toasted him several times during the course of the evening. He denied any plans to return to racing, telling them that he was a pilot first and foremost. Betty beamed throughout the night. They closed St Elmo's in the wee hours.

McKee returned to Allison's on his fourth day home. It was as if he had never left. The plant was extremely busy, much as it was right before the war. Some of his cronies were still there with a lot of new, young engineers fresh out of college. Engine development had escalated during the conflict, with jets now dominating the picture. Allison's entry into this burgeoning field was a new engine designed for the military's recently developed fighter planes, the jet-propelled F-84 and F-89. McKee's assignment was to stay abreast of engine development for the Army, and advise them with regard to suitable plane and engine combinations.

He missed Penny's cheerfulness, but it was great to be home. He maintained his flying skills with bi-weekly trips to Wright Field. He logged several more hours flying a well-worn B-24. On one of these weekends he managed to plunge himself into some really hot water. One Saturday morning, he left Wright Field for a short flight to Indianapolis and return. It was a gorgeous sunny day with no purpose to the flight but to add hours to his logbook. From an altitude of 19,000ft, the familiar "Circle" looked like a bull's-eye in the center of downtown.

Why not? thought McKee.

He turned to a heading of 270° and flew past the Speedway almost to Terre Haute. There, he brought the plane slowly down to 5,000ft as he headed back east. He picked up West Washington Street at the city limits and aimed for downtown. He slowly descended to an altitude of less than 400ft, simulating a typical bombing run. He banked the airplane sharply at the end of Washington Street and entered Monument Circle.

Some of the individuals walking the streets below swore in later affidavits that at times he seemed to dip below the tops of the surrounding buildings. McKee, grinning from ear to ear, was having a great time. He chuckled as he spoke into the intercom. He compared this flight to the bombing raid over Ploesti. As he did so, he brushed the top of the Test building. The contact with the building was duly noted by another eyewitness, who could not believe his eyes. The noise of the four big Pratt and Whitney engines shattered several panes of glass in the nearby Hume-Mansur building. More than a few panic attacks occurred on the street below. Word of the episode preceded him to Wright Field.

"What in the hell were you thinking, Colonel McKee?"

"I guess I got a little carried away, Sir."

"A little? That stunt of yours could have caused a monumental disaster! You're grounded McKee, and if I had my way you'd never fly an airplane again!"

A hearing was held ten days later. McKee was seriously reprimanded and placed on probation. Because of his military record, and the fact his stunt was performed so soon after returning home from the war, he was allowed a significant amount of leeway. The difficult transition from a full-scale war to civilian life was the reason given. The sentence could have been much harsher.

He was allowed to keep his rank and flew again after only two months on the ground. The news media also cut him some slack, mentioning the episode more as a harmless prank. After all, he was one of the nation's top pilots. His buddies at work thought the stunt was hilarious, admiring him for the balls it took to pull it off. Betty only shook her head and asked when he was planning to grow up.

The rest of the winter and spring passed by without incident. McKee never made the effort to contact Viola or his child, and Viola left him alone. The two women had had an earnest and serious conversation prior to his homecoming. Viola agreed to stay out of the picture, wanting McKee to make his own decision regarding visitation or the lack thereof.

In mid-July 1946 McKee received a certified letter from the Army. He was asked to report voluntarily to Miami, Florida, for an important mission. He could choose to ignore the request if he so desired. Little information was given other than that the mission had to do with national interests in the Caribbean. McKee packed his bags that afternoon.

"I gotta go, Betty. Not sure when I'll be back."

"Be careful, you old fool."

Chapter 31

UNDERCOVER IN MIAMI

McKee left for Miami by train. As instructed, he packed only civilian clothes, and looked like an average businessman when he stepped on board. He wore a light brown suit, brown shoes and a white shirt, and carried a small briefcase. There was nothing unusual about his appearance, though he did have a small overnight bag strapped on his shoulder. The Army assured him that he would be picked up on arrival: he was to look for an Army Jeep. No other information was provided.

He was asleep before the train reached Cincinnati. The trip was grindingly slow and would take nearly 36 hours. McKee, not a reader, kept busy by trying to attract the attention of any good-looking woman he spotted. A brunette less than half his age occupied the compartment next to his. McKee noticed her as she boarded, and hung around in the passageway waiting for her to appear. When she finally emerged McKee introduced himself. Her name was Jessica Collins and she was on her way home to visit her parents in Palm Beach. He invited her to dinner that evening. She told him he was old enough to be her father.

"It's not healthy to eat alone," he informed her.

"OK then, but I'm warning you, I'm not cheap."

They walked to the dining car together. As they passed through car after car, they could not help but notice the many prying eyes trying to decide if she was his mistress or his daughter. Her hair without his grey was nearly the same color as his, her blue eyes had a bit more sparkle. They could certainly be related. Both sensed the interest being shown and both relished the attention. Her low-cut dress and bejeweled necklace tended to favor those on the mistress side of the fence, but her childlike smile and braces lent credence to her being his daughter.

As the state of Georgia drifted by, they talked into the early hours of the morning, consuming an entire bottle of the line's best champagne. Jessica didn't seem at all intoxicated after drinking much of the bottle, a feat that surprised even McKee. She was 21 years old and a senior at Vassar. She played on the rugby team and spent the summers during the war in Argentina, where her father maintained a cattle and horse ranch as part of his international holdings. Her family had homes in New England, Europe, Argentina and Florida. McKee realized he was in over his head.

You can't win them all, he reassured himself.

Jessica thanked him at the door of her cabin, gave him a kiss on the cheek, and told him that her father would love to hear his stories.

The train arrived in Miami right on time. The air was already thick, with the temperature hovering near 90° by mid-morning. McKee's shirt looked as if he had just run through a lawn sprinkler as he walked toward the Jeep he found parked by the curb.

"Welcome to the CIG, Colonel McKee."

"Thank you, sir; and what's your name?"

"Longo, Sergeant Longo."

Marveling at the fact that the locals all seemed to be quite comfortable and dry in the stifling heat, McKee, his shirt and pants now both soaked, climbed into the back of the vehicle. Thankfully the ride to the Biltmore Hotel was short. Built by George Merrick and John Bowman in 1926 as part of a luxury chain, the hotel was now under the control of the United States Army and had been converted to a hospital for war casualties.

Unknown to all but a few, some of the rooms upstairs were occupied by a cadre of men operating within the newly developed Central Intelligence Group or CIG, the precursor to the CIA and brainchild of General Eisenhower. McKee was soon to discover what he had gotten himself into.

He was shown to his room, high in the hotel with a spectacular view of the surrounding area. Several large estates were divided by a system of sparkling blue canals. The building stood on the highest point in Dade County, a whopping 16ft above sea level. McKee had some time to kill before dinner and decided to go for a swim. The swimming pool was the largest he had ever seen. When he was finished, he felt clean and refreshed for the first time all day.

Returning to his room, he was surprised to find some nondescript tropical outfits laid out on the bed. They were his exact size. He chose a pair of light tan linen pants and a white Cuban-style shirt to wear with a pair of dark brown sandals. He was to meet the commanding officer for dinner at 8:00pm. He poured himself a whisky from the bottle thoughtfully left on the small table by the window. Ambulances arrived intermittently, unloading the sick and wounded.

McKee was introduced to five men at the dinner table. He learned that each of them was a pilot, and that each had flown bombers during the war. Three had been in the Pacific Theater while the other two had fought in Europe. None of the men was from the same outfit, and none of them knew each other personally. General Zachary Rodine, the group's commander, stood to speak.

"Gentlemen, you have been asked to come to Miami to assist in an operation that will be denied by our government to have ever existed. Officially, the United States is taking a neutral stance in a planned revolt to overthrow President Trujillo in the

Dominican Republic. Unofficially, we want the revolt to succeed. Trujillo has been able to amass quite an air force and, frankly, we're afraid of what he might try to do to his neighbors. The man's a certifiable nutcase.

"We have brought you here to fly supplies, trainees, planes and bombs into Cuba. We will be using B-25s for transport, and all of the flying will be done at night. We may also ask you to deliver a fighter plane or two. You cannot discuss this operation with anyone, and if you are caught, our government will deny any involvement. You will be left entirely to your own devices. Your flight instructions will be delivered six to eight hours before you are to fly. I have nothing else to tell you at this time except good luck and may God be with you. Can we count you all in?"

The men sat in silence. No one spoke. McKee was the first to open his mouth.

"I'm in, General."

The others quickly followed suit. Dessert was served along with another round of drinks. The conversation grew lighter following the commander's address. The men told a few harrowing war stories with exaggerations held to a minimum. They were all decorated airmen, lucky to have made it out alive. None would be overly impressed by a bragging account of heroism from any of the others. McKee couldn't believe his luck – not only to be flying again but to be out of Indianapolis. He had been hoping to fly a B-25. He went to bed smiling, a little hung over when he awoke the next morning shortly before dawn.

The following day, dressed as farm workers, the six men climbed into the back of a rickety, nondescript open delivery truck. They were driven to a remote airfield situated in the middle of the Everglades about 12 miles west of Miami. Each man was leaning casually against the loosely held wooden sides of the truck as they bounced along tracks that in no way resembled roads. There were no signs of any kind to guide them once they were west of the airport. Thick, lush vegetation obscured any chance of seeing more than a few feet in any direction.

After just over an hour, the driver pulled into a clearing that widened considerably as they continued forward. The runway, barren except for lights interspersed along either side, was as long as the one at Shipdham. Three B-25s were parked in a semi-circle on the tarmac. A small lean-to held a short-wave radio set, some well-worn charts, a lounge area with a couch and a couple of chairs, and an oft-used and markedly stained coffee maker. No frills, seat-of-the-pants flying – the way McKee liked it. He was ready to go.

Flight operations were scheduled to begin in two days. General Rodine had arrived by Jeep an hour before the men. He introduced them to the B-25s. Three of the men had previously flown the plane – they would instruct the others. They paired off and walked toward their respective airplanes. Just as one of the men, the one they called Mike, was about to climb into his plane a large coral snake slithered out from behind the nose wheel.

"How many more of those are there?"

"No more than a thousand," said the commander, smiling.

"Shit!"

Mike glanced back toward the snake just as the blade separated its head from its body.

"Nice throw, McKee."

McKee stooped to pick up his pocket knife, a gift from his father on his 16th birthday. He had carried it in his right-hand pants' pocket for years, but this was the first time he had thrown it other than for practice. Only he knew how lucky the throw had been.

I'll just let them keep thinking that-a-way, he thought to himself.

He stuck the knife back in his pocket and hopped up the stairs to the cockpit. The two-engined bomber was less complicated than the B-24. He settled into the co-pilot's seat and began to go over the pre-flight checklist. Mike Bradshaw was to be his pilot and instructor. He had fought in the Pacific, part of the time in Hawaii, most of the time in the Philippines. He knew McKee would need little in the way of instruction, giving him the controls immediately after take-off.

They flew a course to Havana that took them over the Bahamas. The late afternoon storms were yet to develop with only scattered cumulus clouds dotting the cobalt blue sky. The water below was a brilliant turquoise, its depths well delineated by color ranging from light brown in the shallows to an almost blue-black as they skirted the 6,000ft-deep Tongue of the Ocean.

The plane was a few pounds overweight, carrying a mix of common supplies and several heavy wooden boxes full of automatic weapons – ample surplus arms from the war were readily available in the United States. The contents were destined for a small band of revolutionaries training in an area not far from Havana. They were part of a larger organization determined to overthrow the Trujillo dictatorship. The original opposition force began to form in 1941 when a group of exiles banded together in a remote area of the island, calling themselves the Dominican Revolutionary Party. Branches of the organization soon developed in New York, Mexico City and Caracas as well as Havana and two other cities in Cuba. The war curtailed their activities, but once it ended plans for the revolution were put on a fast track. The hiatus, meanwhile, had actually increased the coffers of the revolutionary group, allowing them to build a rather sizable air force as the war progressed.

The planes in their tiny air force comprised both private and military varieties. There were two B-25s and eight P-38 Lightnings, along with a couple of private Cessnas and three Swiss helicopters. Today's mission was to deliver the supplies and guns, then return with six of the young mercenaries to be trained as B-25 pilots back in Florida.

The flight took less than 45 minutes. McKee landed the plane at Teniente Brihuegas, a small airbase outside of Havana, where they were met by four disheveled men in a truck not unlike the one they used for transport in Miami. Few words were spoken as the supplies were unloaded. One of the men, a suspicious-looking type, hastily opened a box of the automatic rifles. He loaded it and fired a short burst into the sky above. The eerie-looking grin on his face bothered McKee.

"Let's get out of here, Mike."

"We have to wait for our six students. Just humor him."

McKee tried unsuccessfully to gain the man's attention. The four exiles spoke only Spanish and were interested solely in themselves and how they appeared wearing the bands of ammunition draped over their shoulders while brandishing their newly acquired automatic rifles. A second truck soon arrived, carrying six eager and equally disheveled-looking young men, none of whom was more than 20 years old. Carrying only backpacks, they filed excitedly into the plane. McKee climbed aboard, firing the engines as soon as he was belted in. Bradshaw waited until the truck with the four now heavily armed exiles rumbled onto the highway. They were smiling and laughing as they drove away, their bodies weighted down with weapons and ammunition.

Bradshaw climbed in and McKee taxied to the end of the runway. McKee, now in the left-hand seat, lifted off over the tranquil waters of Havana harbor. He and Bradshaw had a good idea what the exuberant conversation in the back of the plane was about. Animated and loud, each of the men at one time or another stuck their arms out and made the familiar motion of an airplane in flight.

"Hope they're quick learners," McKee said as he banked the plane toward Nassau.

They landed in Miami at three o'clock in the afternoon. The soon-to-be bomber pilots were confined to the airfield, forced to sleep in small tents hastily erected by the ground crew. McKee and Bradshaw were driven back to the Biltmore along with their comrades who had been engaged in similar missions, dropping off supplies and guns then picking up exiles in either Guantanamo or Santiago de Cuba for flying lessons. They all planned to spend the evening on Miami Beach following a good warm shower. Flying lessons were due to commence in the morning.

The six pilots left the cab at Ocean Drive and 5th. Walking north, they picked an outside bar at one of the swanky new art deco hotels to begin their evening. McKee suggested that with six of them they were not likely to pick up any broads. He and Bradshaw headed on up Ocean.

McKee, now 48, was forced to follow Bradshaw's lead. He was a young-looking 36-year-old with sandy hair, good height and a boxer's chest. McKee didn't particularly care whether he scored or not. He was having fun watching his pal work the room.

They were in the bar of the National Hotel when he met Sally. She was with a girl named Karen who was obviously enamored with Bradshaw. McKee liked her right off. She was a brunette, tanned, and full of energy. She took his hand, leading him to the dance floor. The band was playing Benny Goodman's *Sing, Sing, Sing*.

"You've got to be kidding," he told her as she dragged him onto the floor.

He did the best he could, nearly clobbering a petite blonde dancing nearby. Laughing hysterically, Sally escorted him back to their table.

"You've been at war too long," she told him.

"I'm nearly 50!" he replied.

"I'm 26. Let's get something to drink."

One drink led to another and they lost track of Mike and Karen. McKee thought he remembered them saying something about going to her place a few hours earlier. Sally suggested they grab a cab. She had an apartment off Brickell Avenue. She had left her car at home, riding to the beach with Karen. McKee agreed.

The cab dropped them off sometime around midnight. As McKee stepped from the vehicle the lights went out. Sally and her boyfriend Randy left him lying comfortably beside the curb, kind enough to spare him his clothes but nothing else. Randy placed the blackjack back in the glove box. Karen was unaware of Sally's alternative means of support.

McKee awoke the next afternoon in Jackson Memorial Hospital, a large bump protruding from the back of his head. The doctor released him into Bradshaw's care.

"Sorry, Herschel. I think my night turned out a hell of lot better than yours."

The young Dominican exiles completed their first day of training without Lucky Herschel McKee. They did fine, eager to fly for the cause. Their training would consume the next six weeks. Interspersed with the schooling would be several more supply runs to the island. McKee stayed away from women, deciding he may be too old for that kind of activity. By the time the day was finished, he was too tired to do much of anything anyway. He spent most evenings listening to the younger men talk about their conquests on the beach. He knew he was drinking too much, smoking too much as well. He had taken up cigars since arriving in Miami.

He wrote to Betty on occasion, keeping abreast of the goings on in Indianapolis. He still had not contacted Viola. Linda was now nine years old. With the pilot training ending, plans were in full swing for an invasion of the Dominican Republic, scheduled to take place early in 1947. The students had performed well, only one of them having crashed to his death while flying over Cuba after his graduation. He had persisted in trying to land during a thunderstorm and crashed one of the two B-25s, leaving its wreckage at the end of the runway as a relic and a less-than-subtle reminder.

During the summer McKee and Bradshaw participated in a diversionary flight over Venezuela meant to convince Trujillo that Venezuela was the target and not him. By late summer the number of men assembled in eastern Cuba had tripled. No mention of the assembly of troops ever appeared in any official documents, but in July a communiqué intercepted from the Cuban police listed six airplanes in possession of the revolutionary force: two Lockheed Vegas to be used as bombers, two Cessna C-78s and two Douglas C-47s. The report also mentioned that a larger bomber, a B-24, was expected at any moment.

McKee positioned himself in the familiar B-24 seat. Bradshaw flipped the ignition switches on and the four Pratt and Whitney engines roared to life. They rumbled down the strip west of Miami bound for Cuba. He took the Liberator low over the city, missing the steeple of the Biltmore Hotel by no more than 100ft. The shore was left behind as they flew over Key Biscayne. It was the middle of hurricane season, but the plane was urgently needed for training and to subsequently take part in the Dominican invasion. Where they would get the bombs to fill the bays was still problematic.

So far, the planned invasion was a reasonably well-kept secret outside of Cuba, but on July 25 two members of the Dominican Revolutionary Party blew their cover. They had originally been recruited in Puerto Rico. For whatever reason, they deserted, found their way to Miami and leaked what they knew of the invasion plans to the press. A front-page article appeared the next morning in the *Miami Herald*. Meanwhile, the B-24 continued to make its way to the island.

"This thing's still a piece of shit to fly."

"Tough son-of-a-bitch though," replied Bradshaw.

The landing was planned for ten o'clock that night. It would be darker than dark as there would be no moon visible. Lightning bolts stabbed the ground just beyond the end of the runway as McKee began his descent. Lighted oil drums were all he had to guide him in. The airstrip was unmapped and unnamed. They were somewhere in eastern Cuba, near a place called Cayo Confites. The coordinates they were given were supposed to keep them clear of the mountains. Trying to find the lighted oil drums in the jungle on a stormy night was still extremely difficult.

"There!" Bradshaw shouted.

McKee banked the plane and began a rapid descent. Turbulence from the approaching storm shook them violently. The exiles swore the runway was long enough. McKee thought they must have been smoking something. He touched down with a thud, bounced once, and then settled the plane. Using the brakes and the engine to their maximum, he managed to stop the plane less than five feet from the shore of a small estuary. He and Bradshaw would have to wait until daybreak to return to Miami.

The rain was upon them now, in heavy sheets. The deluge was accompanied by hail and heavy wind gusts that McKee estimated to be over 60 miles an hour. Men recruited for the invasion were trying to sleep in the sand. They had been patiently waiting, living in squalor, for the better part of two months. Their patience was running out. Cuban sympathizers were beginning to fear for their own safety. At least the rain cleared the area of mosquitoes.

The tropical storm blew itself out by the next afternoon. The runway was flooded, while the grating used to provide a suitable surface for the bigger planes was widely separated in some places. Nevertheless, McKee, with Bradshaw seated next to him, took off in the P-38 they had been provided for their return trip. They followed remnants of the storm to Miami. Upon landing, they learned that the B-24 they had so courageously delivered had been confiscated by the Cuban government the very same day. With that news, they headed for the nearest bar.

Chapter 32

THE FAILED INVASION

M cKee and Bradshaw, along with their four CIG flying comrades, continued to carry out missions in preparation for the planned invasion. Postponements were frequent. As the whole process dragged on the situation in Cuba became more and more bizarre. Parts of the government fully supported the revolution, while other parts were busily trying to upend it. The police were continually arresting exiles to confiscate equipment and guns while at the same time the Minister of Sports was raising illegal money for the coup. Corruption was rampant in all branches of the government, including the Cuban armed forces. It was difficult to know who was on what side. Elements of the Army turned their heads while others enthusiastically supported the invasion. The same was true of the Navy, the police department and the customs service. It was not surprising to anyone when the Minister of Sports received a shipment purported to be tennis balls only to find, on opening the boxes, that they contained high-powered machine guns. He was arrested and tried for treason.

America's role in the invasion plans was curious indeed. Officially, the government denied any involvement. However, all of the planes, the guns and the ammunition had been collected and delivered from the United States. Much of it was Army surplus handled by bootleggers. Technicians were sent by the US government to help the exiles with logistics, and pilots like McKee and other types of military personnel were offered as needed. The entire support operation for the invasion had "Made in the USA" stamped all over it.

Even though the plans had been brewing for many months, the invasion began in a disjointed fashion. The order to invade was given on or about September 22, 1947. McKee was among the American pilots who had left Miami and were now operating out of Mariel, helping with logistics, moving supplies and transporting troops to the launching point. Before traveling to Cuba in support of the invasion, he and Bradshaw had been given fake passports. McKee was admitted into the country as Wilfred Mayo. Bradshaw didn't fare much better; his alias was Lucius McElroy.

It became apparent to both men early in the operation that the use of military airplanes was probably a big mistake. The exiles were unable to locate any suitable bomb racks or gun mounts for either the B-24 or the two smaller bombers. They only had a few bombs in their possession to begin with.

"They'd have been better off using cargo planes. They could just roll the bombs out the doors."

"That's true, if they had any bombs to roll," replied Bradshaw.

While the early mobilization was off to a good start, factions within the Cuban Army were still working in opposition. On September 20 the Army seized 13 truckloads of arms and munitions from a farm belonging to the Minister of Education. The very next day the Army raided the posh Sevilla Hotel in Havana, the revolutionary headquarters, grabbing records and cash.

As ships loaded with troops left the shores of Cuba, they were intercepted by factions of the Cuban Navy. 1,500 men were seized on September 25 before they ever boarded. McKee worked to get planes into the air. He managed to get five of them off before Cuban troops raided the airfield and confiscated the remaining planes. He and the other American pilots were hustled out of the area and sent back to Miami. The students they had trained were taken away in trucks to Cuban jails. Of the planes that did take off, three crashed before reaching Haiti; those landing in Haiti were confiscated. The invasion failed before any shots were fired. The total cost was in the millions. Ironically, most of the money spent in support of the invasion had been raised in Cuba.

Later reviews of the ill-fated invasion named three things that stood out. First, with better organization and less interference by Cuban factions the invasion would have had a good chance of succeeding. Second, greed and materialistic issues supplanted the initial idealism of the revolutionary band. Third, there was an assumption on the part of America that the invasion would succeed without having to be openly involved.

With the Dominican effort now history, McKee enjoyed one more night on the town with his comrades before leaving by train for Indianapolis. He didn't have any feelings one way or the other regarding the success of the revolution. He was paid well for his services, was still in one piece, and he was now proficient in flying the B-25. Bradshaw returned to Texas to await another assignment. McKee told Bradshaw he figured this was his last hurrah.

"I'm going to be 50 in six weeks. I'm too old for this shit."

Bradshaw disagreed, telling McKee he thought he was the best pilot he had ever flown with. The two men shook hands and McKee boarded the train.

I hope there aren't any Vassar students on board, he thought as he settled into his cabin.

Just as he was closing the door, he spotted a petite, 30-something blond entering the cabin across the hall, alone. He unpacked his shaving kit and favorite tropical shirt.

"What the hell," he said out loud.

Chapter 33

REALITY AT HOME AND RETURN TO MIAMI

Her name was Mary. She was traveling alone to see her mother in Chicago. She was single, and had just moved to Miami the year before. Her husband had been killed on Omaha Beach. She hadn't really been out with any man for over two years. She made McKee the exception when he offered to take her to dinner. The train ride frightened her a little, not the ride itself, but the fear of traveling alone. McKee appeared to be a safe haven, at least for dinner.

Over wine, they made any talk of the war off-limits. Mary had grown up in Chicago, attending Northwestern University. Her degree was in education. She taught in a public grade school in Coral Gables. Her father had survived World War One but was later killed in a motorcycle crash racing on the dirt at the Illinois State Fair. She remembered the names of some of the drivers McKee mentioned during dinner, names like Roscoe Sarles, Howdy Wilcox and Frank Elliott, the one he mentioned the most.

She missed going to races, there was none in South Florida. She was enthralled with McKee's tales. By dessert they were holding hands across the table.

"It's been a long time for me, Mr McKee."

They walked hand in hand to his cabin. Two couples were having a conversation in the passageway; they waited until they were gone. If there was any trepidation, Mary didn't show it. McKee had a bit of trouble keeping up with her. They slept late, being awakened by the bright sunlight illuminating their two faces. They were still holding hands.

"I think we may have missed breakfast," McKee whispered.

"I'll get us something."

She ducked into her cabin, appearing fresh and prim 15 minutes later. She tapped on McKee's door as she passed by, walking briskly to the dining car. She returned with a tray holding two coffees and an assortment of muffins. McKee was dressed, holding the morning paper when she entered.

"I haven't felt this great for some time, Herschel McKee."

"Me neither," he replied.

The train rolled into Union Station ten minutes late. They said their goodbyes, McKee promising to fly up to Chicago the first chance he got. She kissed him passionately before he stepped from the train. He walked about ten feet, turned, and was about to wave to her again just as Betty, with Lucky in tow, threw her arms around him.

"You're a sight for sore eyes, McKee."

They walked hand in hand to the Cadillac. The day was warm; the top was down.

Not a bad trip home, McKee thought as he pulled up in front of the little bungalow on West Washington Street.

Lucky leaped from the back seat. Betty could not believe how little luggage McKee carried after being gone for so long. She knew his journey was top secret, or so he had said before he left. She figured he'd tell her in good time. The important thing was, he was back.

Feigning fatigue, he went straight to bed after a light supper. The previous night had taken its toll. Betty did not mind. She had waited this long to have him back in her arms, she could wait a few more hours. Her main issue was trying to keep Lucky at bay. He would not leave the tired old pilot alone. McKee eventually fell asleep with Lucky still licking at his cheek.

He and Betty made love sometime around five o'clock in the

morning. After coffee, McKee went through his mail. Betty had sorted out the important stuff. His job at Allison's had been left on hold for the nearly five months he had been gone. He rang them up. John Dempsey, his previous department head, told him to recuperate for a couple of days and then report to his old position.

Amazing company, he thought.

"Not that amazing," Betty informed him, pointing out how closely tied to the military they were.

McKee maintained his reserve status, still traveling to what was soon to be called Wright-Patterson Air Force Base in recognition of Lieutenant Frank Stuart Patterson, son of one of the co-founders of the National Cash Register Company. He had been killed in 1918 during a flight to test a new mechanism for synchronizing machine-gun fire with the rotating propellers of WW1 airplanes. McKee had met him in France, and with his comrades thanked Lieutenant Patterson for being the guinea pig.

McKee now flew conservatively, being mindful of the period he spent on probation. Returning from Dayton one Sunday evening, Betty hit him after dinner right where it hurts.

"Herschel, when are you going to see that child of yours?"

He stood and walked to the garage without saying a word. He jump-started the Harley and took off, not returning for over two hours. When he did, he calmly asked Betty how she knew about Linda.

"You old fool. Viola and I met working for the Red Cross during the war. We've been friends ever since. I know the whole story."

"I'll be damned. And you're over it?"

"Not over it, Herschel. I just accept that you are what you are."

"You're right, you know. I do need to seem 'em both. I'll look her up this week. I promise."

Betty kissed him on the cheek and told him to put the motorcycle back in the garage.

"I am indeed charmed," he mumbled as he put the Harley back where it lived.

On Saturday morning he drove to Viola's as promised, having talked to her for almost two hours over the phone on Thursday. He got the phone number and address from Betty. When he arrived, he was more than a little nervous. Linda was now ten years old, cute as can be. McKee felt a sinking feeling when he realized that he hadn't brought her anything. No little gift, nothing. He tried to give her a hug but she turned away.

"It's going to take time Herschel, lots of time."

Herschel and Viola talked for a time, Linda went outside to play. Viola said she was over him. She told him she realized his place was with Betty as soon as she met her.

"We had fun, Herschel. I'll never forget it. Linda's the perfect child and for that I will always be grateful. Go on now; you owe her more than an occasional check in the mail."

She summoned Linda and then walked the now anxious father and the very hesitant daughter to the car. It was only 50° outside but the sun shone brightly. He put the top down for her. They drove around, conversation at a minimum. He simply did not know what to say. He brought her home in less than half an hour. She remembers him saying no more than a few sentences. She would not see him again for several years to come. He drove away without uttering another word to Viola. He fought the tears that were streaming down his cheeks as he returned home. The task of being a father at this point seemed much too overwhelming. Besides, at some point he would just be leaving again anyway.

Betty welcomed him home with no questions asked and they celebrated Christmas and New Year together. It was now 1948 and life for McKee and Betty gradually settled into a routine. He made the daily trip to Allison's, usually driving the Cadillac. When the weather was good, he would ride the Harley. Public relations appearances grew more numerous as he continued his work developing the jet engine program. Betty continued teaching in the public school system. Their life remained remarkably stable for a period of six years. It was the most stability McKee had ever allowed himself. Betty and Viola continued to meet over coffee on occasion, maintaining their friendship.

McKee's routine was rocked in the early spring of 1954. He left for Allison's on the Harley. It was one of those freakishly warm days that would sometimes occur in February. Lucky chased him to the end of the street as usual. McKee turned right onto Holt Road. Lucky turned to head back home. Less than a block away, he bolted across a neighbor's drive just as a furniture delivery truck was backing out. Lucky was killed instantly. Betty notified McKee at work. She could barely mouth the words.

He raced to the scene and found Betty, who was holding Lucky's head in her lap, sobbing hysterically. The two men in the truck were still there. They were trying to do what they could to comfort her. McKee broke down, something he had not done since the death of his father during the war. He lifted Lucky, carried him home and buried him in the back yard. McKee fashioned a marker that simply read: "LUCKY – The best damn dog in the world."

Two weeks after Lucky's death McKee received another of the familiar-looking certified envelopes from the Army. They were asking him to go to Miami a second time. As usual, little information was supplied. The CIG was now the CIA (Central Intelligence Agency). McKee assumed there was another covert enterprise under way in the Caribbean. The adrenaline began to flow.

Sure enough, the American government was about to finance an invasion of Guatemala. Before World War Two ended, a coup had occurred in Guatemala that resulted in the formation of a pro-Communist government led by a dictator named Juan Jose Ar'valo. Ar'valo did not last long and was succeeded by Jacobo

Arbenz, who held similar political beliefs. When he came to power, Arbenz began to usurp private holdings. One of the companies affected was the United Fruit Company, an American holding. The company appealed to the United States government to do something. They did. Between May 1 and mid-June 1954, the CIA masterminded a successful coup.

McKee's role in the covert activities was to train Guatemalan pilots to fly the relatively new B-26, a light twin-engined bomber with a fairly large bomb-carrying capacity. His students provided successful air cover for a land invasion by 450 troops made up of exiles, mercenaries and Nicaraguans. The training was again carried out in the Everglades, using the same airstrip west of Miami. The United Fruit Company was able to stay in business and the CIA gained confidence in managing covert affairs for the American government in the Caribbean. This time McKee flew back to Indianapolis.

Betty asked no questions regarding where he had been and neither did Allison's. He took up where he left off, continuing to develop jet aircraft engines. In late November he was sent to St Louis to oversee the installation of some new jet engines for Trans World Airlines (TWA). The assignment was expected to take at least four weeks. During the assignment he was required by the Army to attend a meeting in Muskegon, Michigan. With the exception of these types of assignment, his routine was fairly well re-established. While in Muskegon, he was informed by telegram of the delivery of a package he was not expecting.

Chapter 34

GOOD THING IN A SMALL PACKAGE

Baby Lynne Vittorio weighed just seven pounds six ounces. She had brown eyes and dark brown hair. Linda McKee, now 17, had married her high school sweetheart in 1953. His name was Nunzio Vittorio. He was an industrious young man who worked nightly at the Eli Lilly Company in Indianapolis while attending Sacred Heart High School during the day. Lynne Vittorio was born on December 5, 1954. The telegram bearing the news was sent to McKee by Viola two days after the birth. He sent the following letter, not to Viola but to Linda McKee, that same day:

"Dear Linda,

"Received your mother's telegram this afternoon as it was forwarded on from St Louis. I am very happy that you are now the proud mother of a fine girl and I am very proud of you.

"Sorry that I can not be there as I am here in Muskegon, Michigan, for two weeks' duty for the Army provisioning engine conference and I hope to return to St Louis and will drive over to see you on or about the 18th December.

"Hope you are feeling fine and getting over your sickness.

"God bless you with all my love,

"Your Dad,

"Mac."

Linda did not know quite what to think. The brief letter was the first she had heard from him since their short ride in his car seven years before. Now he's all of a sudden paying attention? She folded the letter and placed it inside her diary. She did not show it to her mother or her new husband. December 18 came and went. McKee never showed.

He returned to St Louis from Muskegon to resume his dealings with TWA. He was staying with Frank Elliott, who was not in the best of health. He had been sick for some time and McKee felt the need to spend some time with him; he was not expected to live much longer. They spent their evenings together drinking and reminiscing about the old days. The TWA project took longer than expected and McKee did not return to Indianapolis until February 1955.

He had every intention of visiting his new granddaughter but something always seemed to come up. Linda did not hold her breath. She went on with her life as best she could. She was unable to graduate from high school because of the pregnancy, but once she'd got Lynne through the newborn period she attended evening classes and eventually became an accountant. Nunzio did graduate, and remained at Lilly's until his eventual retirement.

Linda thought it curious that McKee, even though he didn't visit in person, began sending frequent postcards. They would come from places as diverse as California, Texas, Idaho, Canada, the South Seas, Japan, Alaska and Hong Kong. No one, including Betty, had any idea where he was and what he was doing much of the time. He would always brush it off with a comment about "the crazy government".

Chapter 35

JOURNEY'S END

In 1958 news articles began to appear regarding a rebel character who was rampaging his way through Cuba. He led a band of guerilla fighters determined to overthrow the corrupt government of Fulgencio Batista. His name was Fidel Castro. It was the typical Latin American story: the upper class was diminishing in size while at the same time growing much wealthier, while the lower classes, abused to the point of intolerance, began a populist uprising in self-defense.

The American government did not pay too much attention to the young rebel until an encounter occurred between Castro's forces and some American troops who were vacationing at the US Naval base at Guantanamo. Following this brief skirmish, the attention America paid toward Castro grew exponentially.

Castro successfully overthrew Batista in 1959. Many of Cuba's wealthy bailed off the island along with members of the American Mafia. They all took their money with them. As a consequence Castro began a nationalization process to raise money for his regime, the revolution having depleted most of his funds. American businesses were threatened. Within a short time the nationalization process was in full swing and the CIA was called upon to investigate. McKee received another certified letter just before Christmas 1959.

Miami was his destination for the third time. Staying at the Biltmore, now the Medical School campus for the University of Miami as well as a Veteran's Administration Hospital, McKee joined up with his frequent partner in these affairs, Mike Bradshaw. They were to train Cuban pilots to fly the B-26 for an eventual invasion of their own country. This time the US was supporting the previous government.

Castro, who initially was a freelance rebel bent on improving the plight of the poor, eventually aligned himself with the Soviet Union after that government enhanced his war chest with a generous donation of $100 million. The deal gave Russia a significant amount of influence just 90 miles from the state of Florida. Castro became a Communist. McKee, not caring one way or another about the politics, trained his students well. In addition to training pilots, he and Bradshaw would occasionally fly supplies to the island, landing at the American-held base in Guantanamo. Only once was his life endangered.

The delivery flights were always at night. The usual approach was from the sea, but on one particular night McKee had to come in overland. Castro's forces were entrenched a few miles from the base, and as he descended to less than 1,000ft bullets suddenly tore into his left wing. Fuel began to spew from the wing and the port-side engine quit running. Having once been faced with a similar situation in Europe, McKee shut off all fuel flow and was able to land the plane just short of the runway as the wing caught fire. The plane bounced over some rough ground but remained upright. McKee and his co-pilot bailed out when the ground speed decreased to a crawl. The plane and supplies burned as the two men watched from 50 yards away.

When he went to relieve himself following this latest harrowing escape, McKee noticed bright red blood in his urine for the first time. He did not think too much about it, attributing it to the jump from the burning plane. He had landed fairly hard. The blood reoccurred two days later. When it happened a third time he went to see the base medic. He was immediately flown back to Miami.

It was early March 1960. Activity in both Florida and in Cuba had increased substantially. McKee figured something big was about to occur, but he wasn't sure what. Very little was said about Castro and Cuba on the news. Meanwhile he was flown to Walter Reed Army Hospital in Washington DC, where he awaited his diagnosis and news about Cuba. On March 9 he wrote the following letter to Linda;

"Dear Linda,

"The x-rays show a tumor on the left kidney and a hiatus hernia. They will finish my clinical test on Monday then the doctors will evaluate the test, then cut.

"This hospital is the best and the best doctors so I am in good hands. All the high ranks from the President down to me are sent here. I hope to be out by April or May and will pay you and family a visit; not just a few hours.

"Mac."

In late March, President Eisenhower approved a plan to support the development and training of a small band of Cuban exiles to eventually overthrow Castro. By October the plan had expanded to include a full-scale invasion. Air support would be provided by Cuban pilots flying American B-26s, all trained by McKee and Bradshaw and an unknown number of other American pilots working for the CIA. They were to deploy from the base in Guatemala where their advanced training, minus McKee, had taken place.

McKee had a major stroke during the operation to remove his left kidney. The doctors blamed an air embolism, an error during the procedure that sent a bubble of air into his brain. The embolism caused the circulation to the right side of his brain to be momentarily shut off, long enough to destroy millions of nerve cells. He awoke from the surgery partially paralyzed on his left side. He would endure four months of hospitalization in Washington before being transferred to the Veteran's Administration hospital in Indianapolis. He would remain a patient there, undergoing rehabilitation for another six months. He was allowed to go home on February 2, 1961.

He continued to progress and was using a walker well by the end of the month. Betty was by his side most of the time. She took a leave of absence from teaching to spend time working with him. Viola and Linda would visit often, not believing this could happen to Herschel McKee. Lynne, now six years old, would sit on his lap while he told stories. He would often repeat himself, telling the same story just minutes after telling it for the first time. He retired from Allison's. They stuck with him through the entire ordeal. In March, he and Betty traveled to Hawaii. The trip was arranged by the United States Army. He sent the following postcard to Linda on March 15:

"Howdy,
"Long time no see. Well I am on tour in the Islands in the South Seas and will write you. Regards to all,
"Lt. Col. H. J. McKee."

While basking in the sun at the bar on Waikiki Beach, he and Betty heard the news: the invasion of Cuba at the Bay of Pigs on April 17 was an overwhelming disaster. President Kennedy, the broadcast stated, apparently left the exiles without adequate support or defense. Two of the pilots who were flying American B-26s, the broadcast went on to say, defected to the United States; one landed at Miami International Airport. McKee recognized him from his picture in the newspaper delivered to his room the next day. He was one of his students.

"I guess I won't be flying any more," was all he could say to Betty as she finished reading him the rest of the article.

"No, Herschel. I'm afraid your flying days are over." She hugged him as she spoke.

He was now getting around reasonably well, using only a cane. His speech was occasionally slurred, but he was sharp mentally. They remained for six weeks in Hawaii, where he was able to continue rehab at the Navy hospital in Honolulu. They returned to Indianapolis the end of April. He had aged considerably since the operation; his hair was now silver. The doctors told him that they thought the tumor was confined to his left kidney and felt that they had removed all of the cancer. He had lost almost 30lb and most of his strength during the illness. He was facing a fairly grim future.

The first thing he did after returning home was to visit his granddaughter. He would break into tears easily during the day he spent with Lynne and his daughter. Betty had driven him to the Vittorios' home before going on to Viola's to catch up on the latest gossip. Young Lynne turned her head to look quizzically at her mother each time McKee cried. Linda explained how sometimes a person's emotions can become quite labile following a stroke. The visit was the longest McKee had spent with any of his family since leaving for World War Two. Betty picked him up at six o'clock. She relayed the fact that Viola had been diagnosed with breast cancer while they had been in Hawaii.

Chapter 36

GOD SPEED

ost of the men who McKee felt at all close to had died.
Elliot passed away in 1957 while McKee was on assignment
in Japan. All of his friends at Allison's were either retired or dead.
He was never close to his brother, or his sister for that matter, and
he was through with military service. Instead he found himself at
the mercy of three women, a thought that didn't sit all that well
with him. No more motorcycles, he was no longer licensed to
drive a car, and with the exception of the Ed Sullivan Show he
hated television. He continued to smoke cigars, inhaling at least
five a day. He kept his stash in the garage. Betty allowed him a
glass of whisky each evening. As far as he was concerned, his life
had come to a screeching halt. A second stroke occurred in 1963.
Betty had taken him to a reunion of sorts at Wright-Patterson
AFB and it happened during lunch.

The same area of his brain was affected but this time it left him
moribund. What recovery he had evolved slowly over the next two
years. He was transferred to the Veteran's Administration Hospital
in Indianapolis after spending a month in Dayton. Two of the
weeks there had been spent in the intensive care unit. His
emotions were more labile following the second stroke, causing
him to cry with little provocation. He was eventually able to go
home on weekends and could get around with his cane. He was
perpetually sneaking out to the driveway to "work" on Betty's car.

Viola succumbed on June 24, 1964. Betty took Herschel to the
funeral. He sat through most of the service with a blank stare on

his face. It had been more than 18 months since the second stroke and he talked very little. He looked older than his age for the first time in his life. Sitting between Betty and Linda, he openly wept on occasion, his tears bearing no relation to what the minister was saying.

In 1965, becoming too difficult for Betty to care for, he was placed in a nursing home. The police would find him on occasion walking with his cane along nearby streets. When they asked him where he was going he would simply say: "Away." He would then tell them he was escaping from a concentration camp.

The police would take him to Betty's, where he would remain for a couple of days. She would return him to the home when she grew weary. At Betty's he would spend most of his time upstairs, sitting in the old rocker, staring out the window overlooking the small garden. Linda and her daughter would often stop by for a short while when out doing errands. It was during these visits that Lynne at last warmed up to him. She would remain with him until he drifted off to sleep, holding his good hand in hers.

The stories he would try to tell were disjointed and confusing. It was difficult to understand what he was trying to say. She could make out the fact that most of the stories involved racing cars and airplanes, giving Germany hell, living in France, and a woman named Penny who owned a dog named Lucky. Lynne enjoyed the stories regardless of how confusing they were. She knew he had been a hero in the two great wars. She knew also that he had been a wanderer, a philanderer and a thrill-seeker. She wished she could have traveled with him. It was curious, she thought, how he would always seem to smile just before he fell asleep.

Herschel J. McKee died in the nursing home on April 12, 1965. He was buried with honors in Arlington Cemetery along with so many other American heroes. He lies in a nondescript grave in section #37, gravesite #1065.

His ignominious end, as is so often the case, did not do justice to the life he had led. From the day of his birth he was the consummate free spirit. He was guided by an unquenchable thirst for adventure and challenge, untainted by political issues, religious values, or whatever was in vogue at the time. Even though principled, he was loyal only to himself, his country and the men he fought alongside or competed against. For him, women were largely a dalliance. Marrying them seemed to him the highest honor he could bestow.

In an age that sees children still living with their parents well into adulthood, the media bombarding the populace with things to be afraid of, signs warning of every possible danger, safety advocates wanting us all to live in some sort of protected bubble, McKee would not fit in. Perhaps we should all be worried about how mankind will survive another global threat like World War Two with the anxiety-consumed population we now have. Few men like McKee exist these days. Our society discourages them.

McKee drank too much, that we know, but he didn't need a sleeping aid, an anti-anxiety drug or an analyst. He had no fear, no complex neurotic tendencies. He was not foolhardy, far from it. He was phenomenally fatalistic – what will be, will be, was the code he lived by. If a job needed to be done he did it, no questions asked. He concerned himself only with the outcome. Yes, he was, shall we say, somewhat of a "dick off" in his earlier days, but it fit him to a tee. He was not a complex person by any means. He expected others to think like he did. If he had a major fault that was it. From time to time he hurt a lot of people; he didn't mean to, it just happened. But if someone needed help he was there to give it.

Women were hopelessly attracted to him. No one really knows how many relationships he may have had scattered throughout the world. All whom we know about have fond, although some only brief, memories of the man. Three turned up at his funeral: Betty, Susan and even Penny, who managed to make it all the way from England after recognizing his picture on the obituary page of the *Indianapolis Star* – a passenger had left the newspaper on his seat as he boarded a plane at Heathrow. Betty alone managed to hang onto him for the duration. She understood him, required nothing from him, enjoyed him, and took care of him when he needed to be cared for. The following poem was found with her effects when she died in 1979:

GODSPEED

Kiss me; kiss me and go away,
  My eyes will follow after,
Until you're hid by the winding road
  And the wind has stilled your laughter,
I have thrilled to your arms' caress,
  And loved your deep eyes' glow,
Gladly I've lifted my lips to your kiss—
  While there is time—my dear, please go.

You were never meant for my way of life,
  Or content with cottage walls;
Your Gypsy feet need a wide world's space,
  And a starlit dome when darkness falls,
It is afternoon and the sky is red,
  —Be on your way ere the night—
I am strong in the sane cool light of day—
  Don't wait till the stars are white.

—Cynthia Lane

POSTSCRIPT

Herschel's only child, Linda, barely knew her father. He saw her shortly after she was born, then when she was ten years old, when he took her for a very short ride in his car, and once more, briefly, after Lynne was born. She did not see him again until after his stroke. She therefore knew him only vicariously, through newspaper clippings, family photos and family talk. Throughout her life she grabbed everything she could get hold of that had to do with her father. Without her scrapbooks, her mementos and her memories, McKee's story could never have been told. Although she describes him to this day as "a scoundrel" she greatly admires the character that he was. For me, it has been an unbelievable journey. I have lived a large part of my life wishing I was somewhere else. My wife calls me a malcontent. My father called me a second Walter Mitty. I have always read stories of grand adventures and admired the people who experienced them, seemingly without fear of the consequences. We have all enjoyed movies about famous war heroes, daring risk-takers and covert operatives. Herschel McKee was all three. He survived the trenches of World War One. Bullets and bombs didn't kill him during World War Two. Airplane, motorcycle and car crashes didn't kill him, and neither did the Chinese.

He truly was the man who would not die.

INDEX

Folio numbers in italics refer to illustrations